Mariam, the Magdalen, and the Mother

Mariam, the Magdalen, and the Mother

EDITED WITH AN INTRODUCTION BY *Deirdre Good*

INDIANA UNIVERSITY PRESS

Bloomington and Indianapolis

This book is a publication of

Indiana University Press
601 North Morton Street
Bloomington, IN 47404-3797 USA

http://iupress.indiana.edu

Telephone orders   800-842-6796
Fax orders   812-855-7931
Orders by e-mail   iuporder@indiana.edu

© 2005 by Indiana University Press

The paper used in this publication meets the minimum requirements of American National Standard for Information Sciences—Permanence of Paper for Printed Library Materials, ANSI Z39.48–1984.

Manufactured in the United States of America

Library of Congress Cataloging-in-Publication Data

　　Mariam, the Magdalen, and the mother / edited with an introduction by Deirdre Good.
　　　　p.　cm.
　　Includes bibliographical references and index.
　　ISBN 0-253-34533-2 (cloth : alk. paper)—ISBN 0-253-21751-2 (pbk. : alk. paper)
　　1. Mary, Blessed Virgin, Saint.   I. Good, Deirdre Joy.
　　BT603.M27   2005
　　226'.092—dc22   2004021158

1 2 3 4 5   10 09 08 07 06 05

Contents

The Miriamic Tradition

Preface

ↄ

During the Second World War, paintings from London's National Gallery were taken from London and hidden in Welsh mines. At the end of the war Sir Kenneth Clarke, then director of the National Gallery, canvassed the nation to discover which picture should be brought back first to be seen. Everyone requested Titian's *Noli Me Tangere*. Somehow reflecting a national sense of loss and a wistful hope, this depiction of Mary Magdalen's encounter with the risen Jesus resonated with a nation's consciousness. Mary Magdalen[1]—striving to encompass both loss and faithful discipleship—remains a powerful figure in the devotional lives of Christians. This volume articulates a new sight and sound map of Mary Magdalen that problematizes and at the same time enriches the fascination she exerts.

The volume began as a conference. The premise of the conference was that only a variety of authors working from all relevant religious traditions could present a comprehensive and accessible portrait of Mary Magdalen. The conference papers more than justified this expectation. Each essay in this volume offers original scholarship by Jewish, Christian, and Muslim scholars on the religious and prophetic experience of Mary Magdalen and her depiction in Christian art (Miriamic Vision); on aspects of Mary Magdalen's composite identity overlapping with Jewish, Gnostic, early Christian, and Manichaean traditions, together with early Christian, patristic, and Islamic traditions about Jesus' mother (Miriamic Procession; Miriamic Tradition).

A Question of Identity and Previous Scholarship

Mary Magdalen occupies an unusual place in Christian tradition. New Testament accounts of Mary Magdalen reveal a figure quite different from the one that emerges from subsequent Christian tradition, and this contradiction intrigues scholars today. Perhaps most popularly understood as the penitent sinner, or a reformed prostitute, Mary Magdalen figures prominently as the first witness to the resurrection of Jesus, the "apostle to the apostles," the first bearer of the good news. Recently scholars have claimed Mary Magdalen as authority for women's preaching.

The question of identity remains primary in scholarship surrounding the figure of Mary Magdalen, and to be sure, it is not a new question. In 1517 the French Dominican scholar Jacques Lefevre d'Etaples—in opposition to the claim made by Pope Gregory I in the sixth century—concluded in *De Maria Magdalena* that Mary Magdalen and Luke's sinner and Mary of Bethany were not in fact one and the same person. The question of identity arises today in a different form as some scholars ask questions about historical reconstruction and others look more broadly at the cultural and symbolic constructions of gender and sexuality. For example, in her recent book *The Making of the Magdalen* (Princeton 2000), Katherine Ludwig Jansen argues that preachers and moralists of the later Middle Ages invented a Magdalen to address philosophical and social exigencies: the nature of women, their care and custody, and the ever increasing problem of prostitution. Jane Schaberg's *The Resurrection of Mary Magdalene* (Continuum 2002) proposes Mary Magdalen as the successor of Jesus' apocalyptic vision. Most recently, Ann Graham Brock's *Mary Magdalene, The First Apostle* (Harvard 2003) describes the politics of apostolic authority. Peter's prominence may have been at Mary Magdalen's expense. Rather than revisiting her singularity, *Mariam, the Magdalen, and the Mother* argues that the Miriamic roots of her composite identity and prophetic vision are prominent in all religious traditions of the first five centuries of the common era. Moreover, her composite identity is the spark that fired theological imaginations of medieval preachers. As prophet of Jesus' resurrection and ministry, Mariam speaks in sound and song. Texts convey vision through discourse. Some texts (Exodus; Luke) articulate prophecy rationally while others (John; Gospel of Mary) stress vision. These positions and variations of them are reflected in the essays and the contributions of the essays to the issues of how gender and rationality or visionary discourse were related in antiquity.

The first essay, "The Miriamic Secret," explains the name Mariam in Greek and Coptic texts of the first four centuries of the common era. Forms of the name Mariam echo Miriam of Hebrew Scriptures and describe for Semitic hearers both the witness of the risen Lord in John 20 and the singer of the Magnificat in Luke.

The Miriamic Procession

The Miriamic procession is both auditory and visual. From it comes a map of both sight and sound. The sound map starts with the glorious song of Miriam. She sings the ancient "Song of the Sea" in Exodus 15, celebrating Israel's deliverance with music and dance. Her performance on behalf of the nation reflects a female musical tradition identified and described in Professor Carol Meyers's essay "Miriam, Music, and Miracles." This Miriamic strand in the story of ancient Israel not only signifies a special place for women as those who first recognize and give voice to God's salvific deeds but also contributes to a wider understanding of the possibilities for women in Israelite society.

The Miriamic procession continues into the New Testament from the birth stories through the ministry of Jesus and on to the empty tomb and resurrection accounts. Echoes of Miriam's song resonate in the Magnificat, the lament psalms of *Pistis Sophia,* the Manichaean psalms, Peter Abelard's Easter sermon, and medieval and baroque music of the East and West. Refracted images of Miriam's vision appear in the Gospel of Mary and in Christian art.

Mary Magdalen is one of the three women who first discover the empty tomb. Yet John's gospel reports Jesus' appearance to her alone, coupling it with her proclamation of the resurrected Lord to the apostles. In her meeting with Jesus, each calls the other's name: "Mariam!" "Rabboni!" This exchange of names becomes an interchange of sight and sound. We see them side by side. *Noli Me Tangere* is yet another classification of their visible and audible dialogue in Christian art. Professor Antti Marjanen's essay "Mary Magdalene: A Beloved Disciple" explores the special relationship of Jesus to Mary Magdalene in the Gospel of Mary and the Gospel of Philip. Reciprocity extends to others in different traditions. In John, for example, Mary Magdalen is linked with Peter and the Beloved Disciple in John 20 and with Thomas in John 21. Professor Claudia Setzer's essay "Three Odd Couples: Women and Men in Mark and John" indicates that in John, Mary Magdalen exemplifies immediate recognition and faith without signs, in contrast to doubting Thomas. However, John seems to attach less importance to her gender than modern readers do.

As already noted, the writer of Luke's gospel forges aural and literary connections between Miriam and Mary, the mother of Jesus. Professor Mary Foskett's essay "Miriam/Mariam/Maria: Literary Genealogy and the Genesis of Mary in the Protevangelium of James," explores ways in which this gospel and the extracanonical birth story of Jesus known as the Protevangelium of James exploit and subvert ancient images of virginity either to advance or to suppress the Miriamic tradition.

The Miriamic Vision

In "'I have seen the Lord': Mary Magdalen as Visionary, Early Christian Prophecy, and the Context of John 20:14–18," Professor Mary Rose D'Angelo argues a closer continuity between Mary of the fourth gospel and Mary of the Gospel of Mary in that both depict Mary as prophet and originator of mission. Attention to Mary's vision as emblematic of early Christian prophecy helps to eradicate, she proposes, the overly rationalized division between resurrection and ascension proposed by Luke. In conjunction with a prophetic and charismatic Jesus movement, the experience of Mary Magdalen is continuous with the vision of John the seer in Revelation and the new prophets, all of whom saw the risen Lord.

Vision however is not *stasis*. Quite the reverse. Professor Diane Apostolos-Cappadona's essay "On the Visual and the Vision: The Magdalene in Early Christian and Byzantine Art and Culture," is the first to correlate a three-part chronology of Christian iconography outlined by art historians and depictions of Mary in Christian art. She identifies an anonymous group of women processing to the tomb in early third-century frescoes. In the fifth century a discrete Mary Magdalen emerges within the context of "women at the tomb." By the seventh century, she is singular witness and apostle in images that show who she is and what she sees. Here, artistic evidence complements textual arguments for original anonymity and composite identity. In a sight map, Titian's *Noli Me Tangere* may result from the *Chairete* of Byzantine iconography.

The Miriamic Tradition

Professor Stephen Shoemaker's essay "Jesus' Gnostic Mom: Mary of Nazareth and the 'Gnostic Mary' Traditions" argues that ancient Christian traditions (probably from the third century) reveal that there were some in the early church who envisaged Mary of Nazareth as a teacher of secret wisdom who enlightened the apostles. Numerous early Christian apocrypha, including several so-called gnostic texts, include a character known as "Mary," whose identity is usually otherwise unspecified. Generally, this "Mary" appears as an associate, or sometimes as a rival, of the apostles, who is filled with knowledge of the "gnostic" mysteries. Although scholars have persistently identified this Mary with Mary the Magdalen, rather than Mary of Nazareth, this interpretive dogma is based on evidence that is at best inconclusive. This essay reexamines the often overlooked problems with the identification of the "gnostic Mary" simply with the Magdalen, considering the many features of this character's representation that point also to Mary of Nazareth. The traditions of the Virgin Mary's Dormition (her death) in particular present Mary of Nazareth in a light that is strongly reminiscent of the gnostic Mary figure. Thus the gnostic Mary, it turns out, is best understood as a composite figure, drawing on the identities of both the Magdalen and the Virgin (among others), rather than being the representation of a single historical individual.

Subsequent Muslim exegetes of medieval Andalusia argued intensely for the priesthood of Mary, mother of Jesus, and for women who received revelation through the angels or directly from God. Hosn Abboud's essay "'*Idhan Maryam Nabiyya*' ('Hence Maryam is a Prophetess'): Muslim Classical Exegetes and Women's Receptiveness to God's Verbal Inspiration," argues that feminist analysis of the issues of Mary's prophethood not only betrays the androcentric readings projected onto the text by Muslim exegetes of the East but demonstrates the signs of Mary's prophethood (*'alāmāt nubuwwat Maryam*) well established in the Qurānic text. Moreover, this analysis brings to light the importance of the accounts devoted to Mary's story in the Qurānic context or worldview.

Finally Professor Kevin Coyle's essay "Twelve Years Later: Revisiting the 'Mary's' of Manichaeism" identifies different forms of Mary's name (excluding Magdalen) in Manichaean texts and her role as net-caster and hunter or messenger to the eleven.

Book Cover

The back cover illustration is of an altar frontal from Lincoln Cathedral's side chapel at the west end. When I see the frontal I hear weeping. At a remove from John's gospel, sight brings sound. Sight and sound articulate a multivalent and polyphonic name. Together with Titian's *Noli Me Tangere*, the altar frontal creates an inclusio because sight moves from sound to name just as creation through word invites response.

NOTES

1. For the most part this spelling of the name will be used. The Greek spelling of Magdalene (with a final *e*) also appears in this collection of essays.

Acknowledgments

The conference was implemented in cooperation with Rabbi Leonard Schoolman, Director of the Center for Religious Inquiry (CRI), at St. Bartholomew's Church, New York City, in June 2002. For the conference the organist of St. Bart's, Bill Trafka, organized a Choral Evensong with organ and choir to celebrate the feast of Mary Magdalen (transferred). The Rev. Nancy Hanna preached. Without the support of the Rev. Bill Tully, the Rector of St. Bartholomew's Church, and his staff, this collection would not exist. I am profoundly grateful to each of them.

My thanks go to all those who gave papers and presentations at the conference. With the help of Dr. Ena Heller of the American Bible Society, one session of the conference was held at the American Bible Society. I acknowledge with thanks Dr. Heller's generosity and gracious welcome. My gratitude also goes to Julian Sheffield, who suggested the title; to Richard Johnson of Kamera Photographic Studio in Lincoln for the back cover image; and to the Dean and Chapter of Lincoln Cathedral, who gave permission for the altar frontal to appear on the cover.

Abbreviations

AAQ	*American Arts Quarterly*
AASOR	Annual of the American Schools of Oriental Research
ABD	*Anchor Bible Dictionary*
AcOr	*Acta orientalia*
AJA	*American Journal of Archaeology*
ANET	Ancient Near Eastern Texts
ANF	Ante-Nicene Fathers
AnOr	*Analecta orientalia*
ANRW	Aufstieg und Niedergang der römischen Welt
APF	*Archiv für Papyrusforschung*
ARG	Archiv für Reformationsgeschichte
ATR	*Anglican Theological Review*
AusBR	*Australian Biblical Review*
AUSS	Andrews University Seminary Studies
BA	*Biblical Archaeologist*
BARev	*Biblical Archaeology Review*
BASOR	*Bulletin of the American Schools of Oriental Research*
BCE	Before Common Era
BG	Berolinensis Gnosticus
BHS	Biblia hebraica stuttgartensia
Bib	*Biblica*
BIES	*Bulletin of the Israel Exploration Society*
BJRL	*Bulletin of the John Rylands Library*
BR	*Biblical Research*
BZ	*Biblische Zeitschrift*
BZAW	Beihefte zur Zeitschrift für die alttestamentliche Wissenschaft
CBQ	*Catholic Biblical Quarterly*
CE	Common Era
CH	*Church History*
CIG	Corpus inscriptionum graecarum

CIJ	Corpus inscriptionum iudaicarum
CIL	Corpus inscriptionum latinarum
CIS	Corpus inscriptionum semiticarum
EDNT	*Exegetical Dictionary of the NT*
EncIs	*Encyclopedia of Islam*
EncJud	*Encyclopedia Judaica*
Gos. Phil.	Gospel of Philip
Gos. Thos.	Gospel of Thomas
GRBS	*Greek, Roman, and Byzantine Studies*
HTR	*Harvard Theological Review*
HUCA	*Hebrew Union College Annual*
IB	*Interpreter's Bible*
ICC	International Critical Commentary
IDB	*Interpreter's Dictionary of the Bible*
IEJ	*Israel Exploration Journal*
Int	*Interpretation*
ISBE	*International Standard Bible Encyclopedia*
ITQ	*Irish Theological Quarterly*
JAAR	*Journal of the American Academy of Religion*
JAF	*Journal of American Folklore*
JAOS	*Journal of the American Oriental Society*
JAS	*Journal of Asian Studies*
JBL	*Journal of Biblical Literature*
JBR	*Journal of Bible and Religion*
JCS	*Journal of Cuneiform Studies*
JEA	*Journal of Egyptian Archaeology*
JECS	*Journal of Early Christian Studies*
JEH	*Journal of Ecclesiastical History*
JJS	*Journal of Jewish Studies*
JMeH	*Journal of Medieval History*
JMES	*Journal of Middle Eastern Studies*
JNES	*Journal of Near Eastern Studies*
JQR	*Jewish Quarterly Review*
JR	*Journal of Religion*
JRelS	*Journal of Religious Studies*
JSNT	*Journal for the Study of the New Testament*
JSNTSS	*Journal for the Study of the New Testament Supplementary Series*
LCL	Loeb Classical Library
LXX	Septuagint (Translation of Hebrew Scriptures into Greek)
NHS	Nag Hammadi Studies

NovT	*Novum Testamentum*
NPNF	Nicene and Post-Nicene Fathers
NT	New Testament
NTA	New Testament Abstracts
NTAp	NT Apocrypha, Schneemelcher
OT	Old Testament
OTP	OT Pseudepigrapha, Charlesworth
P	Papyrus (followed by a number identifying the papyrus)
PG	Patrologia Graeca, Migne
PJ	Protevangelium of James
PL	Patrologia Latina, Migne
PS	Pistis Sophia
RB	*Revue Biblique*
RevTh	*Revue Thomiste*
RSB	*Religious Studies Bulletin*
SJT	*Scottish Journal of Theology*
TDNT	Theological Dictionary of the NT
TDOT	Theological Dictionary of the OT
TJT	*Toronto Journal of Theology*
TL	*Tidjschrift voor Liturgie*
TLZ	*Theologische Literaturzeitung*
VC	*Vigiliae Christianae*
ZNW	*Zeitschrift für die Neutestamentliche Wissenschaft*
ZRGG	*Zeitschrift für Religions- und Geistegeschichte*

Sigla

[ ] Square brackets in the translation indicate either that the text in square brackets is supported by some manuscripts but not by the majority or that a lacuna exists in the manuscript where writing once existed; the enclosed text has been either restored or left blank by scholars.

( ) Parentheses in the translation indicate material supplied by the translator for the sake of clarity.

Mariam, the Magdalen, and the Mother

1

The Miriamic Secret

DEIRDRE GOOD

*D*escriptions of Mary figures (particularly Mary Magdalen)[1] in the
New Testament and noncanonical texts draw on and are perhaps
even shaped by portraits of Miriam in Jewish and Christian texts
from the Second Temple Period. There are at least two windows through
which we can look at the Miriamic elements in the descriptions of Mary Magdalen and other Marys in the New Testament: names and traits.

Names

As is well known, women appear in the gospel narratives at Jesus' birth,
death, and resurrection. John 20 records a resurrection appearance of Jesus
to Mary Magdalen. Reports of John's version of the resurrection narrative
can be traced back behind the English translations through Latin to the (conjectured) Greek original. We could look at contemporary critical editions of
the Greek New Testament. These editions are scrupulous assessments of the
relative merits of Greek codices, papyrus fragments, and old translations of
the New Testament into Latin, Syriac, Armenian, and other ancient languages
in order to recreate the best Greek text. They are, however, modern reconstructions of conjectured ancient texts rather than actual ancient texts themselves. Accordingly, what is the evidence of ancient texts we do have dating
to the fourth century and earlier?

Among the large codices is Codex Sinaiticus, discovered by Constantin
von Tischendorf. I consulted an edition of that manuscript of the NT, Barn-

abas and the Shepherd of Hermas, published in 1863.[2] Kurt and Barbara Aland regard the text of Codex Sinaiticus (ℵ) "with its numerous singular readings and careless errors" as "highly overrated by Tischendorf" and "distinctly inferior" to that of Codex Vaticanus (B).[3] On the other hand, Professor Stanley Porter (currently principal, dean, and professor of New Testament at McMaster Divinity College, Hamilton, Ontario, Canada) proposed at the 2002 national meeting of the Society of Biblical Literature:

> Whether there should not be a return to use of such a text as Codex Sinaiticus. Rather than being a scholarly construct of the twentieth century, Codex Sinaiticus, along with other ancient manuscripts, constituted an ancient manuscript actually used and revised by various early Christian communities (the various correcting hands of Sinaiticus attest to its use, but also raise a number of important critical issues). Therefore, it provides unparalleled access to an earlier form of the text as used by early Christians.

I would like to use the text of Codex Sinaiticus to establish a fourth-century reading of the New Testament.

The dramatic tale of Tischendorf's discovery of Codex Sinaiticus is told best by himself:

> It was in April, 1844, that I embarked at Leghorn for Egypt. The desire which I felt to discover some precious remains of any manuscripts, more especially Biblical, of a date which would carry us back to the early times of Christianity, was realized beyond my expectations. It was at the foot of Mount Sinai, in the Convent of St. Catherine, that I discovered the pearl of all my researches. In visiting the library of the monastery, in the month of May, 1844, I perceived in the middle of the great hall a large and wide basket full of old parchments; and the librarian, who was a man of information, told me that two heaps of papers like these, mouldered by time, had been already committed to the flames. What was my surprise to find amid this heap of papers a considerable number of sheets of a copy of the Old Testament in Greek, which seemed to me to be one of the most ancient that I had ever seen. The authorities of the convent allowed me to possess myself of a third of these parchments, or about forty-three sheets, all the more readily as they were destined for the fire. But I could not get them to yield up possession of the remainder. The too lively satisfaction, which I had displayed, had aroused their suspicions as to the value of this manuscript. I transcribed a page of the text

of Isaiah and Jeremiah, and enjoined on the monks to take religious care of all such remains which might fall in their way.[4]

In 1859 with the support of the Russian Tsar Tischendorf returned to the monastery of St. Catherine. To his delight, he is once again shown the codex:

> Full of joy, which this time I had the self-command to conceal from the steward and the rest of the community, I asked, as if in a careless way, for permission to take the manuscript into my sleeping chamber to look over it more at leisure. There by myself I could give way to the transport of joy, which I felt. I knew that I held in my hand the most precious Biblical treasure in existence—a document whose age and importance exceeded that of all the manuscripts, which I had ever examined during twenty years' study of the subject. I cannot now, I confess, recall all the emotions which I felt in that exciting moment with such a diamond in my possession. Though my lamp was dim, and the night cold, I sat down at once to transcribe the Epistle of Barnabas.

Eventually the monastery presented the manuscript to the Tsar of Russia as protector of the Greek Church. When the communists took over the Russian government, they had little use for such a Christian manuscript, so in 1933 the Soviet Union sold the manuscript to the British Museum for £100,000.

I consulted an edition of Codex Sinaiticus containing the text of the New Testament, Barnabas, and the Shepherd of Hermas published in 1863. Copyists and readers of John's description of the women at the cross read at 19:25: "Mariam (Μαριάμ) the one of Klopas and Mariam of Magdala" and at 20:1: "On the Sabbath day Mariam of Magdala came early while it was still dark to the tomb and saw the stone rolled away from the entrance to the tomb." At 20:11 the text reads: "Now Mariam (Μαριάμ) stood outside the tomb weeping." As we know, at first she mistakes Jesus for a gardener, and it is only when he speaks that she recognizes the speaker. What does he call her? "Μαριάμ!" She turns to him and says in Hebrew (namely, Palestinian Aramaic rendered into Greek) "Ραββουνι!" The text concludes with the proclamation of Mariam of Magdala to the disciples: "I have seen the Lord!"

How should we render the name Μαριάμ of Codex Sinaiticus into English? In our deliberations we should certainly take into account the Greek translation of Hebrew Scriptures (known as the Septuagint, or LXX) from modern or ancient editions of this text. From these we find that the name

Μαριάμ is always the Greek translation of Miriam, Moses' sister. Take for example the words of Yahweh in Micah 6:4, "For I brought you up from the land of Egypt, and redeemed you from the house of slavery; and I sent before you Moses, Aaron, and Miriam (LXX: Μωϋσῆν καὶ Ααρων καὶ Μαριάμ)." In Greek the names Aaron and Miriam don't decline, but the Greek translator of the Hebrew text has rendered the name Moses into the accusative case. The transliterated Greek reading Μαριάμ occurs throughout the LXX, at Exodus 6:20; 15:20,21; Numbers 12:1,4,5,10,15; Numbers 20:1; 26:59; Deuteronomy 24:9 and 1 Chronicles 5:29, as well as Micah 6:4 discussed above.

The tenacity of this reading can be demonstrated by other renditions of the Greek LXX, for example into Coptic at Exodus 6:20, 15:20, and 21, where the same rendition, Mariam, is constant in the Coptic text.[5] An early Coptic papyrus of Exodus 1–15, Papyrus Bodmer XVI, concludes with the song of Moses (Miriam). The Coptic renders the Hebrew name in Exodus 15:20 **ΜΔΡΙΔΜ** (Mariam) with a corrector's hand adding an ϩ over the letter Δ.[6] Later in the same verse the name is rendered **ΜΔΡΙϩΔΜ**, presumably as the corrector intended. In Philo's first-century allegorical description of Numbers 12:12[7] or Numbers 12:14,[8] the same Greek form appears. Thus, readers of Codex Sinaiticus who knew the Septuagint (and other ancient translations of that text such as the Coptic) would understand the woman of John 20 who encounters the resurrected Jesus to have the same name as the sister of Moses.

Identity and Perception

The question of who Jesus sees in John 20, of what name she has, and of how translators translate that name is one example of what one might call the Miriamic Secret. Why does the Marcan Jesus enjoin secrecy on the part of those healed? Perhaps because Jesus' identity runs counter to their expectations and experience. Demons and others call him Son of God. The disciples' refrain is: "Who is he?" Jesus on the other hand prefers to speak about Son of man. Identity involves perception. Jesus enjoins temporal silence on the part of the healed/reader until perception can be changed.

In Puccini's opera, Turandot keeps all Peking awake to discover, on penalty of death, the anonymous stranger's name. Just before morning, the stranger discloses his own name to her in a declaration of love. To the assembled court later that morning Turandot's declaration that she knows his name can only mean his death for them. However, when she sings instead that his name is "Love!" she has kept both the secret of his name (and thereby his life) and at the same time disclosed her feelings for him. This must have confounded popular perceptions of the ice princess, especially without sleep. So perception of identity varies according to viewpoint.

There are several levels of vision accessible to us in John's text: Who does Jesus see? Who does the omniscient narrator of John's gospel see? Who do scribes copying Greek texts of the NT see? And who do editors of modern critical editions of the Greek NT, translators, and commentators see? Of course, they do not have to see the same thing.

Who does Jesus see? A woman weeping, seeking. Of course we impute to him sight, but in reality the resurrected Jesus speaks to rather than "sees" her and others in John 20–21. Naturally he speaks in Greek: "Woman, why are you weeping? Whom do you seek?" To these questions she responds as if to the gardener: "Sir, if you have borne him away tell me where you have laid him and I will take him." So he tries another language, not Greek but Palestinian Aramaic: "Mariam!" (or "Maria" according to other manuscripts than Codex Sinaiticus, mostly from the Western text tradition, as table 1 indicates).

Who does she see? First, the stone rolled away from the tomb. Then (v. 11–12), two angels in white sitting in the tomb at the head and feet where the body of Jesus had lain. Then, obscurely through her tears—someone she perceives to be the gardener? She speaks to him in Greek: "Sir, if you have borne him away tell me where you have laid him and I will take him." Then after he says her name (in Aramaic rendered into Greek), she addresses him directly in Palestinian Aramaic: "Rabbouni" (as shown in the Targum fragment from the Cairo Genizah).[9]

Who does the omniscient narrator of John's gospel see? For all intents and purposes the narrator and Jesus speak the same language in John 20:1, 11, and 16 by describing and speaking to Mariam if we follow the readings of Codex Sinaiticus, and for v. 11 a corrector of the second-century papyrus P66 containing a text of John's gospel.[10] From a literary point of view, the whole picture of Mariam in the text begins with the story of the sisters Mariam and Martha in 11, and the anointing of Jesus by the same Mariam in 12 (so 11:2). The presence of Μαριάμ ἡ Μαγδαληνή in 19:25 leads directly to her visit to the tomb in 20:1. The literary connections however are manifest in the text: in 11 and 20 (the resurrection stories of Lazarus and Jesus) at least two women with the same name appear. Both weep over a dead man at a tomb; both are consoled (11:31,33; 20:11,15); both accrue followers (11:32,45; 20:18); both experience resurrection (11:43,45; 20:16).

Who do editors of modern critical editions of the Greek NT see in John 20? The editors of the Nestle 27th edition at John 20:1 and 11 judge the Greek text to read first Mary Magdalen and then only secondarily Mariam in the footnotes. But sixteen verses later the same text reads differently:

John 20:16 "Jesus says to her 'Mariam!' Turning around, that one (f.) says to him in Hebrew 'Rabboni' (which means 'teacher')."[11] This latter reading continues in v. 18, wherein Μαριάμ ἡ Μαγδαληνη (attested by P66 ℵ and others) or alternately Μαρία (attested by A D W Bohairic Coptic and others) announced to the disciples, "I have seen the Lord! And he said these things to me." Thus the editors imply that the narrator describes her as Mary Magdalen in vv. 1 and 11, but Jesus identifies her as "Mariam" (v. 16). Having been named such by Jesus, she as Mariam of Magdala announces the good news to the disciples in v. 18. Why does the reading of v. 18 supported by Codex Sinaiticus and P66 not obtain for v. 11 (where the same reading is supported by the same manuscripts but relegated to footnotes)?[12]

Whom do commentators see? Raymond Brown in his commentary on John's Gospel[13] says: "Mary!" He continues: "The best textual witnesses have Mariam here instead of Maria which seems to be the normal form for Mary Magdalene."

He reviews the textual evidence where B = Vaticanus; S = Sinaiticus; A = Alexandrinus; and P = Papyrus #66 dated about 200 CE (table 1).

Thus from earlier commentators such as Archbishop Bernard in 1929 ("Probably the Hebrew form Mariam should be adopted throughout")[14] to modern ones such as Raymond Brown, a consensus exists that Mariam represents the better reading. This is also the reading of Codex Sinaiticus. But what does this name mean?

On the question of meaning, Brown is dismissive: "Since Mariam is closer to Masoretic Hebrew 'Miryam,' some have proposed that John portrays Jesus as speaking to Mary 'in Hebrew,' even as John portrays Magdalene as answering Jesus 'in Hebrew.' The whole theory is dubious on a number of scores." We know that Hebrew names are rendered into Greek as indeclinable nouns:

Gabriel: Γαβριηλ
Moses: Μωϋσεως
Anna: Αννα

Brown points out that in Jesus' time מרים is represented both as Μαριάμ and as Μαρία. He continues by noting that it is not correct to say that Μαρία is a Hellenized form since Jerusalem inscriptions have מרים. E. Y. Kutscher[15] shows that מריה is a back-formation from מרים to מרין due to the fact that ן was understood as an appended nasal.

Table 1.1

John 19:25	Maria B, A	Mariam S
John 20:1	Maria B	Mariam S, A
John 20:11	Maria B, A, P66*	Mariam S P66c
John 20:16	Maria A	Mariam S, B
John 20:18	Maria A	Mariam S, B, P66

Evidence from inscriptions notwithstanding, we are still left with a second-century papyrus (P66) and a fourth-century Greek text (Codex Sinaiticus) for John 20 identifying a woman by the name Mariam, the same form for which occurs in the LXX and elsewhere to describe Moses' sister. This form is also attested in the noncanonical Gospel of Peter 50,1: "Straightway on the Lord's day, Mariam of Magdala, disciple of the Lord."[16]

Luke

In the birth narratives of Luke 1–2 the name Mariam Μαριάμ occurs in the Nestle Greek text. The angel speaks to her (Luke 1:30): "Do not fear Μαριάμ." In modern critical editions of the Greek New Testament for Luke's gospel, no alternative readings in the footnotes are listed.

What does the form of the name mean? The commentaries opine either nothing or something. For example, the most recent commentary on Luke 1–9:50 by Professor François Bovon of Harvard Divinity School[17] argues: Μαριάμ means "Mary." In a footnote he refers to the various ways of spelling Mary's name outlined in an article, "Maria,"[18] by Gerhard Schneider and his own article.[19] In this footnote he documents the two forms for Mary's name found in the NT: Μαριάμ and Μαρία, and adds that "the name Maria came about under the Latin influence of homophony. The use of the form Maria seems to have been preferred in those milieux which were in contact with the Romans, then in Christian families."

It is a matter of perspective. Clearly Luke uses the two forms interchangeably. Use of the name Μαριάμ only in Luke 1–2 and not elsewhere (8:2) might well indicate that Luke is bilingual. We will have to wait until the English edition of volume two of Bovon's commentary to see his explanation of Luke 10:42. In the meantime, all Greek manuscripts including Codex Sinaiticus read Μαριάμ. A unanimity of textual witnesses for Matthew 13:55 also read the name Μαριάμ for the mother of Jesus, presumably for the Semitic audience of Nazarenes in Jesus' hometown (13:54). This is also the reading of the Coptic text of Matthew from Codex Scheide at 13:55.[20]

Tal Ilan offers a different perspective from that of Bovon.[21] Diverse texts, funerary inscriptions, papyrus, and ostraca from 330 BCE to 200 CE, she concludes, indicate that 50 percent of all the women of the time were called Mariamme (Mariam) or Salome. Maria is the shorter form of the first name. Thus all forty-four instances of the first name in whatever form it occurs are listed as Mariamme. These two names were so popular because they were typically Hasmonean: Salome after Queen Salomezion Alexandra and Mariamme after Mariamme the Hasmonean, Herod's beloved wife.

Josephus

Josephus, the first-century historian, uses virtually the same form of the name for the sister of Moses and the wife of Herod the Great: Μαριαμμε or Μαριαμη. *Jewish Antiquities* II, 220, describes the repose of baby Moses in wicker-work made of papyrus, similar in shape to a basket, which his parents put on the river, leaving his welfare in God's hands. "The river received and carried it, and Mariame, the sister of the child, having been bidden by her mother, went along beside him as he was carried to see where the wicker-work would go." As is well known, events in Josephus's *Antiquities* seem to be selective; amongst other missing episodes, nothing of Miriam's leprosy in Numbers 12 is mentioned.

Apocryphal Acts

In the second-century Apocryphal Acts Μαριάμ refers to the mother of Jesus (Acts of Andrew and Matthew 12 quoting Matthew 13:55 with a variant of Μαρία). Is this an echo of Luke 1–2? Acts of Thomas 143 on the other hand refers to Μαρία.

The Acts of Philip and the Martyrdom of Philip[22] in contrast, appear to distinguish between Μαρία the one who bore Jesus (Acts Phil. 6,13,16), and Μαριαμμη or Μαριαμνη described as Philip's sister (Acts Phil. 8,2; Mart. 2,4,6; 21,4; 42,3). Each has different functions. However, occasionally Mariamne takes on Marian traits.

> 94 Now it happened that when the Savior divided the apostles and each went forth according to his lot, that it fell to Philip to go to the country of the Greeks: and he thought it hard, and wept. And Mariamne *his sister* (it was she that made ready the bread and salt at the breaking of bread, but Martha was she that ministered to the multitudes and labored much) seeing it, went to Jesus and said: Lord, don't you see how my brother is

vexed because of this Greek land? 95 And he said: I know, chosen among women; but go with him and encourage him, for I know that he is a wrathful and rash man, and if we let him go alone he will bring many retributions on men. But behold, I will send Bartholomew and John to suffer hardships in the same city, because of the much wickedness of them that dwell there; for they worship the viper, the mother of snakes. And you, Mariamne, change your appearance and your whole female form and go with Philip. And to Philip he said: Why art thou fearful? for I am always with thee. [italics added]

In this passage Mariamne takes the active role and Philip the passive. Is she here taking on an Aaronic role in regard to Philip's Moses-role? She speaks for Philip, who sits mute and despondent, preferring a non-Greek city. Moreover, like her brother, Mariamne speaks Aramaic. Previous scholarship has clarified the connections between Mary Magdalen and Mariamne in regard to both New Testament and heterodox, particularly Gnostic, traditions. Here I am arguing that Mariamne has other more Miriamic traits. At the same time, she is described in Marian terms. Jesus, in response to her request, calls Mariamne "chosen of women."

Mariamne not only has a brother Philip but also Nicanora, a twin sister, both "daughters of the same mother who bore us twins" (Mart. 9). Whether or not Martha is another sister is unclear. Nor is there any clear allusion to John 11. Their roles, however, are different. Mariamne "prepared the bread and the salt at the breaking of bread," while Martha "ministered to the multitudes and labored much." Andrew McGowan, in a book examining the varied and scattered body of evidence for the early use of foods other than bread and wine in Christian ritual meals, suggests that this passage is from a different and more primitive stratum within the Acts of Philip.[23]

Mariamne continues listening to her brother. She speaks Hebrew. Eventually, however, she is martyred; Martyrdom of Philip 1: "And Bartholomew shall go to Lycaonia and be crucified there, and Mariamne's body shall be laid up in the river Jordan."

The Syriac Versions

The Syriac translation of the four gospels probably dates to the late fourth century and forms the basis for the mid-fifth-century Peshitta from the Koine Greek. Without consulting all the critical editions of the Old Syriac, it is nevertheless possible to say provisionally that there is never any variation from the Syriac Mar-yam in every instance of the Greek noun(s) Μαρία or Μαριάμ in the Peshitta.

Mar-yam is the form of Mary's name that was always (as far as we know) used in the old Creeds in the Syriac churches, so perhaps that liturgical usage would have overridden any scribal tendency ever to use a different orthography. Furthermore, since Semitic names are not declined for case, any variation in the ending of a proper name would be quite unusual. The Syriac version of Maria would be Mar-Ya, which is the standard Syriac word for "Lord" and the primary term used in the Peshitta to render YHWH. A Syriac Bible reader would normally understand Mar-Ya as Lord, not as Mary. So with Mar-Ya ruled out, with Mar-Yam well established liturgically, with no custom of variant case endings on proper names, and with Mar-Yam used in Peshitta Exodus for Miriam, it is likely that no Syriac variants of the name Mary/Miriam were ever used in the Bible.

Readers of the Syriac Bible would thus view Mary the mother of Jesus as having the same name as Miriam in Exodus and Mary Magdalene. Where there are three names in English there is one in Syriac. In this respect, the Syriac mirrors exactly the original Palestinian reality: In Palestinian Hebrew or Western Jewish Aramaic, the name of Jesus' mother and the others would have been exactly the same as Miriam in Exodus. The shift from Miriam to "Mary" is a by-product of the move from Hebrew/Aramaic to Greek (and then Latin).

Pistis Sophia

Although there is no scholarly consensus, the text of Pistis Sophia (PS) is conventionally dated to the third century.[24] Three sections of this long work probably correspond to three books; the fourth section is perhaps an independent work. The title probably derives from a passage in Eugnostos (NHC V, 10,11) and the Sophia of Jesus Christ (NHC III, 106,21) identifying the female name of the Savior as Sophia, generator of all, whom some call Pistis.[25] In PS, Pistis Sophia is thus both the female aspect of the Savior and his consort. It is she whose imprisonment and subsequent deliverance the books describe. In form PS, like the Sophia of Jesus Christ, is a (Gnostic) resurrection dialogue between the Savior and the disciples in which past, present, and future events and teachings are clarified. Recent translations of this text identify Maria as the first to engage Jesus in dialogue.[26] However, the Coptic actually names Mariam:

Now it happened when Mariam heard these words as the Savior was saying them, she stared (in a trance) into the air for an hour and said: "My

Lord, command me so that I speak boldly." Jesus the compassionate answered and said to Mariam: "Mariam, blessed one whom I will complete
in all the mysteries of the height, speak boldly, for you are she whose heart
is more directed to the kingdom of heaven than all your brothers."[27]

Bold or confident speech is the goal of ancient rhetorical training and
education and the mark of a free man. From the sixth-century BCE Plato's
Republic 557b to the first-century CE Acts 28:30 it connotes freedom of speech.
Rarely, however, does it describe women's speech (cf. *Elektra* 1055). It is Jesus' response to her request that moves Mariam from mystical trance to articulate words.

Mariam interprets parables of Jesus and the writings of Hebrew Prophets
(Isa. 19) as the disarming of the powerful archons. Philip picks up questioning once he puts down his pen (he has been writing every word). He too
asks for clarity about the bondage of the archons. To both interlocutors, first
to Philip and then Mariam, Jesus explains a strange idea of turning the archons' paths for the salvation of all souls. "But when I had taken a third part
of their power, I turned their sphere to cause them to spend time looking
to the right. I turned their whole path and their whole course and I caused
the path of their course to be accelerated so that they might be purified
quickly and they might go upwards quickly."[28] "Turning" is, I believe, a technical term in PS to describe the orientation of the archons toward divine
revelation. It is similar to the understanding of "turning" in John 20:14, 16
and Revelation 1:12 as explained by Professor D'Angelo in chapter 6 of this
volume.

Mariam asks further questions, in particular, the central one of the text,
namely, how Pistis Sophia herself is in the place of the twenty-four emanations (she has been found below the thirteenth aeon).[29] She clarifies the
laments of Pistis Sophia as the language of the biblical Psalms;[30] she interprets the role of Philip, Thomas, and Matthew as the fulfillment of Deuteronomy 19:15,[31] she identifies the seats of the disciples to the right of Jesus as the
fulfillment of Psalm 81;[32] and she explains biblical phrases "the last will become first and the first will become last" (e.g., Matt. 19:30; 20:16)[33] and Psalm
84:10–11 "Mercy and Truth have kissed each other; and righteousness and
peace have kissed each other."[34] In all these questions and clarifications,
Mariam articulates the plight of the human condition in the fate of Pistis
Sophia, the discovery of self-alienation, its origins, and the means of redemption. To be sure, other disciples and Jesus' own mother Maria also dialogue with Jesus, but no one plays as large a role in the three books as
Mariam.

Traits

There are at least three traits characteristic of Miriam in Second Temple literature and the New Testament:

> she is a sister
> she is a prophet
> and she is disbelieved.

Each of these traits characterizes descriptions of Miriam in Second Temple and rabbinic texts. Each appears in descriptions of Miriamic figures in the New Testament: Mariam in Luke prophesies the forthcoming birth of her child; Mary/Miriam, portrayed as sister of Martha in John, sees the risen Christ and announces this to the disciples. In the longer ending of Mark (16:9) she is disbelieved.

Sister

We can see the first two of these traits in Exodus 15:20: "Then Miriam, the prophetess, the sister of Aaron, took a timbrel in her hand; and all the women went out after her with timbrels and dancing."[35]

The identification of Mariam as a "sister" continues in the Acts of Philip above and in the Gospel of Philip, wherein she is identified as sister, companion, and mother. The Gospel of Philip 59,8–11 explains:

> There were three who always walked with the Lord: Mary (ΜΑΡΙΖΑΜ), his mother; her sister; and Miriam of Magdala (ΜΑΓΑΑΛΗΝΗ), who was called his companion; For Miriam (ΜΑΡΙΖΑΜ) is his sister, his mother and his companion.

Of course the interpretation of this passage is much debated. At face value the text describes three women who share the same name. But the Gospel of Philip is interested in double aspects of human identity (we might say earthly and heavenly), in this case the heavenly counterparts of three women closest to Jesus, all of whom share the same name. Their heavenly identity is that of Holy Spirit or Sophia.[36]

Prophetic Office

Prophecy implies vision. The Lukan identification of Miriam as Jesus' mother alluding to Miriam's prophetic office thus provides Jesus' mother with prophetic abilities we see in Luke 1–2 in the Magnificat and her internal reflection on the words of the angel. We note further that Jesus inherits a prophetic mantle from his mother: in his first sermon for the home crowd at Nazareth in Luke 4, his prophetic message from Isaiah "The Spirit of the Lord is upon me" echoes themes of reversal from the earlier Magnificat.

In the noncanonical birth story called the Protevangelium of James, one passage alone calls Jesus' mother "Mariamme," probably because the passage describes her prophetic abilities (when pregnant). In 17,1–2 Joseph saddles his ass to avoid the embarrassment of enrolling a pregnant wife:

> And he saddled his ass and sat her on it; his son led it, and Samuel [Joseph] followed. And they drew near to the third mile(stone). And Joseph turned round and saw her sad, and said within himself: "Perhaps that which is within her is paining her." And again Joseph turned around and saw her laughing. And he said to her: "Mariamme, why is it that I see your face at one time laughing and at another sad?" And she said to him: "Joseph, I see with my eyes two peoples, one weeping and lamenting, and one rejoicing and exulting."

In this passage, use of a different form of the name signifies prophetic activity because the form of the name connects it to that of Miriam. Alternate forms of the name continue as late as the eleventh- and twelfth-century Old English Gospel of Pseudo-Matthew to indicate prophetic activity:

> Sancta Marian . . . is called star of the sea because the star of the sea shows where east and west, where south and north are to seafaring people at night. In the same way therefore the right way to eternal life was shown by the holy virgin Sancta Marian to those who sat in darkness for a long time and in the shadow of death.[37]

The prophetic role of Miriam and Aaron is seen in their critique of Moses in Numbers 12:1–2: "Miriam and Aaron spoke against Moses because of the Cushite woman whom he had married, for he had married a Cushite woman; and they said, 'Has the Lord indeed spoken only through Moses? Has he not spoken through us also?' And the Lord heard it."

Upon this passage Philo comments that when Miriam spoke against Moses, sense perception was shameless and bold in daring to find fault with Moses.[38] Here Miriam's prophetic gifts are labeled "sense perception" and of lesser value compared to *Nous*, or rational thought, particularly when challenging male prophetic activity. Elsewhere, however, the same allegory is used to Miriam's advantage. She personifies: "sense perception made pure and clean. For it is right with both mind and sense to render hymns and sing blessings to the Godhead without delay."[39] Here the sense perception of a woman is linked to *Nous* when praising God in Exodus 15:20 but lesser perceptivity when critiquing male prophets. The biblical text constrains Philo to praise Miriam's prophetic role.

Amongst early Christian writers 1 Clement 4,11 describes the zeal (or jealousy) of Aaron and Mariam in their critique of Moses.

Pseudo-Philo in the second-century Latin translation of a Hebrew text known as *Biblical Antiquities* 9,10 speaks of Miriam's prophetic office after the time of the New Testament:

> The spirit of God came upon Miriam one night, and she saw a dream (*Et spiritus Dei incidit in Mariam nocte, et vidit somnium*) . . . and reported it to her parents in the morning, saying, "I had a vision this night, and behold a man was standing in a linen garment and he said to me, 'Go and say to your parents, "Behold the child who will be born of you will be cast forth into the water; likewise through him the water will be dried up. And I will work signs through him and save my people, and he will exercise leadership always."'"[40]

Miriam's parents do not believe her prediction that their unborn child will save his people. Their disbelief recalls Abraham's response to the prediction of Isaac's birth (23,5) and anticipates the disbelief associated with the birth stories of Samson and Samuel. Without the benefit of the Hebrew midwives of the Hebrew Bible, Jochebed hides the infant in her womb for three months. When concealment is no longer possible, the prenatally circumcised newborn is placed on the riverbank in an ark constructed by his mother. Moved by her dreams, Pharaoh's daughter comes to bathe in the river, finds the baby, recognizes him as a Hebrew, and immediately begins to nurse him.

The disbelief of parents in birth stories is echoed in the words of Mariam to the annunciation recorded by Luke: "How can this be, seeing I have not known a man?" However, I would argue this is part of a broader Miriamic theme since another echo of a disbelieving reaction to a prophetic announcement is likewise found in the reaction of the disciples to the words of Mary Magdalene in the longer ending of Mark.

Another prophetic aspect of Miriam's role is described in the third- or fourth-century CE midrash Exodus Rabbah 1.22. Commenting on the verse "And his sister stood afar off" (Exod. 2:4), the midrash says:

> Why did Miriam stand afar off? Rabbi Amram in the name of Rab said: Because Miriam prophesied, "My Mother is destined to give birth to a son who will save Israel," and when the house was flooded with light at the birth of Moses, her father arose and kissed her head and said: "My daughter, your prophecy has been fulfilled." This is the meaning of: "And Miriam the prophetess, the sister of Aaron, took a timbrel" (Ex 15:20); "The sister of Aaron but not of Moses?" [She is so-called] because in fact she said this prophecy when she was yet only the sister of Aaron, Moses not having been born yet. Now that she was casting him into the river, her mother struck her on the head saying: "My daughter, what about your prophecy?" This is why it says "And his sister stood afar off" to know what would be the outcome of the prophecy.[41]

Is it possible that the description of the women in Mark 15:40 alludes to this action of Miriam? "There were also women looking on from afar, among whom were Mary Magdalene, and Mary the mother of James the younger and of Joses, and Salome."[42]

In Coptic texts discussing or alluding to biblical women prophets the question is again simply how the name Mariam (Coptic **ⲘⲀⲢⲒϨⲀⲘ**) should be translated and what it means. In the Coptic Gospel of Mary, for example, the name occurs at 9,21; 10,1,7; 17,7; 18,1; and the title at the end of the text: **ⲠⲈⲨⲀⲄⲄⲈⲖⲒⲞⲚ ⲔⲀⲦⲀ ⲘⲀⲢⲒϨⲀⲘⲘ**. Two passages indicate Mariam's prophetic abilities and the reaction of disbelief. I surmise that both prophetic abilities and the reactions of disbelief are Miriamic traits, familiar from the biblical account. First comes vision and then opposition. Gospel of Mary 10:[43]

> Mariam said to them: "I will now speak to you of that which has not been given to you to hear. I had a vision of the teacher and I said to him: 'Lord, I see you now in this vision.' And he answered: 'You are blessed, for the sight of me does not disturb you. There where is the *Nous* (Mind, Intellect), lies the treasure.'"

After the vision comes the opposition in Gospel of Mary 17:

> Having said all this, Mariam became silent, for it was in silence that the Teacher spoke to her. Then Andrew began to speak and said to his broth-

ers: "Tell me, what do you think of these things she has been telling us? As for me I do not believe that the Teacher would speak like this. These ideas are too different from those we have known." And Peter added: "How is it possible that the Teacher talked in this manner with a woman about secrets of which we ourselves are ignorant? Must we change our customs and listen to this woman? Did he really choose her and prefer her to us?" 18 Then Mariam wept and answered him: "My brother Peter, what can you be thinking? Do you believe that this is just my own imagination, that I invented this vision? Or do you believe that I would lie about our Teacher?" At this Levi spoke up: "Peter, you have always been hot-tempered, and now we see you repudiating a woman just as our adversaries do. Yet if the Teacher held her worthy, who are you to reject her? Surely the Teacher knew her very well, for he loved her more than us. Therefore let us atone, and become fully human (*Anthropos*), so that the Teacher can take root in us. Let us grow as he demanded of us, and walk forth to spread the gospel, without trying to lay down any rules and laws other than those he witnessed."

No one knows more about the Gospel of Mary than Professor Karen King.[44] So let me point out only that in addition to the Miriamic traits of name, prophetic vision, and subsequent opposition, Mariam in 18,2 identifies Peter as "my brother." To be sure, Mariam herself (9,14) and Andrew (17,11) address the group as "brothers." But Peter speaks to her directly: "Sister!" (10,1) and she calls him "My brother Peter!" (18,2). Other disciples address each other directly by name (Levi to Peter at 18,7) but not as brother. Of course the text as we have it is fragmentary, but in its present form we have Mariam and Peter addressing each other as brother and sister when Peter wishes to hear her vision and when she defends it. Behind this I see echoes of Miriam as sister of Moses acting in concert with Aaron (Levi in Gos. Mary?).

Another text connecting a Miriam figure (Coptic ⲘⲀⲢⲒⳌⲀⲘⲘⲎ) to Peter in a context of prophetic utterance is found in the Psalms of Heraclei-des discussed by Professor Coyle in chapter 10 of this volume.

The primacy of Mary Magdalene in the proclamation of the resurrec-tion has been affirmed from the late third century onward: Joseph's Bible Notes (*Hypomnestikon*) 152 list the ten epiphanies of the Lord to his own af-ter he was raised from the dead as "First, to Maria and her companions at the tomb; second to Kephas alone."[45]

The prophetic role of Mariam as a composite figure with traits of Luke 1–2 in addition to prophetic vision continues in the fifth-century *Questions of Bartholomew,* wherein Jesus answers Bartholomew's questions but then vanishes. As they are in Chritir with Μαρία Bartholomew asks Peter, Andrew, and John (2,1) to join him in asking Mariam "she who is highly favored, how she conceived the incomprehensible or how she carries him who cannot be carried or how she bore so much greatness." However, in the event Bartholomew alone asks this question. Mariam answers: "Do not ask me concerning this mystery. If I begin to tell you, fire will come out of my mouth and consume the whole earth." However, not wishing to deny the apostles a hearing, Mariam first prays to the Creator of the Universe to be allowed to speak to the apostles.

Having first arranged the apostles in various supporting positions around her as she sits on the ground, so as to prevent the loosening of her limbs when she begins to speak, she tells the story of a theophany promising that in three years she would conceive a son and "through him the whole world shall be saved. As she was saying this, fire came from her mouth and the world was on the point of being burned up. Then came Jesus quickly and said to Μαριάμ: 'Say no more today or my whole creation will come to an end.'"

To be sure, others have noticed the Miriamic secret. One of the first people to observe a connection between the Hebrew prophet Miriam and the Mariam of John 20 was the thirteenth-century Parisian Peter Abelard in his thirteenth sermon for Easter. Peter notes the prophetic office of one and the apostolic office of the other; to both the Lord revealed mysteries that they disclosed in words:

> The pages of the Old, as much as of the New Testament bear witness to the extent to which exultation of the paschal solemnity concerns the devotion and the honor of women. For just as the Pascha was first celebrated in Egypt by the people of God, and that night its faithful were set free through the drowning of the Egyptians, not men alone but women also gave praise to the Lord with hymns of thanks, as Exodus tells us. For there it is written: Then Moses and the sons of Israel sang this hymn to the Lord.

> There is also said concerning the hymn of the women: "For Maria the prophetess, the sister of Aaron, took up a timbrel in her hand. And all the women went out after her with drums and with chorus with which they sang saying: Let us sing to the Lord. . . ." Now listen carefully to the manner in which the song of the women depicts such a great mystery. For here Maria who led the singing of that chorus of women, must be understood to have been a virgin, since it does not say that she had a husband. And she had other privileges as well, not only that of singing

is recorded, as did Moses and the people, but she is also said to have been a prophetess, and to have held a timbrel in her hand. How is a prophet to be understood unless as one who saw? When she sang her vision, that is her revelation, she revealed also through her words the mysteries which the Lord had shown her.

Peter Abelard infers that the second Mary or Miriam alludes to the first:

Let us turn then to the New Testament, and here there is a Maria and with her were other women and this other Miriam had with her devoted women to whom the Lord first showed the joy of his resurrection (*et in hac Maria et caeteris cum ea feminis alteram Mariam, et cum ipsa devotas feminas, quibus primum Dominus suae resurrectionis gaudium exhibuit*). Let us understand this thoroughly and note how many details are closely fitting. For the one is recorded as a prophet, the other is called apostle of the apostles (*apostolorum apostola*). The one took up a corporal drum, the other had one which was spiritual. And as she was the more devoted to the living Lord, she was the more afflicted by his death, and was as one done to death. Therefore she deserved first to enjoy the consolation of the resurrection, since hers was the greatest affliction and grief at his death. She is said to be the apostle of the apostles, that is to say, the herald of the heralds, because the Lord first directed her to the apostles so that she might proclaim the joy of resurrection to them. That Maria was the first to sing to the others her song, and before the others she is first empowered in the joy of her resurrection. And she was first to sing proclaiming that which she was first to see. After her, this resurrection joy was given to other women, before it was given to the apostles, to the men. Thus the Lord said, directing the apostles, "Go and tell my brothers that they should go to Galilee." It is thus ludicrous to imagine that there might be an order (*ordo*) thought more blessed or more honorable. For in the Old Testament the Pascha is told in advance to men but it records that thereafter women sang. In our Pascha, however, that is the day of the Lord's resurrection, the song of rejoicing at the appearance of the resurrection is made known to women before the men. For the Hebrew Pascha, a Greek term, is called in Latin a passing over. In the old Pascha, the Lord crossed over Egypt, and killed the firstborn, and set his people free through the crossing of the Red Sea. And so the feast is known by the name of Pass-over. It is not inappropriate that the present Pascha, that is to say the day of the Lord's resurrection, is so-called. For this is the change in human nature from mortality to immortality, from corruption to incorruption which passing over and movement is in Christ.[46]

Abelard concludes that men and women will be freed of their gender and will resemble the phoenix, symbol of Christ.

Conclusion

I hope the Miriamic secret is no longer a secret. What does the occurrence of the name Μαριάμ found in the Greek translation of Hebrew Scriptures and in the Greek of Philo of Alexandria, Josephus, Clement of Rome, the Gospel of Peter, the first-century P66, the fourth-century Codex Sinaiticus, the fifth-century Questions of Bartholomew; the Latin of Pseudo-Philo's *Biblical Antiquities;* and the Coptic of the Gospel of Mary and Pistis Sophia mean? And in sources I have not discussed, such as Greek inscriptions? Is it just an alternative spelling of "Mary" that has been ignored and deemed insignificant? Or something else? And what does the preservation and recurrence of this name mean for the interpretation of Mary of Nazareth or Mary Magdalen? I am arguing that it signifies Miriamic traits of prophetic vision and authority and that it warrants a retranslation of the name where the Greek text reads "Mariam." This translation is more faithful to the Greek. Moreover it renders the name of Jesus' mother and the first apostle of John's gospel in a way that identifies these figures as Semitic rather than Latin, that is, not European. By way of analogy, one can see the profound effects of translating Romans 16:7 correctly to reflect the presence of a woman apostle, Junia, before Paul. Yet there is more. To hear the name of Jesus' mother as Miriam or the resurrected Jesus' cry to Mary in the garden as "Mariam!" is to be drawn into the world of the text and to hear it as the text's authors intended the name to be heard. That we experience it as different is a consequence of our preference for Latin. Everett Fox has given us a model as Martin Buber and Franz Rosenzweig did before him. Now we must begin to do for the New Testament what they did for the Hebrew Bible. And then in the call of parents for their daughters in our playgrounds we will hear a world from which we have hitherto been severed.

NOTES

1. For the most part this spelling of the name will be used.
2. *Codex Sinaiticus* (Lipsiae: F. A. Brockhaus, 1863). The facsimile edition is He-

len Lake and Kirsopp Lake, *Codex Sinaiticus Petropolitanus,* 2 vols. (Oxford: Clarendon, 1911–1922).

3. Kurt and Barbara Aland, *The Text of the New Testament* (Grand Rapids, Mich.: Eerdmans, 1987), 107.

4. Constantin von Tischendorf, *When Were Our Gospels Written? An Argument by Constantine Tischendorf—With a Narrative of the Discovery of the Sinaitic Manuscript* (New York: American Tract Society, 1866).

5. Melvin K. H. Peters, ed., *A Critical Edition of the Coptic (Bohairic) Pentateuch,* vol. 2: *Exodus* (Atlanta: Scholars Press, 1986), 15, 42.

6. *Bibliotheca Bodmeriana: La collection des Papyrus Bodmer,* vol. 6 (Muenchen: K. G. Saur, 2000).

7. *Legum Allegoria (Allegorical Interpretation)* I.76.6 (hereafter *LA*).

8. *LA* II.66.4.

9. Matthew Black, *An Aramaic Approach to the Gospels and Acts,* 3rd ed. (Oxford: Clarendon Press, 1967), 21.

10. *Bibliotheca Bodmeriana,* vol. 2.

11. λέγει αὐτῇ Ἰησοῦς Μαριάμ στραφεῖσα ἐκείνη λέγει αὐτῷ Ἑβραϊστί ραββουνι (ὁ λέγεται διδάσκαλε).

12. P66 at John 20:11 actually reads Μαριάμ with the last letter raised not for space reasons but perhaps added by a corrector. *Bibliotheca Bodmeriana,* vol. 2, 143.

13. Raymond Brown, *The Gospel of John,* vol. 2 (New York: Anchor Bible/ Doubleday, 1970), 990.

14. Archbishop J. H. Bernard, *A Critical and Exegetical Commentary on the Gospel according to St. John,* vol. 2 (New York: Charles Scribner's Sons, 1929), 632.

15. E. Y. Kutscher, *Scripta Hierosolymitana,* vol. 4: *The Language of the 'Genesis Apocryphon': A Preliminary Study,* in *Aspects of the Dead Sea Scrolls,* ed. C. Rabin and Y. Yadin (Jerusalem: Magnes of the Hebrew University, 1957), 1–35.

16. Ὄρθρου δε τῆς κυριακῆς Μαριάμ ἡ Μαγδαληνή, μαθήτρια τοῦ Κυρίου.

17. François Bovon, *Luke* 1 (Philadelphia: Fortress, 2002).

18. Gerhard Schneider, "Maria," in *EDNT,* vol. 2 (Grand Rapids, Mich.: Eerdmans, 1991).

19. "Le privilège pascal de Marie-Madeleine," *New Testament Studies* 30 (1984): 58–59, n.1.

20. *Das Matthäus-Evangelium im Mittelägyptischen Dialekt des Koptischen (Codex Scheide)* (Berlin: Akademie Verlag, 1981), 86.

21. Tal Ilan, "Notes on the Distribution of Jewish Women's Names in Palestine in the Second Temple and Mishnaic Periods," *JJS* 40 (1989): 186–200.

22. *Acta Philippi,* 2 vols., ed. and trans. F. Bovon, B. Bouvier, and F. Amsler (Turnhout: Brepols Publishers, 1999).

23. Andrew McGowan, *Ascetic Eucharists: Food and Drink in Early Christian Ritual Meals* (Oxford: Clarendon, 1999), 118–25.

24. For discussion, see W. Schneemelcher, ed., and R. McL. Wilson, *New Testament Apocrypha,* vol. 1: *Gospels and Related Writings,* 5th ed. (Westminster: John Knox, 1991), 361–69; Deirdre Good, "Pistis Sophia," in *Searching the Scriptures,* ed. Elisabeth Schüessler Fiorenza, vol. 2: *A Feminist Commentary* (New York: Crossroad, 1994), 678–707.

25. Douglas M. Parrott, ed., *Nag Hammadi Codices III,3–4 and V,1 with Papyrus Berolinensis 8502,3 and Oxyrhynchus Papyrus 1081, Eugnostos and the Sophia of Jesus Christ,* Nag Hammadi Studies 27 (Leiden: Brill, 1991), 116–17.

26. Violet MacDermot, *The Fall of Sophia: A Gnostic Text on the Redemption of Universal Consciousness* (Great Barrington, Mass.: Lindisfarne, 2001).

27. PS Book 1,17. Coptic text in Carl Schmidt, ed. *Pistis Sophia,* translation and notes by Violet MacDermot, NHS 9 (Leiden: Brill, 1978), 26. Translations from the Coptic are my own.

28. PS 1,27.

29. PS 1,30.

30. PS 1,33.

31. PS 1,43.

32. PS 1,45, 50.

33. PS 1,52.

34. PS 1,60, 62.

35. LXT Exodus 15:20 λαβοῦσα δε Μαριαμ ἡ προφῆτις . . .

36. For discussion, see Jorunn Jacobsen Buckley, *Female Fault and Fulfilment in Gnosticism* (Chapel Hill: University of North Carolina Press, 1986), 105–25.

37. Mary Clayton, *The Apocryphal Gospels of Mary in Anglo-Saxon England* (Cambridge: Cambridge University Press, 1998), "The Gospel of Pseudo-Matthew," 164.

38. *LA* II.66–67.

39. Philo *Agr.* 80; "pure and clean" refers to Num 12:14–15.

40. Pseudo-Philo's *Biblical Antiquities,* in James H. Charlesworth, ed., *Old Testament Pseudepigrapha,* vol. 2 (Garden City: Doubleday, 1985).

41. *Midrash Rabbah,* vol. 3, trans. and ed. H. Freedman and M. Simon (London: Soncino, 1961).

42. Mark 15:40: Ἦσαν δὲ καὶ γυναῖκες ἀπὸ μακρόθεν θεωροῦσαι ἐν αἷς καὶ Μαρία [ℵ A D L and western witnesses] [Μαριάμ C W Θ 0184 syh] ἡ Μαγδα—ληνὴ καὶ Μαρία ἡ Ἰακώβου τοῦ μικροῦ καὶ Ἰωσῆτος μήτηρ καὶ Σαλώμη.

43. I follow the numbering of Anne Pasquier's edition, *L'Évangile selon Marie* (BG 1) (Québec: Les Presses de L'Université Laval, 1983), which counts the first six missing pages and which is widely used. However, Karen King's numbering is different because it doesn't count the first six missing pages: see Karen King, *The Gospel of Mary of Magdala* (Santa Rosa, Calif.: Polebridge Press, 2003).

44. On p. 205, n. 58, King discusses the question of identity. But the title of the book and the late appearance of this note indicate that for her the issue is resolved.

I am arguing that the form of the name in Gos. Mary, together with traits of prophet, sister, and reaction of disbelief, signal the presence of Miriam.

45. Robert Grant and Glen Menzies, *Joseph's Bible Notes (Hypomnestikon)* (Atlanta: Scholars Press, 1996).

46. My thanks to the Rev. Alistair Stewart-Sykes for his translation of this sermon.

The Miriamic Procession

2

&

Miriam, Music, and Miracles

CAROL MEYERS

Introductory Comments: Miriam, Prophecy, and the Song of the Sea

Miriam is a unique figure in the Hebrew Bible. As the first woman to be designated by the term *prophet* (Hebrew *nĕbî'â*), she becomes the paradigmatic female prophet of ancient Israel, much as Moses serves as the archetype of the male prophetic tradition.[1] Her importance in the Hebrew Bible is signified by the fact that she is the only female figure to appear in five different biblical books.[2] In addition, she is noteworthy as one of the few female figures in the Hebrew Bible who is not identified in terms of her marital or maternal status. That is, we are never told that she is "wife of" or "mother of" someone.[3] Yet, we do learn indirectly—in genealogical passages in Numbers and 1 Chronicles, and not in the exodus tale itself—that she is the daughter of Amram and Jochebed and thus the sister of the two figures most prominently linked with traditions about the beginnings of Israel, namely, Moses and Aaron.[4] In the narratives of the exodus tradition, the three of them form a trinity of leadership that Miriam asserts in her famous challenge to Moses' role: "Has the Lord spoken only through Moses?" (Num. 12:2; cf. Mic. 6:4).

Whether she is a historical figure and how much of the tradition about her is authentic can never be decided. The majority of scholars would probably attribute an authentic core to the exodus traditions, which have reached their present form through a long and complex transmission process.[5] Thus it is unlikely that the story of Israelite liberation from Egyptian bondage is historical in the usual sense of that term. Yet the canonical image of Miriam as one who challenges authority and who becomes a spokesperson for God

27

cannot easily be turned aside. She is part of a master narrative that becomes foundational for Judeo-Christian ideas of human suffering and divine redemption. Aside from the question of historicity, the Miriamic materials and other similar texts in Hebrew Scripture can provide important insights into female prophetic traditions. More specifically, they reveal the presence of a gender-specific tradition, grounded in musical performance, in ancient Israel.

Miriam's association with music begins with the biblical attribution to her in Exodus 15:20 and 21a of the so-called Song of Miriam:

> (20) Then the prophet Miriam, the sister of Aaron, took a drum[6] in her hand; and all the women went out after her, with drums and with dancing.
> (21a) And Miriam sang for them,
> (21b) "Sing of Yahweh, for he has triumphed gloriously,
> (21c) Horse and rider, he has hurled into the sea."

At first glance, that song seems to consist of a single poetic verse, 15:21b–c. This verse follows the well-known description, which we shall examine below, of Miriam and a cohort of female musicians performing with drum, dance, and song. In reality, however, that one biblical verse is not simply a shorter version of the extended song in Exodus 15:1b–18, which seems to be attributed to Moses in 15:1a ("Then Moses and the Israelites sang this song of Yahweh"). Rather, verse 21 (b–c) is likely the Song's opening verse; as such it also served as the title, according to the ancient practice in Semitic antiquity of titling poems or other literary works by their first words or line.[7] Thus the title is provided, with the imperative of the verb "to sing," in relation to Miriam, after the account of the song being sung by Moses and the Israelites, who collectively say, "I will sing. . . ."

In considering the relationship between vv. 1b–18 and v. 21 with regard to Mosaic and Miriamic authorship, one is looking at one of the oldest passages in the Hebrew Bible, which for the moment I shall call the Song of the Sea, thereby sidestepping the thorny issue of whose song it is. Indeed, its metrical style and strophic structure, with many examples of repetitive parallelism, fit extremely well into the pattern of old Canaanite poetry, thus making this archaic poem a unified composition that is arguably the oldest literature in the Hebrew Bible.[8] That fact along with its content— celebrating God's salvific deeds in behalf of Israel—make it one of the most important passages of Hebrew Scripture. It thus seemed inconceivable to generations of (male) biblical scholars that the poem could have originated with women.

Interpretive tradition thus favored the apparent canonical attribution of the longer poem to Moses, with the single verse (v. 21) allotted to Miriam deemed a faint female echo of the rousing male original. Miriam and her companions, it was thought, sang that one verse antiphonally at the end of each strophe of the eighteen-verse poem linked to Moses.[9]

A crack in this androcentric reading of Exodus 15, favoring male creativity and prophecy over that of women, appeared more than fifty years ago in the joint Ph.D. dissertation of Frank Moore Cross and David Noel Freedman, two leading students of W. F. Albright and reigning experts to this day in the field of ancient Hebrew poetry. Their joint doctoral dissertation included a chapter on Exodus 15 that was published separately as a journal article.[10] The first sentence of that article presciently reads, "It seems fitting to designate the hymn in Exodus 15 as 'The Song of Miriam.'" Cross and Freedman were not influenced by feminist inclinations; first-wave feminist biblical study by then was dormant, and second-wave feminist scholarship would not yet emerge until almost two decades later.[11] Rather, their attribution of the poem to Miriam was the result of their assessment that the tradition ascribing the poem to Miriam was superior to the tradition attributing it to Moses. They point out that "it is easy to understand the ascription of the hymn to the great leader. It would be more difficult to explain the association of Miriam with the song as a secondary designation."[12] They also demonstrated that it most closely resembles, in terms of its being a song of triumph, another passage of archaic Hebrew poetry attributed to a woman, namely, the Song of Deborah in Judges 5. In so doing, they acknowledge that female authorial creativity is indeed possible for the biblical world.

Decades later, Phyllis Trible presented the case for Miriamic attribution more directly. She asserts:

> the very retention of a Miriamic ending . . . argues for both its antiquity and authority. So tenacious was the tradition about Miriam that later editors could not eliminate it altogether. In fact, once upon an early time, before editors got jobs, the entire Song of the Sea, not just the first stanza, was ascribed to Miriam and the women of Israel. Later, redactors (editors) who were intent on elevating Moses took the song right out of her mouth and gave it to him—to Moses, the inarticulate one—in company with the sons of Israel. Thus they constructed an ending for the Exodus story that contradicted the older tradition. Unable to squelch the Miriamic tradition altogether, the redactors appended it in truncated form (Exod 15:20–21) to their preferred Mosaic version. . . .

This entire exercise ended up both preserving and destroying the woman's story. It kept Miriam but diminished her importance. And it heightened the apotheosis of Moses.[13]

Trible reaches her apt conclusion by applying a hermeneutics of suspicion to her consideration of the Exodus 15 materials.

Several years later, her conclusion as well as that of Cross and Freedman gained credence from another study, a literary analysis by Gerald Janzen that sees the verses ascribed to Miriam as an analepsis.[14] By analepsis, he means the temporary withholding of important information in order to present it later for some desired effect.[15] In his view, the song that Moses and the Israelites sing in vv. 1b–18 thus constitutes a response to that already sung by Miriam and her female companions. Among the features that led Janzen to this conclusion are the fact that Miriam and her cohort are said to sing for "them" (masculine plural), denoting Moses and the Israelites, whereas Moses and the Israelites sing to Yahweh. Miriam's song begins with a masculine plural imperative, likewise indicating that the women are providing the hymnic material to Moses and the rest of the people. In short, Moses and all the others are responding antiphonally to the composition of Miriam, which she sings along with her troupe of dancing musicians.[16]

Another possibility, which does not preclude the suggestions already noted, is that put forth by Fokkelein van-Dijk-Hemmes. She points out that the material in vv. 20–21 forms a conclusion to the Song of the Sea, and thus to the entire exodus story, for in the very next verse (23) the trek across the wilderness begins. By ending the exodus account with the performance of women, an *inclusio* is formed. Women's actions that dominate the beginning of the exodus narrative in Exodus 1 and 2:1–10 are balanced by women's actions at its ending in Exodus 15:20–21.[17]

Susan Ackerman has provided a historical rather than a literary perspective in a recent article. She suggests that the fact that the Bible could admit of the possibility of women assuming the role of prophet can be understood as stemming from a phase of liminality in the life story of the Israelite community. Gender conventions that would otherwise have restricted women from leadership positions would have been suspended in such destabilized situations.[18] Although her supposition that gender conventions would normally have precluded female prophetic positions may be challenged in the light of other mentions of female prophets at other points in Israel's story, her association of female prophetic activity with ruptures in historical continuity, with the exodus being the prototypical example, is certainly relevant to the Miriamic tradition.

A final piece of evidence that supports the case for Miriamic authorship of the Song of the Sea comes from the Dead Sea Scrolls. This new information is found in a recently published group of fragments, which is part of a set of manuscripts that Qumran scholars call the Reworked Pentateuch.[19] These fragments, dating to about 75–50 BCE, contain material that differs from the Masoretic text. Poorly preserved though they are, eight lines of poetic text have survived as Miriam's Song and represent the survival of at least one manuscript tradition preserving Miriam's own song.[20]

These examples of pre-feminist as well as feminist biblical scholarship are important in reclaiming a tradition of female creativity in ancient Israel. That tradition has been obscured by centuries of interpretation characterized by androcentric biases that ignored such possibilities for women in the biblical world. I will come back eventually to what may be meant by Miriam's musical chant, but first I want to add another kind of witness to the likelihood that calling Exodus 15 the Song of Miriam is more accurate than attributing it to her more famous brother. That witness comes from probing into women's musical traditions in the biblical world.

Miriam the Musician

The narrative introduction to the Song of Miriam in Exodus 15:20 situates the poetic verse—or verses if we accept the preceding nineteen verses as authentically Miriam's—in a social context. Miriam does not simply proclaim the words attributed to her. Rather, she does so in a public event that can be termed a performance, that is, a formal presentation before an audience. The biblical text mentions three aspects of the performative tradition: (1) *drum,* specifically a handheld frame drum; (2) *dance,* probably ecstatic body movements accompanying the highly emotional nature, to be considered later, of the performative event; and (3) *song,* or more likely chanting, given the rhythmic rather than the melodious or harmonious nature of Hebraic musical tradition.[21]

These three aspects of the Miriamic musical tradition in the Hebrew Bible arguably constitute a performance genre that can be associated with women.[22] Two main lines of evidence, which will be considered in turn, support that contention. The first is a series of biblical passages that directly or elliptically mention drums, dancing, and song in association with women. The second is the discovery of a corpus of archaeological artifacts that link the only one of those three features that exists in the realm of material culture—namely, drums—with female musicians.

Before examining these two lines of evidence and then considering the social implications of a female musical genre, it is important to note several aspects of ancient Hebraic instrumental music. The Hebrew Bible actually has a rich vocabulary of musical terms, especially ones denoting musical instruments. Dozens of different musical instruments are mentioned in the Bible; and the Bible itself may have had its own classificatory system according to sociomusical function.[23] However, such classifications contain so many doublings and overlaps that a more observer-imposed scheme, based on how sound is produced, is more useful.[24] This system divides the musical instruments of the Bible into four categories:

1. *chordophones,* or stringed instruments, of which the Bible mentions at least nine different kinds;
2. *aerophones,* or wind instruments, of which a dozen or so appear in Hebrew Scripture;
3. *idiophones,* or instruments that produce sound by parts moving against other parts (such as rattles and cymbals), of which five different ones are named; and
4. *membranophones,* or percussion instruments, with only one biblical example.

The biblical word for drum is *tōp* (plural *tuppîm),* an onomatopoeic term related to other Semitic words for drum (Assyrian *tuppu,* Ugaritic *tp,* Aramaic *tōp,* Arabic *duff;* cf. Sumerian *dup* or *tup*) as well as Greek *tupanon* (or *tumpanon*) and Latin *tympanum.* English versions of the Bible (see n. 6) render the term variously as timbrel, tambourine, tabret, timbre, and drum. The first four of these are lexically related to *tōp* but are anachronistic translations in that they refer to an instrument with metal jingles that was probably not invented until the Roman period or later. The term *tōp* most likely refers to a small handheld percussion instrument. Although none of the biblical texts that mention it provide a description, archaeologically retrieved information as well as representations in ancient art suggest that it consisted of a round wooden frame, about twenty-five to thirty centimeters in diameter, with a skin or hide—or two parallel hides—stretched over it.[25] The presence of only one kind of percussion instrument in the Hebrew Bible is surprising, given the variety within other instrument types as well as the considerable range of membranophones of varying sizes and shapes mentioned in ancient Near Eastern texts and depicted in Egyptian and Mesopotamian art.[26] The association of that instrument with women, and perhaps only women, thus has implications for the role of women in Israelite musical performance traditions.

Biblical Texts Mentioning the Drum-Dance-Song Genre

The hand drum is mentioned in sixteen passages in the Hebrew Bible. In eleven cases, the drum is part of an ensemble. That is, it is mentioned together with other instruments, most prominently the lyre, but also with as many as six or seven different instruments.[27] A good example is one of the songs of praise for God in the book of Psalms:

> Praise Yahweh!
> . . . .
> Praise him with blasts of the *horn;*
> Praise him with *harp* and *lyre!*
> Praise him with *drum* and dance;
> Praise him with *lute* and *pipe!*
> Praise him with clanging *cymbals!*[28]

This text apparently comes from what we might consider a religious context, whereas some of the other texts mentioning drums along with other instruments indicate a secular setting. The texts do not specify whether the musicians are male or female. Indeed, assumptions that men were the musicians may be unwarranted for every biblical passage in which ensembles appear, given extra-biblical artistic evidence for female ensembles. Groupings of instruments (or ensemble playing) were apparently common in ancient Israel/Canaan/Phoenicia[29] and are depicted in ancient Near Eastern art, with two notable examples representing female musicians. A bowl found in Cyprus shows a group of musicians, presumably Phoenician; it depicts three women—one playing a double flute, the second a harp, and the third cymbals.[30] And an ivory box, probably Phoenician in origin or inspiration, from Assyria has three women carved in relief on the side—one plays the double flute, the second a frame drum, and the third a stringed instrument.[31]

The other five instances in which the word for the frame drum appears all involve that instrument alone, and in each case the musicians are women. The Miriam text in Exodus 15 is of course the most notable of these, and "drum" is found twice in that passage. The other texts are Judges 11:34, the end of the sad tale of Jephthah's daughter; 1 Samuel 18:6, in a narrative about David before he becomes king; and Jeremiah 31:4, an oracle of hope and consolation to those who survive the destruction of Judah and Jerusalem. What is notable about these additional passages is not only that they pair women with drums and dancing, but also that in two of them (1 Sam. 18:6 and Jer. 31:4)—and probably in the third (Judg. 11:34) by inference—song also appears. One other text, Judges 5:1, perhaps is another example, with Deborah's song elliptically invoking the image of drum and dance accompanying the song.[32] Taken together, these texts specifying drum-dance-song seem to represent a distinct women's tradition of musical performance. Archaeological evidence supports such a possibility.

Archaeological Evidence for Women and Drum

The ancient art of coroplasty (the modeling of clay figures or statuettes) seems to have flourished in Palestine in the period of the Hebrew Bible. Although a comprehensive catalogue of Palestinian terracottas does not exist, the discovery of small clay figurines from virtually every site with Iron Age settlements has long been noted. Among the corpus of ceramic rendering of humans at Palestinian sites, figures of females are most common. The identity of these figures is difficult to establish. Many archaeologists have been quick to label them as fertility figurines and/or as representations of Asherah, Astarte, or some other female deity.[33] Others, noting the lack of insignia or decoration typically used to signify deities in coroplastic art, contest such a notion.[34] The fact is that within the general category of small clay statues of females, there are significant variations with respect to style, size, techniques of manufacture, decoration, pose, accompanying objects, and other aspects of form.

Within this plethora of gynomorphic terracottas, one particular type is notable in relation to the Miriamic music tradition and the other passages mentioning women and drums. The statuettes of this type, like almost all of the terracottas of the larger group to which they belong, are small objects, ranging from eight to twenty centimeters in height. They feature a standing female figure holding a disc-shaped object in front of her, usually perpendicular to her body. The object rests on one of her hands, and her other hand is pressed against the flat side of the disc.[35] Because many similar terracotta figures (of both males and females) are holding a musical instrument, such as a lyre, harp, or double flute—all part of Israelite musical tradition—the females holding discs can be identified as women playing drums. The discs depict the hand-held frame drum, and they should not be confused with the tambourine, probably not yet invented. Nor should they be confused with cymbals, which are also depicted as discs but with the hands on either side of the disc rather than with one on the side and one below.[36] Indeed, once it is understood, by attending to the hand positions, which figurines represent cymbalists and which represent drummers, it becomes clear that virtually all of these small terracottas of figures playing the frame drum depict female musicians.

The handheld frame drum is quite uniformly represented in these terracottas, despite differences in the level of artistry, detail, and decoration.
Most Iron Age examples are constructed of a wheel-made base, which forms
a trumpet-shaped pedestal or skirt, to which has been attached either a mold-
formed or hand-modeled head. The hands, arms, and hand drum are all hand
modeled. Although some crude examples are entirely handmade, most
show the use of a potter's wheel and/or a mold, thus indicating workshop
production.

Most of these terracottas are made of the typical buff-colored or reddish-
colored clays that are typical of east Mediterranean deposits. Some figures
are entirely undecorated, but most have simple black and/or red painted lines
to indicate stripes or patterns on the woman's dress, which is otherwise quite
simple, lacking flounces, ruffles, pleats, drapings, or other embellishments.
The face is sometimes colored red, as may be the drum. And the hair, which
is either braided or loose and shoulder-length, with bangs lying evenly across
the forehead in both cases, is often colored black. The rather plain hairstyle
indicates that the figurines are depicting a woman's own locks and not a head-
dress or hairpiece. Both the simplicity of dress and hairstyle and the utter
lack of adornments such as jewelry or headpieces support the notion that
these figures represent humans and not deities or even elite females, who
are often signified by such items of decoration.

Establishing that these figurines represent an Israelite cultural tradition
is somewhat problematic. Although female terracottas in general have been
widely found, in both sacred and domestic contexts, at Palestinian sites of
the Iron Age (i.e., the period of the Hebrew Bible), the female drummer is
not as ubiquitous at such sites as are the nude figurines. Moreover, because
so many examples are in museums and were acquired through the antiquities trade and not legitimate excavations, their provenance is uncertain. Those
that have been found in legitimate excavations tend to be from Cyprus or from
coastal Palestinian sites such as Achziv,[37] Tyre, Shiqmona, and Kharayeb. Yet,
although there have been considerably more examples found in Cyprus than
in the Levant, there is reason to believe that many aspects of the tradition of
small terracottas actually originated in Palestine or Syria.[38] That is, the thematic as well as the technical inspiration for the Cypriot forms is likely to
have originated in Syria-Palestine in the Iron Age and apparently found fer-
tile ground in the indigenous coroplastic and religious tradition of Cyprus.
This is especially so for the terracottas depicting women playing the hand
drum, for that membranophone, as Braun states in his exhaustive study *Music in Ancient Israel,* is of local Palestinian provenance and "represents a characteristic product of the musical world of ancient Israel."[39]

In sum, biblical texts—those mentioning the drum-dance-song genre—and also archaeological artifacts point to the existence of a specifically female musical tradition in ancient Israel.[40] Moreover, the fact that men are not specifically mentioned as drum players in the Bible, when coupled with the fact that men are not depicted playing that instrument in the terracotta tradition, makes it plausible that every place in which drums appear in biblical texts involves the presence of female percussionists. At the very least, the existence of a female musical genre has implications for reconstructing female roles in Israelite society.

Implications for Women's Social Roles

Analyzing the social dynamics of a women's musical genre is informed by two developments in contemporary scholarship: one in the discussions of *performance* and, more specifically, of women's performance; and the other in the study of the *professional* aspect of women's expressive activities in traditional societies.

In the study of *performance,* western values have tended to view women's expressive forms as less important than men's forms. The aesthetic productions in both art and music that have been most valued formally and publicly have been those of men, and this is especially true for the far less visible activities of women in premodern societies.[41] But now, several decades of ethnomusicological research with feminist concerns—that is, research that recognizes the existence and validity of women's musical productions across cultures—not only have brought recognition to many little-noticed female expressive traditions[42] but also have examined the relationships between music, gender roles, power, and status.[43]

The public aspect of women's performance groups in ancient Israel is a significant factor in considering the social dynamics. Performance, after all, is a two-part phenomenon: first, and this will be considered later, the creation of an artistic production outside the public eye; and second, an artistic event involving performer(s), expressive genre, setting, and audience. The public setting and audience is an activated instance of skill and creativity and also establishes a performer-audience communicative flow that can have a favorable impact on women's status in society. An expected and delivered performance, as was the case for the Israelite women carrying out the drum-dance-song genre, has the ability to transform social relations. In anticipation and delivery of the performance, the women who sang with dance and drums would have exerted social control because of the intrinsic aesthetic appeal of the event and also because of its political and religious function.[44]

The control over the audience because of the general rhetorical power of any performative act contributes to the status of the performers, subverts or suspends normal hierarchies favoring males, and may thereby become a strategy for some kinds of wider informal control.[45] In short, a female performance genre in ancient Israel signifies an area of prestige and, occasionally, of attendant social power for these female musicians.[46]

The *professional* aspect of these performance activities has another dimension, the internal or private aspect—a process outside the public eye—that also is understood better now as the result of feminist scholarship. The existence of a single-gender group with public performance goals meant that women in that group were members of a professional association that can be termed a "guild." Although this designation sometimes indicates a formal union of people in the same trade or craft,[47] I use it here in its general sense, denoting any association of people for the promotion of common interests. As such, it is an appropriate term for recognizing a group of professional women in ancient Israel, whose services were provided as needed to the Israelite populace. Such groups may not have enjoyed the same kind of explicit recognition that accompany groups, such as soldiers or priests, that originate in state institutions; but their professional expertise nonetheless provided expected services and, as already indicated, contributed to the community power of the female participants.

The internal dynamics of such groups, which are also especially important in considering a premodern society, are not usually recognized.[48] The existence of a group of professional musicians meant that expertise had to be obtained through training as well as experience. Knowledge of the techniques, songs, compositional procedures, and instruments would have depended on the transmission of a corpus of information from one practitioner to the next. The ability of women to perform thus would have entailed regular interaction in practice, training, and composition sessions. In these gender-specific groups, women exercised exclusive control over themselves and their worlds, with some of them functioning as leaders and mentors. Such guilds have their own hierarchies and values, affording internal prestige to the participants in relation to their competence and accomplishments within the group as well as in public performance.[49] Women in such groups experience a sense of power rather than powerlessness.[50] Indeed, anthropological research has shown that women who have formal social ties with other women—who work with them in groups—have much greater opportunities for enhanced status than women without such ties.[51]

Clearly this close examination of the Miriamic tradition exemplified in the drum-dance-song genre reveals otherwise invisible aspects of women's lives in ancient Israel. As is the case with other aspects of gendered behaviors in premodern societies, recent research seeking to recover emic perspectives tends to challenge preconceived Western notions about male dominance in traditional communities.[52] But there is still more to the Miriam topos to be considered. The drum-dance-song genre appears in very specific circumstances; thus another look at the biblical passages that explicitly or implicitly mention it is in order, especially as those texts may inform the Mary Magdalene tradition of the New Testament.

Miriam and Miracles

The paradigmatic appearance of the drum-dance-song genre is, of course, the Song of Miriam. The setting of that song is integrally related to the function of this performative genre in the exodus account. The same is true for the other passages in which it appears in Hebrew scripture. Thus I will now consider the "historical"-literary context of the Exodus text and the other ones, mentioned earlier, that depict this gender-specific musical performance genre.

1. Exodus 15. The poetic Song of Miriam (and Moses) interrupts the prose account of the exodus. This well-known and foundational narrative describes the Israelite departure from Egypt after extraordinary diplomatic efforts on the part of Moses to secure permission from the pharaoh. It then presents the even more dramatic story that constitutes the culmination of the exodus. The pharaoh changes his mind and attempts to recapture the fleeing Israelites. In this final twist to the exodus tale, the armies and the chariots of the pharaoh are totally destroyed. A military crisis evokes panic and a cry for help, and the Israelites are spared through the gracious intervention of Yahweh as the waters of the Reed Sea (Red Sea) engulf the menacing Egyptian forces.[53] The saga of liberation is brought to a spectacular close with the Song of Miriam, where only poetry can supply the emotional exultation aroused by the sense that a miracle has occurred—that Yahweh has entered the human arena with a salvific act.[54] Only poetry, typically chanted in rhythmic music in ancient Semitic culture, would have had the possibility of expressing the sense of deliverance against enormous odds.

2. Judges 11. The sad tale of Jephthah's daughter is vivid and disturbing because it ends in the death of the young woman. Modern readers, unaware of the ancient Semitic ideology of war and of vows, tend to be so shocked by the way a father's vow has gone awry that they pass by the situation that provoked the infamous vow and subsequent death of the maiden. As an unlikely leader, Jephthah rises to the occasion of dealing with the military threat

posed by the Ammonites. The Ammonites were one of several national groups east of the Jordan; they appear in the biblical record as enemies of the Israelites, with one of their leaders called Nahash, "Snake," a name no doubt reflecting Israelite opinion of a threatening group.[55] The fact that Jephthah makes a vow that he will sacrifice whoever will come to greet him should he return home victorious is an indication of the desperate plight of the Israelites. Human sacrifice in the ancient Near East seems to have occurred only in times of an enormous crisis.[56] Thus the deliverance of Jephthah's troops from what was apparently a vastly superior fighting force seems unimaginable. But Yahweh intervenes—"Yahweh gave them into his hand (v. 32)"—and thus an emotional poetic response by a female performer was the culturally appropriate act for acknowledging the miraculous salvific intervention of Yahweh in human affairs. The unnamed daughter of Jephthah comes out to greet her father "with drums and with dancing" (v. 34). Song is not mentioned, perhaps because no snippet of the words of her greeting has survived in the text, but its presence can be assumed as part of the genre.

3. 1 Samuel 18. David's rise to power is narrated in a substantial narrative block, 1 Samuel 16 to 2 Samuel 5, which is known as the History of David's Rise.[57] David emerges as the central character of this narrative unit. The pivotal event signifying David's charismatic and military abilities is the David and Goliath episode set forth in legendary detail in chapter 17. Goliath is described at some length, with his extraordinary height and elaborate armor and weaponry meant to show that he was far superior to the young, unprotected, and virtually unarmed David. All the Israelites flee in fear when they see the Philistine champion. In other words, the odds are stacked against David. Yet he prevails because, as David anticipates, "Yahweh . . . will save me from the hand of the Philistine" (17:36). It is no wonder, then, that women come out, after his miraculous victory over the gigantic enemy warrior, with "singing and dancing . . . and with drums" (18:6). Moreover, the narrative is interrupted with a poetic couplet, a fragment of the song. Again, the emotion of poetry bursts forth, as sung by female performers following divine intervention in human affairs.

4. Jeremiah 31. This chapter, with the preceding one (ch. 30), is the centerpiece of a long section (chs. 26–36) of the second part of the book of Jeremiah. It depicts a return to Zion and a utopian restoration for the entire people in the eschatological future. The journey home is presented as a second exodus (31:2); Yahweh again will "save" Israel by overcoming "all of the nations among which I scattered you" (30:11). Female Israel[58] responds to God's miraculous delivery of the dispersed survivors of the Babylonian conquest and exile by dancing with drums (31:4), whereupon Yahweh instructs

the female celebrators of God's intervention to "sing aloud with gladness" (31:7); the ensuing poem is perhaps meant to be the song of the female performer, none other than Zion herself.

5. Judges 5. This chapter presents a long poem that may be one of the oldest extant Israelite literary compositions. Indeed, its impressionistic and parallelistic style, like that of Exodus 15, is much like earlier Ugaritic poetry.[59] The poem is attributed to Deborah, along with her general Barak, perhaps echoing the way Miriam's Song in Exodus is taken over by a male counterpart. The context here—an outpouring of song after a military success— typically evokes a woman's performance genre and thus makes the addition of Barak a suspect accommodation to the androcentric interests of the Deuteronomic historian, who provides the superscription announcing the song that follows. The context is perhaps the most dramatic battle scene in the book of Judges. It certainly is the one that involves the largest number of Israelite troops, drawing militia from at least eight Israelite tribal groups, who face a coalition of Canaanite kings with an enormous (900) contingent of chariots. Again, the odds are against a positive outcome for the outnumbered and outmatched Israelite muster. Both the prose (in ch. 4) and poetic (ch. 5) versions of this apparently doomed attempt of the Israelites to overcome the enemy make it clear that the outcome, in which the Israelites are saved, is the result of Yahweh's intervention. The prose account simply claims, "on that day God subdued King Jabin of Canaan" (4:23), whereas the poetic account attempts to capture the emotional experience of having God's earth-shaking and miraculous involvement be the reason for the Israelites to escape disaster.

These passages have in common a context of unexpected military victory, a component that has given rise to the term "victory song" to describe the genre that appears in these examples of women performing with dance, drum, and song.[60] I have no argument with that designation, but I fear that it may obscure the fact that the victories are not the ordinary military successes of an established army. In each instance, the victories—of unarmed, outnumbered, underequipped, or otherwise disadvantaged Israelites—are attributed to ahistorical, miraculous circumstances, namely divine intervention in human affairs. And female humans respond with poetic song and movement that celebrate redemption. In other words, when a miracle occurs, "the causal connection between heaven and earth becomes visible and immediate, as explosive contact is made between heaven and earth. . . . Only poetry [i.e., song] can convey the mystery of the miraculous and its meaning"[61] for those who experience divine salvation.

The Miriamic paradigm of a female performance tradition involves a specific context and content. The context represents the emotional performative response to the experience of being saved; only God could have achieved the positive outcome. And the content—the words of the songs, insofar as they are preserved in these biblical texts—announces the conclusion that Yahweh is responsible for the miracle. The poetic songs are in a sense the product of the divine spirit, and they represent theological statements about divine salvific power. If the consensus that the poetry preserved in the songs of Miriam and the others of this genre are among the oldest biblical texts, then the first biblical "theologians" may have been women: Miriam and the other female musicians of ancient Israel.

One further feature of the literary presentation of the performances in the texts described above is noteworthy. In Exodus 15:20, Judges 11:34, 1 Samuel 18:6, and Jeremiah 31:4, the text reports that the performers "went out" and then sang their songs.[62] The use of such a verb is most likely a cliché—formulaic language used to announce this performance genre.[63] This cliché was apparently part of the literary tradition of the early Jewish community in Palestine. The author of the first-century BCE book of Judith[64] portrays Judith and the women of her community celebrating the miraculous conquest of the Assyrians by singing with dancing and drums (Jth. 15:12–16:1). The text indicates that, for this performance, Judith "went" out before all the people (15:13).

A century or so later, in the early Christian community, two gospel writers proclaim that Mary Magdalene "went out" to announce the miraculous appearance of the risen Jesus (Mark 16:8 and John 20:18). The Greek verbs are equivalent to the Hebrew ones for the performers of the drum-dance-song genre. The Mary Magdalene passages may thus be two more scriptural instances of a cliché embedded in the Israelite genre of women announcing a miracle. What better paradigm could there be than this Miriamic one for the witness of Mary Magdalene to the miracle of the risen Lord!

NOTES

1. This is the claim of Phyllis Trible, "Miriam," in *Women in Scripture: A Dictionary of Named and Unnamed Women in the Hebrew Bible, the Apocryphal/Deuterocanonical Books, and the New Testament*, ed. Carol Meyers, Toni Craven, and Ross S. Kraemer (Boston: Houghton Mifflin, 2000), 127, and "Bringing Miriam Out of the Shadows," *Bible Review* 5 (1989): 25.

2. The books are Exodus, Numbers, Deuteronomy, 1 Chronicles, and Micah. In contrast, another prominent woman, Sarah, is mentioned only in Isaiah in addi-

tion to her frequent appearances in the Genesis narratives. For a recent and detailed study of all the Miriam texts, see Ursula Rapp, *Mirjam: Eine feministisch-rhetorische Lektüre der Mirjamtexte in der hebräischen Bibel,* BZAW 317 (Berlin: de Gruyter, 2002); her exegeses are useful, but her conclusions about context are less persuasive.

3. Post-biblical sources are apparently uncomfortable with her lack of wifely and motherly credentials. In rabbinic tradition she marries Caleb and begets Hur and is ultimately an ancestor of King David. See Babylonian Talmud *Soṭa* 2a and *Exodus Rabbah* 1.17, and the comments of Naomi Graetz, "Did Miriam Talk Too Much?" in *A Feminist Companion to Exodus to Deuteronomy,* ed. Athalya Brenner, Feminist Companion to the Bible, vol. 6 (Sheffield: Sheffield Academic Press, 1994), 234–35.

4. Num. 26:59; 1 Chron. 6:3. Although Miriam is not mentioned by name in the narrative in Exodus 2 about the sister of Moses helping to rescue the infant endangered by the Pharaoh's decree, her appearance in those two genealogical passages with her two brothers, Aaron and Moses, supports the notion that it is Miriam who is the unnamed sister in Exodus 2. The brief genealogy in Exod. 6:14–25 (see v. 20) mentions Aaron and Moses as children of Jochebed and Amram but omits Miriam.

5. For a compelling and balanced discussion of the historicity issue as well as the problem of dating the exodus, see Carol A. Redmount, "Bitter Lives: Israel in and out of Egypt," in *The Oxford History of the Biblical World,* ed. Michael D. Coogan (New York: Oxford University Press, 1998), 79–121. See also the helpful discussion of the nature of the biblical narrative of the Exodus in *Now These Are the Names: A New English Rendition of the Book of Exodus,* translated with commentary and notes by Everett Fox (New York: Schocken Books, 1986), xxix–xxxi.

6. The Hebrew word *tōp* is often mistranslated "tambourine" (NRSV) or "timbrel" (NJPS) when in fact it designates a hand drum. See below. The translation of biblical texts in this article is the author's.

7. E.g., the so-called Epic of Creation from ancient Mesopotamia is better known by its opening words, *Enuma Elish* ("When on High . . ."). So Bill T. Arnold and Bryan E. Beyer, eds., *Readings from the Ancient Near East* (Grand Rapids, Mich.: Baker Academic, 2002), 31.

8. Such is the opinion of most scholarship, following Frank Moore Cross, "The Song of the Sea and Canaanite Myth," in *Canaanite Myth and Hebrew Epic* (Cambridge, Mass.: Harvard University Press, 1973), 112–44. However, a minority voice sees Exod. 15:1–21 as a unified composition originating in the Second Temple Period; see Martin L. Brenner, *The Song of the Sea: Exod 15:1–21* (Berlin: Walter de Gruyter, 1991).

9. So, inter alia, Umberto Cassuto, *A Commentary on the Book of Exodus,* trans. Israel Abrahams (1951; reprint Jerusalem: Magnes Press, 1983), 182. Even more recent commentaries sustain that view; Terence Fretheim (*Exodus* [Interpretation: A Bible Commentary for Teaching and Preaching (Louisville: John Knox Press, 1991)], 161) supposes, although Miriam's song may have come first, Moses' song is an expansion of a shorter female song. The scholarship on this issue up to the 1980s is summarized in Rita Burns, *Has the Lord Spoken Only through Moses? A Study of the*

Biblical Portrait of Miriam, SBL Dissertation Series 84 (Atlanta: Scholars Press, 1987), 11–40.

10. Frank M. Cross, Jr., and David Noel Freedman, "The Song of Miriam," *JNES* 14 (1955): 237–50. The dissertation, *Studies in Ancient Yahwistic Poetry,* was submitted to Johns Hopkins University in 1950 and later published as SBL Dissertation Series 21 (Missoula, Mont.: Scholars Press, 1975).

11. For a summary of feminist biblical scholarship in the United States, see Alice Ogden Bellis, "Feminist Biblical Scholarship," in *Women in Scripture: A Dictionary of Named and Unnamed Women in the Hebrew Bible, the Apocryphal/ Deuterocanonical Books, and the New Testament,* ed. Carol Meyers, Toni Craven, and Ross S. Kraemer (Boston: Houghton Mifflin, 2000), 24–32.

12. "Song of Miriam," 237. In an article written a half century later, Freedman sees Miriam's role as secondary but attributes that to a later editor who "wanted it clearly understood that Moses . . . composed and performed this dramatic song"; see "Moses and Miriam: The Song of the Sea," in *Realia Dei: Essays in Archaeology and Biblical Interpretation in Honor of Edward F. Campbell Jr. at His Retirement,* ed. Prescott H. Williams Jr. and Theodore Hiebert (Atlanta: Scholars Press, 1999), 70–71.

13. Phyllis Trible, "Bringing Miriam out of the Shadows," *Bible Review* 5 (1989): 19–20; see also Athalya Brenner, *The Israelite Woman: Social Role and Literary Type in Biblical Narrative,* Biblical Seminar 2 (Sheffield: Sheffield Academic Press, 1985), 52.

14. J. Gerald Janzen, "Song of Moses, Song of Miriam: Who Is Seconding Whom?" *CBQ* 54 (1992): 211–20.

15. Citing the work of Gérard Genette (*Narrative Discourse: An Essay in Method* [Ithaca, N.Y.: Cornell University Press, 1980], 40), who defines analepsis as an allusion to a previous event—"any evocation after the fact of an event that took place at an earlier point in the story."

16. Janzen, 193.

17. Fokkelein van Dijk-Hemmes, "Some Recent Views on the Presentation of the Song of Miriam," in *A Feminist Companion to Exodus to Deuteronomy,* ed. Athalya Brenner, Feminist Companion to the Bible, vol. 6 (Sheffield: Sheffield Academic Press, 1994), 203.

18. "Why Is Miriam Also among the Prophets? (and Is Zipporah among the Priests?)," *JBL* 12 (2002): 47–80.

19. The fragment is presented in detail in Sidnie A. White, "4Q364 and 365: A Preliminary Report," in *The Madrid Qumran Conference,* ed. J. Trebolle Barrera and L. Vegas Montaner, Studies in the Text of the Desert of Judah 11 (Leiden: Brill, and Madrid: Editorial Complutense, 1992), 222–24.

20. See George J. Brooke, "The Long-Lost Song of Miriam," *BARev* (1994): 62–65. The content of those lines, which praise God for saving Israel and also for exalting a female (Miriam?) in so doing, is similar to the theme of the Song of Hannah in 1 Sam. 2:1–2 and Jth. 16:6–7, in which divine salvation is echoed in the exaltation of a female figure.

21. Eric Werner, "Music," in *IDB*, vol. 3 (New York: Abingdon, 1962), 466; cf. Sol B. Finesinger, "Musical Instruments in the Old Testament," *HUCA* 3 (1926): 23.

22. This connection was first pointed out to me by Eunice Poethig, who graciously shared with me her discussion of this subject in an excursus to her 1975 unpublished M.Div. dissertation, "The Woman of Israel as Oral Traditioner," at McCormack Theological Seminary. However, acknowledgment of Miriam's song as one of any number of genres of women's music, in which composition as well as performance is attributed to creative females, appears already in Shelomo Dov Goitein, "Women as Creators of Biblical Genres," *Prooftexts* 10 (1988): 1–33. This article was originally published in Hebrew in 1957. For a comprehensive study of women's voices in Hebrew scripture, see Athalya Brenner and Fokkelien van Dijk-Hemmes, *On Gendering Texts: Female and Male Voices in the Hebrew Bible*, Biblical Interpretation Series 1 (Leiden: Brill, 1993).

23. Some would suggest three sociomusical categories: sacerdotal, levitical, and lay or secular; see Edith Gerson-Kiwi, "Musique dans le Bible," in *Dictionnaire de la Bible*, suppl. vol. 5 (Paris: Létouzey et Ané, 1957), 1411–68, and, for a variation, Hanoch Avenary, "Jüdische Musik," in *Die Musik in Geschichte und Gegenwart: allgemeine Enzyklopädie der Musik,* ed. 1, vol. 7 (Kassel: Bärenreiter-Verlag, 1968), 224–32.

24. See Alfred Sendrey, *Music in Ancient Israel* (New York: Philosophical Library, 1969), 262–63, and more recently Joachim Braun, *Music in Ancient Israel/ Palestine,* trans. Douglas W. Stott (Grand Rapids, Mich.: Eerdmans, 2002), 11–12. These musicological classificatory systems are based on the work of Erich M. Hornbostel and Curt Sachs, "Systematik der Musikinstrumente," *Zeitschrift der Ethnologie* 46 (1914): 553–90.

25. See the discussion in Braun, *Music,* 29–30. As a frame drum, the *tōp* is thus distinguished from the tubular or vessel drum, which is made by stretching a skin over a hollow body of any shape or size.

26. Sendrey, 40–97; Moshe Gorali, "Musical Instruments in Ancient Times," *Ariel* 29 (1971): 70; Joachim Braun, "Musical Instruments," in *Oxford Encyclopedia of Archaeology in the Near East,* vol. 4 (New York: Oxford University Press, 1997), 73–74.

27. Braun, *Music,* 165–80.

28. Ps. 150:1,3–4. Note the association of drum with dance. Emphasis is the author's. Other passages in this ensemble tradition are Gen. 31:27; Isa. 5:12; 24:8; 30:32; Ps. 81:3–4; 149:3; Job 21:12; 1 Sam. 10:5; 2 Sam. 6:5; 1 Chron. 13:8.

29. Braun (*Music,* 180) calls these ensembles the "eastern Mediterranean orchestra," because they are widely found, rather than "Phoenician orchestra" or "Canaanite orchestra," designations he finds too narrow.

30. Friedrich Behn, *Musikleben im Altertum und frühen Mittelalte* (Stuttgart: Hiersemann, 1954), pl. 33, no. 76.

31. Richard D. Barnett, "The Nimrud Ivories and the Art of the Phoenicians," *Iraq* 2 (1935): 189, pl. 26.

32. Studies of the way traditional songs are composed and performed suggest an organic composition-performance tradition, with movement (dance) and rhythm

(drums) along with words constituting a compositional whole. See, e.g., Alfred B. Lord, *A Singer of Tales* (Cambridge, Mass.: Harvard University Press, 1960), and Ruth H. Finnegan, *Oral Poetry: Its Nature, Significance, and Social Context* (Cambridge: Cambridge University Press, 1977).

33. E.g., Raz Kletter, *The Archaeology of the Judean Pillar-Figurines and the Archaeology of Asherah*, BAR International Series 636 (Oxford: Tempus Reparatum, 1996); James R. Engle, "Pillar Figurines of Iron Age Israel and Asherah./Asherim" (Ph.D. dissertation, University of Pittsburgh, 1979); Othmar Keel and Christoph Uehlinger, *Gods, Goddesses, and Images of Gods in Ancient Israel*, trans. Thomas H. Trapp (Minneapolis: Fortress Press, 1996).

34. E.g., James B. Pritchard, *Palestinian Figurines in Relation to Certain Goddesses Known through Literature*, American Oriental Studies 24 (New Haven, Conn.: American Oriental Society, 1943), recognizes the propensity of scholars to associate these objects with so-called mother goddesses and is wisely cautious in his study of the figurines. See my discussion of one set of such terracottas in "From Household to House of Yahweh: Women's Religious Culture in Ancient Israel," in *Congress Volume Basel 2001*, ed. André Lemaire, Vetus Testamentum Supplements, vol. 92 (Leiden: Brill, 2002), 285–87.

35. For photographs of a classic example of this type, and references to other examples, see Carol Meyers, "A Terracotta at the Harvard Semitic Museum and Disc-Holding Figures Reconsidered," *IEJ* 37 (1987): 116–22. There are also illustrations of this type and related ones in John Myres, *Handbook of the Cesnola Collection of Antiquities from Cyprus* (New York: Metropolitan Museum of Art, 1914). A comprehensive corpus of Cypriot examples is found in Vassos Karageorghis, *The Coroplastic Art of Ancient Cyprus*, vol. 5A: *The Cypro-Archaic Period Small Female Figurines: Handmade/Wheelmade Figurines* (Nicosia: A. G. Leventis Foundation, 1998), 68–75, pls. 46–55, and Jacqueline Karageorghis, *The Coroplastic Art of Ancient Cyprus*, vol. 5B: *The Cypro-Archaic Period Small Female Figurines: Figurines Moulées* (Nicosia: A. G. Leventis Foundation, 1999), 191–212.

36. These discs are often referred to as tambourines in the literature, perhaps because of an old translation tradition that has not been corrected in light of archaeomusicological data. Similarly, instrumentalists holding a disc that is not supported on one hand are sometimes called drum-players when they should more accurately be labeled cymbalists. For a complete discussion, see Carol Meyers, "Mother to Muse: An Archaeomusicological Study of Women's Performance in Ancient Israel," in *Recycling Biblical Figures: Papers Read at a NOSTER Colloquium in Amsterdam, 12–13 May 1997*, ed. Athalya Brenner and Jan Willem Van Henten, Studies in Theology and Religion, vol. 1 (Leiden: Deo Publishing, 1999), 50–77.

37. The Achziv examples were excavated in the 1940s and have only recently been fully published. See Michal Dayagi Mendels, *The Achziv Cemeteries: The Ben-Dor Excavations, 1941–1944* (Jerusalem: Israel Antiquities Authority, 2002), 145–62.

38. See, for example, the claims of Frieda Vandenabeele, "Has Phoenician Influence Modified Cypriot Terracotta Production?" in *Early Society in Cyprus*, ed.

Edgar J. Peltenburg (Edinburgh: Edinburgh University Press in association with the National Museum of Scotland and the A. G. Leventis Foundation, 1989). See also the description of some of these figures as being in the "Syrian" or "Egypto-Syrian" mode in Jacqueline Karageorghis, *La grand déesse de chypre et son culte,* Collection de la Maison de l'Orient Méditerranéan Ancien 5, Série Archéologique 4 (Lyon: Maison de l'Orient, 1977), 210. The "Egypto-" designation may be related to the appearance of the hand drum, played by female musicians, in Egypt in the New Kingdom.

39. At 30, 125.

40. Because of the widespread discovery of the female drummer terracottas in Cyprus and the Levant, this genre would hardly have been limited to Israelite culture but rather may have been part of a wider musical tradition in the east Mediterranean. See H. Louis Ginsberg, "Women Singers and Wailers among Northern Canaanites," *BASOR* 72 (1938): 13–15.

41. So Marta Weigle, "Women as Verbal Artists: Reclaiming the Daughters of Enheduanna," *Frontiers* 3 (1978): 1–9.

42. See, for example, Ellen Koskoff, ed., *Women and Music in Cross-Cultural Perspective* (New York: Greenwood Press, 1987); Rosan A. Jordan and Susan J. Kalčik, eds., *Women's Folklore, Women's Culture,* American Folklore Society, New Series 8 (Philadelphia: University of Pennsylvania Press, 1985); and Kimberly Marshall, ed., *Rediscovering the Muses: Women's Musical Traditions* (Boston: Northeastern University Press, 1993).

43. Examples of such approaches are John Kaemmer, *Music in Human Life: Anthropological Perspectives on Music,* Texas Press Source-books in Anthropology (Austin: University of Texas Press, 1993), and Judith Lynne Hanna, *The Performer-Audience Connection: Emotion in Metaphor in Dance and Society* (Austin: University of Texas Press, 1983).

44. This will be considered in more detail in the next section of this essay.

45. See Roger D. Abrahams, "Introductory Remarks to a Rhetorical Theory of Folklore," *JAF* 81 (1968): 143–48, and Terri Brint Joseph, "Poetry as a Strategy of Power: The Case of Riffian Berber Women," *Signs* 5 (1980): 418–34. See also Weigle, 5.

46. Peggy R. Sanday, "Female Status in the Public Domain," in *Women, Culture, and Society,* ed. Michele Z. Rosaldo and Louise Lamphere (Stanford, Calif.: Stanford University Press, 1974), 192–93, points out that in general, whenever women group together for whatever purpose, the status of such women within the society tends to be relatively high.

47. Guilds is used in that sense by Isaac Mendelsohn in his classic study of "Guilds in Ancient Palestine," *BASOR* 80 (1940): 17–21.

48. Musical performers are just one example of the many such professional groups that would have existed in ancient Israel. For a discussion of other such groups, see Carol Meyers, "Guilds and Gatherings: Women's Groups in Ancient Israel," in *Realia Dei: Essays in Archaeology and Biblical Interpretation in Honor of Edward F. Campbell Jr. at His Retirement,* ed. Prescott H. Williams Jr. and Theodore Hiebert (Atlanta: Scholars Press, 1999), 161–70.

49. The internal dynamics of performance groups, as well as the public aspect, represent differences from or changes in expected hierarchies. This phenomenon has larger theoretical implications, probably meaning that it is not accurate to designate ancient Israel or any other such traditional society as patriarchal, with an overarching hierarchical structure. Instead, the concept of "heterarchy," which allows for different systems of ranking, according to age, gender, profession, etc. in a diverse whole, fits more accurately the nature of complex pre-modern societies. See the discussion of the heterarchy model in Carol Meyers, "Hierarchy or Heterarchy? Archaeology and the Theorizing of Israelite Society," W. G. Dever Festschrift (as yet untitled), ed. Seymour Gitin, J. Edward Wright, and J. P. Dessel (forthcoming).

50. So Jordan and Kalćik, "Introduction," in *Women's Folklore, Women's Culture,* xii.

51. Michele Z. Rosaldo, "Women, Culture, and Society: A Theoretical Overview," in *Women, Culture, and Society,* ed. Michele Z. Rosaldo and Louise Lamphere (Stanford: Stanford University Press, 1974), 36–37.

52. Challenge to existing notions of gendered behavior is a methodological consideration with important results for determining gendered aspects of power in ancient Israel; see Carol Meyers, "Having Their Space and Eating There Too: Bread Production and Female Power in Ancient Israelite Households," *Nashim: A Journal of Jewish Women's Studies* 5 (2002): 14–44.

53. Although the Reed Sea (Red Sea) episode in some way marks the beginnings of the wilderness wanderings, it is perhaps better to see it as the culmination of the deliverance sequence of Exodus 1–14; so Walter Houston, "Exodus," in *The Oxford Bible Commentary,* ed. John Barton and John Muddiman (Oxford: Oxford University Press, 2001), 76.

54. So Fox, 81.

55. Nahash fights against King Saul, according to 1 Sam. 11:1–12; see Larry G. Herr, "Ammonites," in *Oxford Encyclopedia of Archaeology in the Near East,* vol. 1 (Oxford: Oxford University Press, 1997), 103–105.

56. Alberto R. W. Green, *The Role of Human Sacrifice in the Ancient Near East,* American Schools of Oriental Research Dissertation Series 1 (Missoula, Mont.: Scholars Press for the American Schools of Oriental Research, 1975). Another biblical example, 2 Kings 3:26–30, likewise involves a desperate military predicament.

57. Jakob H. Grønbæk, *Die Geschichte vom Aufstieg Davids (1. Sam. 15–2. Sam.5): Tradition und Komposition,* Acta Theologica Danica 10 (Copenhagen: Munksgaard, 1971).

58. Like Hosea and Ezekiel, Jeremiah deploys the marriage metaphor, with Israel as Yahweh's wife/bride. The language of 31:3–5 echoes the "bride" language of 2:2 and 3:1–10. So Kathleen M. O'Connor, "Jeremiah," in *The Oxford Bible Commentary,* ed. John Barton and John Muddiman (Oxford: Oxford University Press, 2001), 513; cf. Angela Bauer, *Gender in the Book of Jeremiah: A Feminist Literary Reading* (New York: Peter Lang, 1999).

59. See Susan Niditch, "Judges," in *The Oxford Bible Commentary,* ed. John

Barton and John Muddiman (Oxford: Oxford University Press, 2001), 181. She draws upon the work of Frank M. Cross, "Prose and Poetry in the Epic and Mythic Texts from Ugarit," *HTR* 67 (1974): 1–15.

60. Suggested by Eunice Poethig, "The Victory Song Tradition of the Women of Israel" (Ph.D. dissertation, Union Theological Seminary, 1985).

61. David Noel Freedman, "Pottery, Poetry, and Prophecy: An Essay on Biblical Poetry," *JBL* 96 (1977): 20.

62. The verb in each case is a form of yṣ'.

63. So William Propp, *Exodus 1–18: A New Translation with Introduction and Commentary,* Anchor Bible 2 (New York: Doubleday, 1998), 547.

64. A late Hasmonean date (ca. 76–67 BCE) seems likely, with the mention of Judith in the late-first-century CE work 1 Clement providing a *terminus ante quem;* see Denise Dombkowski Hopkins, "Judith," in *Women's Bible Commentary,* expanded ed., ed. Carole A. Newsom and Sharon H. Ringe (Louisville: Westminster John Knox Press, 1998), 280–81.

3

Mary Magdalene, a Beloved Disciple

ANTTI MARJANEN

*A*mong those second- and third-century Christian texts in which Mary (Magdalene)[1] figures as an important character there are two that describe her special position by stating that the Savior loved her more than the rest of the disciples. In the Gospel of Mary, this characterization of Mary is articulated by Levi, one of the male disciples of Jesus, after the disciples have hotly debated whether the instructions imparted to Mary during a private appearance of the risen Jesus to her correspond to the teachings of the Savior known by the male disciples (18,14–15).[2] In the Gospel of Philip, the status of Mary as the beloved disciple of Jesus is recognized by her envious male colleagues, who demand that he explain why she has gained this special position among the disciples (63,30–64,9).[3] In both of these writings the position of Mary as the beloved disciple serves specific functions that I hope to elucidate, but before I do this it is useful by way of comparison to look at some other early Christian texts that refer to the beloved disciples and see what functions and roles they have or do not have in these texts.

A "Beloved Disciple" as the Founder and Leader of a Christian Community

It is a commonplace that in the Christian writings of the first three centuries, and even more so in later apostolic legends, the earliest followers of Jesus, the apostles, were regarded as founders and leaders of Christian

churches and communities. This is already attested in the New Testament:
Peter, James the Just, and John the Zebedee, the pillars of the Jerusalem
church, as well as Paul, the missionary to the Gentiles, are notable examples
of this phenomenon (Gal. 2:7–9; 1 Cor. 3:10; Matt. 16:17–19; Gos. Thom. 12).
In his *Ecclesiastical History*, Eusebius does not confine the missionary activity of Peter and John only to Jerusalem, but he knows of traditions that introduce Peter as the founder of the bishopric in Antioch (*Hist. eccl.* 3.36.2;
cf. Origen, *Hom. Luc.* 6; *Ps.-Clem. Rec.* 10.69–72) and John as the missionary and founder of the first churches in Asia Minor (*Hist. eccl.* 3.1.1; cf.
Clement of Alexandria, *Quis div.* 42.2). In addition, Eusebius is aware of traditions according to which Thomas proclaimed the gospel and evidently established the first churches in Parthia, Andrew in Scythia (*Hist. eccl.* 3.1.1),
and Bartholomew in India (*Hist. eccl.* 5.10.3).[4] These observations invite us
to ask whether the fact that an apostle is designated as a founder or leader
of a Christian community is motivated by the fact that this particular apostle is regarded as a "beloved disciple" of Jesus.

If the texts dealing with Mary Magdalene are excluded at this point, it
is to be noted that there is no text in which the "beloved disciple" motif is
explicitly connected with one's gaining or assuming a leadership role.[5] Yet
some scholars have insisted that the "beloved disciple" of the Gospel of John
should be seen not only as the founder of the Johannine community but
also as its (first) leader.[6] As a decisive argument they refer to the final chapter of the gospel, in which the discussion about the destiny of the "beloved
disciple" has been taken to have been written in order to deal with the per-
plexity the death of the leader of the community has occasioned. This argument is not very convincing, however. First of all, it is not clear at all that
this text reflects the bewilderment caused by the death of a leadership figure.
Rather, it seems to be related to the discussion about the delay of the parousia.[7] The redactional comment on the reply of the risen Jesus to the question of Peter in John 21:23 stresses that the Johannine community should
not panic even if the "beloved disciple" has passed away before the return
of Jesus. The loss of a founder or a leader is not an issue. Secondly, although
the "beloved disciple" can be regarded as the mediator and the guarantor
of the Johannine tradition, and thus as an opinion leader (see below), it is
by no means certain that he was regarded as the founder and the (first) leader
of the Johannine community. As a matter of fact, the twenty-first chapter
of the gospel seems to attribute the leadership role to Peter, who is described
as the shepherd of the flock (21:15–17), despite the fact that he is not considered to be the one beloved by Jesus but to be the one who is expected to
love Jesus more than others. In light of this evidence, it is not necessarily to

be expected that the Mary texts in which she is characterized as a "beloved disciple" would grant her a leadership role, but if they do they appear to be quite exceptional.

A "Beloved Disciple" as a Person of Deeper Understanding

If there are no clear examples of "beloved disciples" assuming a leadership position in second- and third-century Christian texts, there are several texts in which a "beloved disciple" demonstrates or receives a special ability to understand Jesus and his message. It is frequently implied that the object of perception is a special, even a secret, revelation. In the so-called Second Apocalypse of James in the Nag Hammadi Library, the Savior calls James the Just as his beloved (Coptic: *merit*) and grants him a gift of deeper understanding: "My beloved! Behold, I shall reveal to you those things that neither [the] heavens nor their archons have known" (56,16–20). Also in the First Apocalypse of James, James the Just is praised for his understanding of the message of the Savior (29,4–5). Even though he is not called the "beloved (disciple)" in the extant part of the text, it is quite obvious that he has to be regarded as one since the way he is described closely follows that of the Second Apocalypse of James. In both writings James and the Savior for example kiss and embrace each other as an indication of their special relationship (1 Apoc. Jas. 31,4–5; 32,6–8; 2 Apoc. Jas. 56,14–16). In the so-called Secret Gospel of Mark the writer refers to a young man who is depicted as a special favorite of Jesus. This "beloved disciple" is led by Jesus to "the mystery of the kingdom of God."

In a third-century document Questions of Bartholomew, the protagonist of the text, the beloved Bartholomew, receives the promise from Jesus that he will get to know everything he wishes and even that which he does not know to ask (Quest. Barth. 1,5). In a Nag Hammadi tractate, the Apocryphon of James, two disciples, James and Peter, are portrayed as "beloved ones" who because of their knowledge and understanding can become "the cause of life for many" (10,29–34). In Pistis Sophia I–III, too, the designation "beloved" is used of several disciples who impress with their perception, including Philip (PS 75,2–3), John (PS 129,8), James (PS 149,7; 175,3), and Matthew (PS 161,22–23).[8] In the fourth book of Pistis Sophia the term "beloved disciple" no longer refers to a single special disciple but it is directed to all of the disciples since they all have been given the promise of "all mysteries and all knowledge" (PS 358,12–15). All of these texts suggest that the "beloved disciples," irrespective of whether the writers refer to a single one or whether many or all disciples are styled "beloved," serve as the prototypes of Jesus' followers who have or who are granted the extraordinary capacity both to grasp and to interpret the spiritual truths imparted by Jesus.

A "Beloved Disciple" as the Mediator and the Guarantor of a Special Revelation

A "beloved disciple" not only has a special ability of comprehension but also is assigned the task to act as mediator and authenticator of the message he or she has received. The classic example is the "beloved disciple" of the Gospel of John. In John 21:24 the "beloved disciple" is pictured as the one who by writing down the teachings and deeds of Jesus (or at least a small portion thereof) conveys them to later readers and makes it possible for them also to believe. At the same time, his/her special relationship as the closest disciple of Jesus and as an eyewitness makes him/her the guarantor of the truthfulness of the account. In this way the "beloved disciple" is also an opinion leader, although not necessarily seen as a person exercising supreme authority within the community.

A task of handing on the special revelation of Jesus is also given to James, the special confidant of the risen Savior in the First Apocalypse of James (36,15–38,11). He is the first one in a long chain of transmitters through whom the secret message is conveyed to further generations of hearers or readers. Unlike the "beloved disciple" in the Gospel of John, James is not the one whose task is to write down the teachings of Jesus. There is another non-canonical text, however, in which James is pictured as the one whose specific assignment is to note down the revelations of Jesus. In the Apocryphon of James, in which James is styled as a "beloved disciple," he is said to have written two secret books, one containing revelations imparted to him alone, the other one to both him and Peter. In Pistis Sophia I–III, too, there are two "beloved disciples," Philip and Matthew, who are given the task to write down the words and the deeds of Jesus (PS 71,18–22).[9]

As previously stated, the revelations "beloved disciples" receive and mediate are often secret. Usually they also have to be kept secret. Often this means that the revelation is transmitted only to a chosen group, to those who know how the message should be perceived. In the Apocryphon of James, the narrator of the text, James, warns his addressee not to disclose the secret revelation contained in the book to too many since it was not even divulged to all of the twelve. The revelation was meant only for those who can believe its message (1,8–28). This sort of language seeks to explain why the book had not gained wide publicity despite its ostensibly ancient character and why it had a limited readership. A similar discussion is found in the Questions of Bartholomew. In that text Bartholomew explicitly asks (4,66–68):

> Lord, may I reveal these mysteries to every man? (67) Jesus answered him: Bartholomew, my beloved, entrust them to all who are faithful and can keep for themselves. For there are some who are worthy of them; but there are also others to whom they ought not to be entrusted, for they are boasters, drunkards, proud, merciless, idolaters, seducers to fornication, slanderers, teachers of falsehood, and doers of all works of the devil, and therefore they are not worthy that they should be entrusted to them. (68) These things are also to be kept secret because of those who cannot contain them. For all who can contain them shall have a share in them.[10]

In these texts a "beloved disciple" is not only a revealer and a mediator of the secret teachings but also their guardian. His/ her task is to discern those who are worthy of them and to whom they can be delivered.

A "Beloved Disciple" as a Lover of a Teacher

The term "beloved disciple" can also imply that the love relationship between the teacher and the disciple is not simply nonsexual. Since this option has been suggested in connection with those texts in which Mary has been called the disciple "Jesus loved," it is important to ask whether the study of comparative material contains features that could support this kind of thesis.

It is interesting to note that in Greek philosophical schools a teacher could be styled as "lover" (erastēs) and a disciple as "beloved" (erōmenos).[11] Even though there is no reason to think that these designations always or often presupposed an erotic or a sexual relationship between the teacher and the disciple, it was not fully excluded either. Plutarch (Moralia 448E) gives us to understand that the use of the term erōmenos instead of mathētēs tends to imply that a pupil has a sexual relationship to his teacher. Is this possible in early Christian texts as well?

As far as the mere terminology is concerned one can at least say that the term erōmenos does not occur in Greek Christian texts to describe a "beloved disciple." This would suggest that in Christian texts the love relationship between the teacher and the disciple is not perceived in sexual terms. There is one Christian text, however, in connection with which the issue of a possible sexual character of the love relationship between Jesus and a "beloved disciple" has been raised. The text is the so-called Secret Gospel of Mark, which describes a nocturnal encounter between Jesus and a scantily dressed young man who is said to have loved him. It is the time of the meeting and the reference to the peculiar clothing of the young man that suggests to some scholars a sexual dimension in the encounter between the two men portrayed in the text.[12]

The significance of the undeniably extraordinary details of the story should not be overemphasized however. The point of the text is not that Jesus is teaching his disciple erotic skills, that is, the mystery of love, but, as the text says, "the mystery of the kingdom." The fact that the instruction takes place in the night does not stress its erotic nature but underscores the secret character of the teaching. In other words, the "beloved disciple" of the Secret Gospel of Mark is introduced into deeper spiritual wisdom that is not meant for every follower of Jesus. Based on this observation one can conclude that those Christian texts that introduce a "beloved disciple" do not generally lend support to an assumption that the love relationship between Jesus and his "beloved disciples" could have had sexual undertones.

Let us now move to the two texts that present Mary Magdalene as a "beloved disciple." They shall be examined in light of the four central themes in the other texts that referred to a "beloved disciple," although the order of the treatment will be different. Let me still emphasize one further point: the purpose of the following sections is not to settle historical questions but to see how Mary Magdalene is viewed in the texts and symbolic worlds of the Gospel of Mary and the Gospel of Philip.

Was Mary Magdalene Jesus' Lover or the Most Perceptive Disciple?

The fact that Mary Magdalene has more often than her male colleagues provoked a notion that the love relationship between Jesus and her is of a sexual or even marital nature depends not only on her sex but also on the way Jesus' and her relationship is described in the texts. Not only do the Gospel of Philip and the Gospel of Mary say that Jesus loved her very much, but the Gospel of Philip also states that she was the companion (*koinōnos* or its Coptic equivalent *hōtre*) of the Savior (59,6–11) and that he "[used to] kiss her [often] on her [mouth]" (63,35–36).[13] In the case of the Gospel of Mary Jesus' love for Mary can hardly be interpreted in terms of a sexual relationship. That Jesus loved Mary more than the rest of the disciples, as

Levi puts it in the text (18,14–15), simply indicates her favorite position as a disciple who was in a special way equipped to receive and interpret authoritative revelations.

The characterization of Mary in the Gospel of Philip is more complex in many respects. To be sure, the fact that Jesus is said to have loved Mary Magdalene more than the other disciples finds its explanation also in the Gospel of Philip in her ability to understand Jesus better than do her (male) colleagues. When they ask Jesus why he prefers her to them (63,37–64,2) he says to them: "Why do I not love you like her? When a blind man and one who sees are both together in darkness, they are no different from one another. When the light comes, then he who sees will see the light, and he who is blind will remain in darkness" (64,5–9).[14] But what should one conclude from Mary's status as Jesus' companion and the kisses between her and Jesus?

The term "companion" (koinōnos and its Coptic equivalent hōtre) can be used in several ways. It can connote an illegitimate sexual partner, for example. Since the word in the Gospel of Philip always appears in a positive sense, this meaning of the word is to be excluded. Koinōnos can also denote a marriage partner, a wife. This interpretation of the term is unlikely too. The Gospel of Philip frequently speaks about someone's wife; however, it never employs koinōnos in this sense, but always a more common Coptic word, shime. Hence, the use of the word koinōnos seems to imply that the companionship between Mary and Jesus is not to be viewed in terms of a sexual or marital relationship but in terms of a spiritual relationship. But what about the kisses? Do they not speak against this assumption?

The kisses do not have to be perceived from the perspective of a sexual partnership.[15] First, in other contemporary religious writings there are plenty of examples where kissing functions as a metaphor for transmitting a special spiritual power.[16] Second, in the only other passage in the Gospel of Philip where kissing is referred to it is mentioned without concrete sexual implications, as a metaphor of spiritual nourishment (58,30–59,6). Third, the altercation between the (male) disciples and the Savior in Gospel of Philip 63,37–64,9 suggests that kissing is not to be understood as an expression of sexual love. The question of (male) disciples shows that the relationship between Jesus and Mary Magdalene is viewed in such a way that also male disciples can be jealous of her. In addition, when the (male) disciples ask why the Savior loves Mary more than the others, they do not point to any sexual motives but to her spiritual capacity to see better. Fourth, in the Second Apocalypse of James, which is the most interesting parallel to Gospel of Philip 63,34–37, it is said that when the risen Lord wanted to disclose his most secret mysteries to James he kissed him and called him his

"beloved" (2 Apoc. Jas. 56,14–20). In that context kissing is clearly a symbolic act that demonstrates James's privileged standing. In light of these observations, the reference to Jesus kissing Mary in the Gospel of Philip is best
expounded as having no sexual connotation but as being an indication of
her supreme position as a disciple whose spiritual perception excels that of
the others.[17]

Mary's status as Jesus' *koinōnos* is thus not a role of a lover. Neither is
she to be regarded as a wife, but as a spiritual companion. In this way Jesus
and Mary constitute a spiritual consortium that, in Valentinian terms, provides the prototype of the union between Christ and his Church that mate-
rializes when the spiritual elect are united with their angelic counterparts in
the realm of light (Gos. Phil. 58,10–14).[18]

Mary Magdalene as the Mediator and the Guarantor of a Special Revelation

Although the Gospel of Philip emphasizes the extraordinary spiritual
perception of Mary Magdalene, it nowhere refers to a special revelation obtained by her. Nor is Mary Magdalene described as a guarantor or a mediator of the traditions preserved in the Gospel of Philip. This is in line with
the tendency in the Gospel of Philip according to which Mary is the confidant
of Jesus during his earthly life, whereas the male disciples are jealous of her
position and only after the resurrection gain a better understanding of deeper
spiritual mysteries. After the resurrection, it is the collective witness of all
the apostles and their followers by means of which the teachings of Jesus
found in the Gospel of Philip are authenticated and mediated to further generations (74,17–18; 81,1–14).[19]

In the Gospel of Mary the situation is different. Mary is pictured both
as the one who receives a special, authoritative revelation cast in the form
of a vision and as the one who as the special favorite of Jesus guarantees its
truthfulness. In this way the Gospel of Mary can be clearly linked with those
texts in which a "beloved disciple" serves as an authenticator of the tradition underlying a text on which a community bases its understanding of its
faith.[20]

The peculiar thing in the Gospel of Mary is that in the text world of the
writing the position of Mary is questioned. The readers are informed that
Mary's revelation is given a cold reception among the male disciples, especially by Peter and Andrew, who seriously doubt whether the risen Savior
could have revealed something like that, especially to a woman and in a vision (17,10–22). The fact that the revelation obtained by Mary is not accepted

without reservations suggests that the author of the text is addressing an audience that is skeptical about the ideas related to Mary Magdalene of the text. In this situation it may not be accidental that Peter, probably representing skeptical voices, in inviting Mary to reveal some special teachings of the Savior does not characterize her as a "disciple Jesus loved" but as the one whom "the Savior loved more than the rest of women" (10,2–3). To balance this the author needs to introduce Levi into the narrative after Mary's speech and its critical reception by the other male disciples. Levi supports Mary, and his defense is based on the fact that the Savior knew Mary very well and loved her not only more than the rest of women but more than the other disciples (18,12–15). According to Levi, she is the "beloved disciple" who is the best choice for the task of receiving and authenticating the authoritative revelation of the Savior.[21]

Mary Magdalene and the Question of Leadership Roles

Usually the "beloved disciple" motif is not connected with the question of leadership roles in early Christian communities. The Gospel of Philip does not seem to be an exception in this regard. Mary Magdalene is not portrayed as a paragon of a Christian leader in that writing. Rather, she is a prototype of a Christian who perceives deeper spiritual truths, to the extent that she together with Jesus can be seen as the symbol of the Church uniting with Christ in the final consummation in the realm of light.

Again, the Gospel of Mary discloses a somewhat different picture. The conflict between Mary and the male disciples, Peter and Andrew, which has a central role in the plot of the writing, brings a new feature to the "beloved disciple" motif. Here it also has to do with the question of spiritual leadership. While validating Mary's teaching and her privileged status against accusations launched by Peter that the Savior would not have revealed such a special revelation to a woman that he did not tell to his male disciples, the Gospel of Mary affirms the legitimacy of women's leadership role. As succinctly put by Karen King, Mary and her defender Levi "represent those Christians who question the validity of any apostolic authority that challenges the truth of their own experience of the Living Lord; for them, apostolic authority is not based simply on being one of the Twelve or on gender but on spiritual qualifications. Women who have those qualifications may exercise legitimate authority."[22] It is therefore worth noting that immediately after the risen Jesus departs from his disciples and before Levi grants a formal justification to her position as a spiritual authority Mary herself already takes the place of the leader and consoles and encourages her desperate colleagues (9,12–24).

Although the leadership role is questioned by Andrew and Peter, the support of Levi again returns it to Mary at the end of the gospel.

Conclusion

The two texts in which Mary Magdalene features as a "beloved disciple" draw a somewhat different picture of her. In the Gospel of Philip, she is a "beloved disciple" in whom the most dominant feature is connected with her ability to see and to understand spiritual realities. As a special consort of Jesus she also becomes a prototype for seeking unification with the realm of light. Mary Magdalene in the Gospel of Mary seems to expand the notion of a "beloved disciple" to a new direction. She is no longer a mere authenticator of an authoritative tradition, an opinion leader, but a supreme spiritual authority who is courageous enough to challenge old traditions if they tend to discourage and intimidate the followers of the Savior because of irrelevant issues, such as gender or restraining rules (18,7–21). It is the "beloved disciple" of the Gospel of Mary who better harmonizes with essays in this collection. As a receiver of a special divine revelation and as a spokesperson for a subdued group, namely women, Mary Magdalene of the Gospel of Mary joins in a long-standing prophetic tradition. And as a favorite disciple of Jesus she assumes the role of an apostle, along with the others who have mediated the message of the risen Lord.

NOTES

1. Whether Mary is Magdalene, as I assume (A. Marjanen, *The Woman Jesus Loved: Mary Magdalene in the Nag Hammadi Library and Related Documents*, Nag Hammadi and Manichaean Studies 40 [Leiden: Brill, 1996]; A. Marjanen, "The Mother of Jesus or Magdalene? The Identity of Mary in the So-Called Gnostic Christian Tradition," in *Which Mary? The Marys of Early Christian Tradition*, ed. F. Stanley Jones, SBL Symposium Series 19 [Atlanta: Society of Biblical Literature, 2002], 31–41), or the mother of Jesus or a composite figure (see S. Shoemaker, "Rethinking the 'Gnostic Mary': Mary of Nazareth and Mary of Magdala in Early Christian Tradition," *Journal of Early Christian Studies* 9 [2001]: 555–95; S. Shoemaker, "A Case of Mistaken Identity? Naming the Gnostic Mary," in Jones, *Which Mary?* 5–30) does not affect the argumentation.

2. For the Coptic text and an English translation of the Gospel of Mary, see Robert McL. Wilson and George W. MacRae, "BG,1: The Gospel according to Mary," in *Nag Hammadi Codices V,2–5 and VI with Papyrus Berolinensis 8502,1 and 4*, ed. Douglas M. Parrott, Nag Hammadi Studies 11 (Leiden: Brill, 1979), 453–71.

3. For the Coptic text and an English translation of the Gospel of Philip, see Bentley Layton and Wesley W. Isenberg, "Tractate 3: The Gospel of Philip," *Nag Hammadi Codex II,2–7 together with XIII,2*, Brit. Lib. Or.4926(1), and P.Oxy. 1, 654, 655*, vol. 1: *Gospel according to Thomas, Gospel according to Philip, Hypostasis of the Archons, and Indexes*, ed. Bentley Layton, Nag Hammadi Studies 20 (Leiden: Brill, 1989), 129–217.

4. For the apostles as missionaries, founders, and leaders of early Christian communities in early Christian traditions, see, e.g., Walter Bauer, "The Picture of the Apostle in Early Christian Tradition: 1. Accounts," in *New Testament Apocrypha*, vol. 2: *Writings Relating to the Apostles, Apocalypses, and Related Subjects*, ed. E. Hennecke and W. Schneemelcher, trans. R. McL. Wilson (London: SCM Press, 1965), 35–74.

5. The term "leader" is not used here of an opinion leader in general but in the narrow sense of the word, referring to a person exercising supreme authority within a group or community.

6. For the discussion, see Ismo Dunderberg, "The Beloved Disciple in John: Ideal Figure in an Early Christian Controversy," in *Fair Play: Diversity and Conflicts in Early Christianity—Essays in Honour of Heikki Räisänen*, ed. Ismo Dunderberg, Christopher Tuckett, and Kari Syreeni, Supplements to *NT* 53 (Leiden: Brill, 2002), 243–69. Some scholars suggest that the "beloved disciple" in the Gospel of John is Mary Magdalene. Most recently this is done by Esther A. de Boer, "The Gospel of Mary: Beyond a Gnostic and a Biblical Mary Magdalene" (dissertation, University of Kampen, 2002), 149–74. Despite her sometimes ingenious attempts to overcome the interpretive problems related to the identification of the "beloved disciple" with Mary Magdalene, such as the grammatical masculinity of the disciple "whom Jesus loved" and the obvious distinction between the "beloved disciple" and Mary Magdalene both at the cross and at the empty tomb, de Boer's thesis remains unconvincing.

7. Dunderberg, 250.

8. In the present article, the references to Pistis Sophia are made according to Carl Schmidt and Violet MacDermot, *Pistis Sophia*, Nag Hammadi Studies 9 (Leiden: Brill, 1978). The first number gives the page number of the Coptic text; the second number refers to the line.

9. Thomas is the third writer, but he is nowhere in the writing explicitly called "beloved."

10. The translation is derived from Felix Scheidweiler, "The Questions of Bartholomew," in *New Testament Apocrypha*, vol. 1: *Gospels and Related Writings*, 5th ed., ed. W. Schneemelcher, trans. R. McL. Wilson (Louisville: Westminster John Knox, 1991), 539–53.

11. Sjef Van Tilborg, *Imaginative Love in John*, Biblical Interpretation Series 2 (Leiden: Brill, 1993), 85–87.

12. This possibility was already suggested by Morton Smith, the first editor of the Secret Gospel of Mark; see Morton Smith, *Clement of Alexandria and a Secret Gospel of Mark* (Cambridge, Mass.: Harvard University Press, 1973), 251. Although

Smith primarily saw in the text a description of "a baptism administered by Jesus to chosen disciples, singly, and by night" he also thought that the union the baptism symbolized "may have been physical."

13. The lacunae of Gos. Phil. 63,35–36 can be plausibly reconstructed on the basis of the traces of the words and the discussion on Mary Magdalene and the function of the kisses in Gos. Phil. 59,3–9; for the arguments, see Silke Petersen, "*Zerstört die Werke der Weiblichkeit?" Maria Magdalena, Salome und andere Jüngerinnen Jesu in christlich-gnostischen Schriften,* Nag Hammadi and Manichaean Studies 48 (Leiden: Brill, 1999), 145–47; Jane Schaberg, *The Resurrection of Mary Magdalene: Legends, Apocrypha, and the Christian Testament* (New York: Continuum, 2002), 154.

14. Some scholars have insisted that the passage of the blind and one who sees does not belong together with the previous text dealing with the discussion between Jesus and his disciples about the relationship of Jesus to Mary Magdalene; see, e.g., Hans-Martin Schenke, *Das Philippus-Evangelium (Nag Hammadi-Codex II,3),* Texte und Untersuchungen 143 (Berlin: Akademie-Verlag, 1997), 336. For the arguments to the contrary, see Marjanen, *Woman Jesus Loved,* 163–64.

15. The following arguments derive from Marjanen, *Woman Jesus Loved,* 158–59.

16. Cf., e.g., *Jos. Asen.* 19,10–11; *Odes Sol.* 28,6–7; *Disc. 8–9* 57,26–28.

17. Schaberg, 155, insists that asking whether the kissing is an expression of "a spiritual love between a master and a disciple, or an erotic love creates a false dichotomy," but does not present any real arguments that would in the context of the Gospel of Philip speak for a more inclusive interpretation of the love relationship between Jesus and Mary Magdalene.

18. For the idea of the final spiritual consummation in Valentinianism and in the Gospel of Philip, see Marjanen, *Woman Jesus Loved,* 160–62. For the use of kisses in connection with the (Valentinian) eschatological reunification of the emanations with the Father in the realm of light, see also Gos. Truth 41,34–35.

19. For a more extensive presentation of this view, see Marjanen, *Woman Jesus Loved,* 165–69.

20. Unlike many other texts introducing a "beloved disciple," the Gospel of Mary does not appropriate the secrecy motif. Although Mary's revelation is received in a private vision, it is proclaimed openly, at first to the other disciples and later on to other people.

21. As has been cogently demonstrated by Karen King, "The Gospel of Mary," *Searching the Scriptures,* vol. 2: *A Feminist Commentary,* ed. Elisabeth Schüssler Fiorenza (New York: Crossroad, 1994), 601–34, there is another feature in the gospel that seems to serve the author's desire to bolster the truthfulness of Mary's teaching in the eyes of the readers. It is the connection between the teaching of the risen Savior at the beginning of the text and the revelation obtained by Mary after his departure. Although the fragmentary nature of the Gospel of Mary does not give a full possibility to assess all the links between the two, some of them are quite conspicuous. The ascent of the soul that Mary's vision describes is a concrete illustration of the

restoration of the soul to its root (7,17–20). The right answers presented by the soul to the worldly powers are made possible by the true self-knowledge that Jesus' view of salvation implies. The soul's dialogue with the third power about the dissolution of everything (15,21–16,1) seems to presuppose Jesus' prior teaching on that topic (7,3–8). All this seems to suggest that the author wants to defend Mary's teachings by demonstrating their affinity with Jesus' own ideas.

22. King, "Gospel of Mary," 623–24.

4

Miriam/Mariam/Maria: Literary Genealogy and the Genesis of Mary in the Protevangelium of James

MARY F. FOSKETT

o read the second-century extracanonical text the Protevangelium of James is to encounter a Mary who is altogether familiar and unfamiliar. What the title Protevangelium of James conceals, its alternative title, *Genesis Marias, Apokalypsis Iakob,* or "Birth of Mary, Revelation of James" reveals: the subject of this early Christian text is Mary, the mother of Jesus. As the text details the story of Mary from her origins and birth to her childhood and youth, her "marriage" to Joseph, her virginal conception, and the birth of her child, it maintains a steady focus on Mary rather than her son. And while it is obvious that the anonymous author of the Protevangelium of James (hereafter called PJ) drew heavily upon the traditions concerning Mary and the infancy of Jesus narrated in the opening chapters of Matthew and most especially Luke, it is also clear that much of what PJ says about Mary is without parallel in the New Testament. For not only is the Mary of this text (whose provenance is exceedingly difficult to determine) a virgin when she conceives her firstborn child, she remains a seemingly intact virgin even after giving birth.[1] It is to this text, then, not Matthew and Luke, that we can properly apply the phrase "virgin birth."

Thus the virgin of the PJ stands apart from her canonical portrayals. Indeed, the very aim of PJ is to praise both Mary and her extraordinary virginity. To readers of the Gospel of Luke, then, the Mary of the Protevangelium of James is, as is commonly found with all family resemblances, both very much like her canonical namesake and very much unlike her.[2] Moreover, when we consider how the Lukan Mary bears the marks of her own biblical namesake, Miriam, we can begin to trace both the literary genealogy that connects the Hebrew prophet to the canonical Mary and her extracanonical counterpart and the literary permutations that partly wrest from the protagonist of the Protevangelium the heritage of her foremothers.

Miriam/Mariam

The Lukan mother of Jesus is appropriately introduced early in this gospel, in the infancy narrative. Having recounted the miraculous pregnancy of Mary's elder kinswoman, Elizabeth, Luke turns his attention to Mary's even more unusual story: "In the sixth month the angel Gabriel was sent from God to a city of Galilee named Nazareth, to a virgin betrothed to a man whose name was Joseph, of the house of David; and the virgin's name was Mary" (Luke 1:26–27). From the very first, we know her name—Mary, or Mariam, the Greek equivalent of the Hebrew Miriam. Thus the Lukan mother of Jesus carries the name of the first woman prophet of the Jewish and Christian scriptures. While one might at first think this merely a coincidence (after all, couldn't many a Jewish woman have been named Mariam?), a close reading of the text shows that it is much more than that. For it is not only Miriam's name, but her prophetic vocation as well, that echoes throughout Luke's story. As Phyllis Trible has argued, the Lukan mother of Jesus figures prominently in the Miriamic procession as "Miriam *rediviva*."[3] Just as it is Miriam to whose lips we rightly ought to attribute the Song of the Sea (Exod. 15:1–18), it is Mariam, in Luke's gospel, who sings the Magnificat. Owing to the Magnificat's prophetic boldness, New Testament interpreters have identified Mary, the mother of Jesus, as a prophet in her own right. It is Trible, however, who has made explicit the hymn's Miriamic character. She writes, "We all know that the Song of Hannah (1 Samuel 2) provides vocabulary and themes for the Magnificat, but few of us know that the Song of the Sea, the Song of Miriam (Exodus 15), does the same."[4] In the tradition of Miriam's song, which celebrates and signals the liberation of the Hebrew people from Egypt, so is the Magnificat also a song of deliverance. Reading the two hymns side by side, Trible exposes the resonance between them:

> SS: I will sing to the Lord, most glorious deity.
> M: My spirit rejoices in God my Savior.
>
> SS: Thy right hand, O Lord, glorious in power;
> Thy right hand, O Lord, shatters the enemy.

M: God has shown strength with the divine arm, has
Scattered the proud in the imaginations of their hearts.

SS: Pharaoh's chariots and his hosts God hurled into the sea.
M: God has put down the mighty from their thrones.[5]

As Trible has made undeniably clear, it is not only biblical tradition, but
also Miriamic tradition in particular, that lends shape to Luke's portrayal of
Mary. Furthermore, when one looks beyond Mary to the rest of the gospel,
this same tradition is found at the core of Jesus' ministry and mission. Following Trible's lead, we can hear Miriamic themes reverberating throughout Luke's story of Jesus. The themes of deliverance laid out in the Magnificat
("God has put down the mighty from their thrones, and exalted those of low
degree; God has filled the hungry with good things, and the rich God has
sent empty away" [Luke 1:52–53]), form the very center of Jesus' inaugural
sermon: "The Spirit of the Lord is upon me, because God has anointed me
to preach good news to the poor. God has sent me to proclaim release to the
captives and recovery of sight to the blind, to set at liberty those who are
oppressed, to proclaim the acceptable year of the Lord" (Luke 4:18–19). In
Jesus' voice one can hear echoes not only of Isaiah, but of Miriam and
Mariam, too.

Mariam's hymn also echoes throughout the Lukan beatitudes: "Blessed
are you poor, for yours is the kingdom of God. Blessed are you that hunger
now, for you shall be satisfied. . . . But woe to you that are rich, for you have
received your consolation. Woe to you that are full now, for you shall hunger"
(Luke 6:20–25). Thus the entirety of Luke's gospel, including the portrayal
of Jesus' primary mission, is shaped by the prophetic vision that Mary utters, one that is itself rooted in the traditions of her ancient foremother,
Miriam. In this way, the Lukan Mary clearly honors her literary and theological genealogy to reveal her place in the Miriamic procession.

Mariam/Maria

Before turning to a discussion of how the heroine of the Protevangelium
of James fits into this same genealogy, let me recount PJ's plot for readers
who may be unfamiliar with this apocryphal text. The narrative, widely read
and probably dating to the mid second century, begins by focusing first on
Mary's parents. Mary's father, Joachim, a figure significant enough to be included "in the records of the twelve tribes of Israel" is introduced as "a very
rich man" (1,1–2). Yet despite the piety and wealth of Joachim and his wife,

Anna, they suffer from the stigma of infertility until God answers their prayers for a child.

In a brief annunciation scene, an angel of the Lord appears to Anna, saying that she "will conceive and give birth, and your child will be spoken of in all the world" (4,1; cf. Luke 1:31). Anna vows to bring the child as a "gift to the Lord my God, and it will serve him its whole life" (4,2). After she gives birth, she asks the midwife, "What have I delivered?" When she hears the response, "a female," Anna exclaims, in an obvious adaptation of Luke 1:46, "My soul has been magnified this day" (5,6), and she names the baby Mary.

Almost immediately after she is born, the child demonstrates exceptional physical growth and agility. Mary's parents raise her at home for her first three years, and they ensure the child's purity by confining her to a bedchamber-turned-sanctuary where nothing profane or unclean touches her. When Mary turns three, Joachim and Anna bring her to the temple. In contrast to her former home environment, she moves about freely here, quite at home in this most sacred of spaces, where she is "fed like a dove, receiving her food from the hand of an angel" (8,2).

All goes seemingly well until Mary reaches the age of twelve and is forced to leave the temple "lest she pollute the sanctuary of the Lord our God" (8,3–4). The priests' sudden concern for the purity of the temple suggests the imminent onset of the young girl's menarche, a phenomenon that would render both her and the temple unclean (Lev. 15:19–33). The text's recourse to Jewish custom when other aspects of the temple cult have been ignored only underscores the degree to which sexuality figures as the primary cause of crisis. The problem is not the temple. The problem is Mary.

After the high priest, Zechariah, prays for divine guidance, Mary, the "virgin of the Lord," is entrusted to the care of the aged widower Joseph, who takes Mary into his keeping (9,7–11) but soon leaves to go build houses. One day, while drawing water outside, Mary is greeted by an unidentified voice: "Greetings, favored one! The Lord is with you. Blessed are you among women" (11,2). In a variation on Lukan tradition, the virgin is disturbed because she can't discern where the voice is coming from. Retreating indoors, she is encountered by an unnamed angel (contra Luke's Gabriel) who tells her that she "will conceive by (the Lord's) word" (11,5). Mary is doubtful, wondering not whether she will conceive, but whether she will actually give birth in the manner usual for (all other) women (11,6).

After Mary consents to the divine message, she visits Elizabeth. In contrast to Luke's account, not only does Elizabeth refrain from praising Mary for having believed God's word, but Mary utters no joyous response to her kinswoman. Far from glossing over this departure from Lukan tradition, the narrator underscores the distinctive rendering of this scene by commenting specifically that Mary has forgotten the mysteries that the angel revealed to her (12,6).

When Joseph returns home from his building projects to find Mary in her sixth month of pregnancy and unable to explain its origin, he is anguished, frightened, and accusatory. After weeping bitterly, Mary at last speaks—and asserts her innocence. Like her canonical counterpart, she implies that she is yet a virgin, but when Joseph asks from whence her pregnancy comes, Mary can only declare her ignorance. Soon enough, others notice Mary's pregnancy, and both Joseph and Mary are tested and vindicated by an obscure drink test that confirms that they are indeed "intact" (*holokleros*, 16,5).

As in Luke's gospel, Mary travels with Joseph to Bethlehem in order to be enrolled in the emperor's census. When it comes time for her to give birth, Joseph goes in search of a Hebrew midwife, leaving Mary alone in a cave. He and the midwife return just in time to witness the phenomena that accompany Jesus' birth. A cloud overshadows the cave and as it withdraws, an intense light appears inside. As the light dims to reveal a newborn baby, the midwife proclaims a miracle: a virgin has given birth (19,18).

Sure enough, a postpartum gynecological exam confirms Mary's condition. Refusing to believe the midwife's astounding claim, another woman at the scene, Salome, examines Mary with her hand (20,2; cf. 19,19). In a scene that recalls Thomas's testing of Jesus (John 20:25), Salome's hand bursts into (clearly punitive) flames. When she picks up the newborn and is immediately healed, Salome rejoices that the child has been born to be king of Israel (20,10). Although the scene ends in language that praises the child, its weight rests on this final confirmation of Mary's extraordinary virginity.

In the final scene in which she appears, Mary acts to protect the baby from Herod's murderous rage by wrapping him in strips of cloth and hiding him in a manger. With this final harmonization of the canonical infancy narratives, PJ concludes its praise of Mary.

Even as brief a synopsis as this demonstrates PJ's literary dependence on the earlier canonical gospels. PJ's protagonist is clearly intended to correspond directly with the Lukan Mary. With such a clear connection in place, one might expect to see PJ's Mary giving voice to the same Miriamic tradition evidenced in Luke's narrative. Yet such is clearly not the case. Not only does Mary not give voice to the Magnificat, she hardly carries any voice at all. Rather than standing squarely in the prophetic tradition of her foremothers, the Mary of the Protevangelium is mostly situated at quite a distance from it.

The first hint of discontinuity emerges at the very opening of the narra-

tive. Whereas the Lukan Mary bears little social status, Mary is a figure of elevated standing throughout PJ. The gospel mentions only a few details concerning the circumstances in which we find Mariam, and almost nothing is
said of her family and kin.[6] In contrast, the Jacobean Mary is born into a
wealthy family, a great deal is made of her parents' standing within Israel, and
the text repeatedly details the circumstances in which she lives and the characters with whom she interacts. Because of these differences from Luke, interpreters have long read the Protevangelium as an apologetic piece that aims
to defend Mary against the kind of slander reflected in Celsus's *True Doctrine*.
The text implicitly refutes ancient claims that Mary was of little or no social
status, that she had to work with her hands at weaving in order to earn a badly
needed income, and that she was publicly exposed as an adulteress.[7]

That Mary differs from her Lukan counterpart is also made evident by
her name. Except for a single scene and variant readings that are scattered
and few, Mary bears the name Maria, rather than the name of her foremother,
Mariam. The author of PJ retains Mary's Lukan identity but little of her Miriamic heritage. Largely absent are the prophetess, the Magnificat, and the celebration of a people's deliverance. Indeed, the same kind of editorial hand
that took the Song of the Sea from Miriam's lips and placed it on Moses' can
be detected throughout PJ.[8] Fragmentary echoes of the praise that the Lukan
Elizabeth offers Mariam and that Mariam sings to God are placed here on
the lips of male priests (PJ 7,7; 12,2). Even when Mary is elevated as an object
of praise (as when the priest exclaims, "Mary, the Lord God has extolled your
name and so you will be blessed by all the generations of the earth," 12,2),
such exaltation costs Mary much of her Miriamic inheritance.

The narrative's only significant allusion to the Miriamic dimension of
Mary's portrayal is found in variant renderings of an enigmatic scene (PJ
17,1–11) that precedes the narration of Jesus' birth.[9] The critical texts of Tischendorf and de Strycker, which have served successively as the standard
Greek editions of the Protevangelium, each incorporate Miriamic references
in the single scene that casts Mary as a visionary. Mary is called *Mariam* (Tischendorf) and *Mariamme* (de Strycker). Unlike the few sporadic and seemingly random references to Mariam that occur in Tischendorf, the conver-
gence of Miriamic appellations by two critical texts in the same scene
deserves attention.

The occurrence of *Mariamme* in de Strycker's text accompanies Mary's
only demonstration of prophetic vision and speech in all of PJ:

And so (Joseph) saddled his donkey and had (Mary) get on it. His son
led it and Samuel brought up the rear. As they neared the three-mile

marker, Joseph turned around and saw that she was sulking. And he said to himself, "Perhaps the baby she is carrying is causing her discomfort." Joseph turned around again and saw her laughing and said to her, "*Mariamme*, what's going on with you? One minute I see you laughing and the next minute you're sulking."

And she replied, "Joseph, it's because I imagine (*blepo en tois ophthalmois mou*) two peoples in front of me, one weeping and mourning and the other celebrating and jumping for joy."

Halfway through the trip *Mariamme* said to him, "Joseph, help me down from the donkey—the child inside me is about to be born." (PJ 17,5–9)

As Ronald F. Hock notes in his commentary and critical translation of the Protevangelium, in this sequence Tischendorf also calls Mary by the name of her Hebrew foremother: "And *Mariam* replied . . . Halfway through the trip *Mariam* said to him" (PJ 17, 9–10). Thus both texts demonstrate that though it is certainly marginalized, Miriamic tradition is not *entirely* suppressed in PJ.

Maria is Mariamme/Mariam when she is momentarily identified as a seer (*blepo en tois ophthalmois mou*). Here she is visited by revelation and utters an insight that serves as the counterpart to Simeon's programmatic prophecy in Luke 2:34.[10] Thus in this instance alone, PJ reassigns to a female figure prophetic insight that Luke attributes to a male character. The tradition knows Miriam and her visionary legacy well enough to make effective use of it in one scene while omitting it from the rest of the narrative.

The Virgin(s) Mary

Thus important differences emerge in the portrayals of the Lukan Mariam and PJ's Maria. One is a prophet in her own right who introduces the central themes of Jesus' later ministry. The other is the largely silent but greatly revered object of praise. Having seen a disparity in the degree to which each stands in the Miriamic procession, we now consider the continuity and discontinuity of another dimension of their portrayals, namely, the identification of each as a *parthenos,* or virgin. The virginity of the Lukan Mary is surely the primary interest and concern of the Protevangelium. Yet as PJ develops this aspect of Mary's portrayal into a full-blown narrative about her, it not only expands the significance of, but also changes, the very virginity it attributes to its protagonist. Whereas virginity need be only a temporary condition of the canonical virgin, it is an absolute state that defines and distinguishes the Jacobean Mary. Mariam and Maria are virgins *differently*. And it is virginity, or rather the way in which each narrative exploits particular images of virginity, that holds at least one key to understanding how these texts alternatively sustain and suppress the procession of Miriamic tradition.

That virginity is somehow connected to the Miriamic dimension of Mary's portrayal is evidenced by a gap in the Lukan narrative that scholars as varied as Peter Brown, Raymond E. Brown, and Turid Karlsen Seim have observed. Prophecy, especially as prophetic speech, is a prominent theme in the books we call Luke and Acts. Yet although the prophetic Spirit is said to be poured out "upon all flesh" (Acts 2:17–21)—daughters as well as sons, and female as well as male slaves—Luke limits his portrayal of female prophetic activity to only seven characters in his two-volume saga. Interestingly, each of the seven women is either a virgin (see again Mary's Magnificat), a widow (Luke 2:36–38), or a woman well advanced in age (Luke 1:18). Despite the programmatic function of prophetic activity, only the widow, Anna, and Philip's four virgin daughters are explicitly identified as female prophets (*propheteuousai*, Acts 21:9). Thus Luke's narrative suggests not only that the Spirit's interaction with women is limited, but that it is predicated upon the absence of female erotic activity. As Seim notes, "In Luke-Acts chastity is never explicitly stated as a prerequisite for revelations by the Spirit or the gift of prophecy. . . . It is, however, remarkable that out of the seven concrete cases of prophesying women who are mentioned in Luke-Acts . . . six are said to be chaste."[11] Moreover, when Mary gives voice to the Magnificat, the single extended speech in all of Luke-Acts attributed to a female character, she is a virgin. After she gives birth to Jesus and is called no longer virgin but mother (*meter*), she is rendered silent and left only to ponder in her heart all that she sees and witnesses.

The ancient association of virginity and prophecy is well attested. Jewish, so-called Pagan, and Christian witnesses lend evidence to the belief that "abstinence from sexual activity, and especially virginity, made the human body a more appropriate vehicle to receive divine inspiration."[12] While it would be misleading to contend that either virginity or sexual renunciation was seen as essential to prophecy, literary evidence does suggest that virginity supplied the seer with a certain advantage. Prophecy was seen as a highly charged physical phenomenon analogous to, but not synonymous with, sexual union. As Dale Martin suggests in his study of prophecy in the Corinthian church, "the physiology of prophecy could be analyzed by analogy with the physiology of sex, because prophecy was thought of as the penetration of the body of the priestess by the god or some other, perhaps inanimate, invading force."[13] Moreover, the prophetic availability of women "was a physiological fact, anchored in the very nature of female flesh."[14] Women, whose flesh was considered cooler, moister, and more porous than that of men, were considered more penetrable. In addition, one need only recall ancient models of female anatomy and images of prophecy at the famed Delphi (in which a virgin prophetess was seated over the oracular tripod) to see the provocative symmetry of a virgin's upper mouth that opens to speak for, and a lower orifice that opens to receive, the spirit of a male god.

Thus the inconsistency between Luke's emphasis on a generalized outpouring of the prophetic Spirit and his very limited portrayal of female prophecy may be owing, in part, to such ancient economies of prophecy and physiology. Despite the openness of his stated theological program, cultural images of virginity may be exerting their influence. Seen in this light, Mary's virginity advances her prophetic role and her Miriamic heritage. But the virgin who utters the Magnificat is rendered silent and decidedly less Miriamic once she takes on the role of wife and mother.

In contrast to Luke, PJ's author exercises another choice altogether by supplanting virginity's prophetic connotations with another ancient image associated with virginal status, namely purity. In ancient discourse, virginity and sexual abstinence were often associated with moral or cultic purity. Occasionally expected of laity, limited periods of abstinence were more often associated with priests who needed to prepare themselves for their sacred duties. Requisite extended virginity, as in the case of certain priestesses, indicated a kind of discrete and exceptional purity possessed by the priestess. Such virginity, as in the case of the Vestal Virgins, whose purity was said to have reflected the sanctity of the fire and the objects they handled in the course of their ministrations, was particular and distinct.

According to Mary Beard, one sees "the boundary between virginity and non-virginity" being negotiated in the ancient question of whether virginity, in and of itself, was sufficient evidence of the kind of chastity that a priestess was to exhibit.[15] The disputes detailed in the elder Seneca's declamations give the reader reason to observe that, in the context of priesthood, being a virgin was to imply more than virginity. It was to signal exceptional purity. Throughout the declamations, the lines between virginity, chastity, and purity remain ill defined and closely aligned, with each connoting the other. Such semantic blurring lies at the heart of a legal process that "enquires into a woman's ancestors, her body, her life" (*Contr* 1,2,11).[16] A priestess not only had to provide evidence of her purity through her conduct and her choices, she had to physically embody virginity, chastity, and purity—the tripartite requisite of women seeking the priesthood.

So-called Pagan, Jewish, and Christian narratives also underscore the relationship between virginity and purity. The thematic function of sexual self-control in the ancient novels is well known. In texts such as Joseph and Asenath, the Acts of Paul and Thecla, and the Acts of Peter, virginity is associated with moral and spiritual purity. As a virgin who chooses to remain spiritually and physically chaste, Thecla commits herself to the perpetual preservation of her virginity. And in the Acts of Peter, virginity so embodies purity that its loss signals nothing less than absolute defilement. Indeed, it is better for a virgin to die than to fall victim to sexual violation. Here the virgin's body is valued *insofar as it is pure.* Thus in both ancient discourse and narrative, virginity could function as both a means and sign of purity.

Interpreters have noted the degree to which the Protevangelium repeatedly aims to demonstrate Mary's remarkable purity. Like the Vestal Virgins of respectable parentage who go to live at the temple at the age of six and whose bodies are of sound condition (*Attic Nights* 1,12), Mary, the healthy three-year-old daughter of righteous and wealthy parents, is brought to live in the "temple of the Lord" (PJ 7,1–10). Living in the temple, eating a special diet, and interacting only with the religious elite, Mary is portrayed as a holy child. Thus the narrative attributes to Mary the priestly requisites of physical soundness, chastity, and purity—but refrains from ascribing to her the duties and privileges of the priesthood.

As she departs from the sheltered life of the temple, it is the designation "virgin of the Lord" that most sets Mary apart, that expresses her purity, and that distinguishes her from among other women. The virgin belongs to the Lord—thus she is given to Joseph as a ward, not as a wife. As a sacred object that is dedicated to the Lord, celebrated by the people, and protected (mostly) by men, she resembles more a cult object than a priestess in whose care the sacred things are placed.

The nature of Mary's virginity is most revealed in the annunciation and birth of her son. Again, here she asks not *how* she will conceive, but whether she will give birth in the manner of other women (PJ 11,6). The virgin's question exposes her concern for her bodily integrity—and it is to *this* question that the angel responds, "the power of God will overshadow you" (PJ 11,7). As readers well know, God makes good on the divine promise. Mary most certainly does not give birth as other women do, but only as a most exceptional virgin can.

Thus Mary's virginity is a concrete expression of her purity. Her purity is worthy of praise and honor, but it is a purity that is ascribed and then well guarded, rather than achieved. By elevating Mary, or rather Maria, as an object of devotion and exaltation, PJ takes the Lukan Mary's virgin identity and spins it in a new direction, one that leads away from Miriam and toward the very roots of later Mariological development. Mary retains her virginity and her prominence, but loses much of her voice and that of her foremother.

Therefore as readers consider the Miriamic tradition and how it is carried forth or not by subsequent Marys, we would do well to examine not only who each of these Marys is, but also what has been given to her and what has been taken away. To do that, after all, is to honor and give voice anew to Miriam herself. For both attempts to diminish her voice and resistance to such suppression lie at the heart of her legacy and procession.

NOTES

1. This essay makes use of Ronald F. Hock's commentary and critical translation of the Protevangelium of James. Noting the multiple problems raised by the precise dating, authorship, and provenance of the text, Hock observes: "The question of provenance for the Infancy Gospel of James is the most difficult to answer, and perhaps only negative answers are possible . . . it may be best at present to withhold judgment on the matter of provenance, at least until new evidence of arguments are forthcoming" (*The Infancy Gospels of James and Thomas,* The Scholar's Bible [Santa Rosa, Calif.: Polebridge Press, 1995], 12–13).

2. My argument here draws and builds upon my previously published work. For extended discussion of the differences between the portrayal of Mary in the Protevangelium of James and in Luke-Acts, the various images associated with virginity in antiquity, and the significance of some of these as they relate to the Protevangelium of James and Luke-Acts, see Mary F. Foskett, *A Virgin Conceived: Mary and Classical Representations of Virginity* (Bloomington: Indiana University Press, 2002).

3. Phyllis Trible, "Eve and Miriam: From the Margins to the Center," in *Feminist Approaches to the Bible: Symposium at the Smithsonian Institution, September 24, 1994, sponsored by the Resident Associate Program; Phyllis Trible, et al.,* ed. Hershel Shanks (Washington, D.C.: Biblical Archaeology Society, 1995), 23.

4. Ibid., 22.

5. Ibid.

6. Joel Green, "The Social Status of Mary in Luke 1.5–2.52: A Plea for Methodological Integration," *Bib* 4.73 (1992): 457–72.

7. See, for example, P. A. van Stempvoort, "The Protevangelium Jacobi, the Sources of Its Theme and Style and Their Bearing on Its Date," in *Studia Evangelica III,* ed. F. Cross, TU 88 (Berlin: Akademie Verlag, 1964), 410–26.

8. Trible, "Eve and Miriam," 17.

9. Hock, 61–63.

10. As Hock notes, "The idea of two peoples seems to come from Gen. 25:23, but the weeping and celebrating likely derives from Luke 2:34, where Simeon says that Jesus will cause the fall and rising of many in Israel" (63).

11. Turid Karlsen Seim, *The Double Message: Patterns of Gender in Luke-Acts* (Nashville: Abingdon Press, 1994), 180. In his monumental study of the canonical infancy narratives, Raymond E. Brown momentarily pondered a possible connection between sexual status and prophecy in Luke in a significant footnote: "We may speculate whether in Luke's view the celibate state had something to do with the ability to prophesy. The four daughters of Philip who prophesy are unmarried" (*The Birth of the Messiah: A Commentary on the Infancy Narratives in the Gospels of Matthew and Luke,* 2nd ed., Anchor Bible Reference Library [New York: Doubleday, 1995], 467 n. 68).

12. Peter Brown, *The Body and Society: Men, Women and Sexual Renunciation in Early Christianity* (New York: Columbia University Press, 1988), 67.

13. Dale B. Martin, *The Corinthian Body* (New Haven, Conn.: Yale University Press, 1995), 241.

14. Ibid., 242.

15. Mary Beard, "Re-reading (Vestal) Virginity," in *Women in Antiquity: A New Assessment,* ed. Richard Hawley and Barbara Levick (London: Routledge, 1995), 172.

16. Seneca (the Elder), *The Elder Seneca: Declamations in Two Volumes,* trans. M. Winterbottom, Loeb Classical Library (Cambridge, Mass., and London: Harvard University Press and Heinemann, 1974).

5

Three Odd Couples: Women and Men in Mark and John

CLAUDIA SETZER

*I*ndividual women meet Jesus in both public and private settings in the gospels. Here I will examine three instances where women's encounters with Jesus appear in tandem with his encounters with men. These paired scenes act as reflections or photographic negatives of one another. Because these encounters yield richer results when read in pairs, and because these are often unlikely pairs, I call them "three odd couples."[1] Perhaps also oddly to some, in all three cases, the women are the "winners," the exemplary ones compared to the men.

First I will look at these three examples and how they seem to work, doing a feminist-literary interpretation that builds on the work of many feminist scholars. Then I will do a bit of creative betrayal, and turn the interpretation back on itself to ask what are the assumptions at work in these feminist readings? How much are we reading in our own preconceptions about women and men, power, status, Jewish culture, and the earliest Jesus movement? In turning the stories a different angle, I hope to train more light on them.

Mark 7: The Syro-Phoenician Woman

In this wonderful story three players appear in succession. Three groups or people question Jesus or want something from him. First the Pharisees, with some scribes, ask why the disciples are eating with hands *koinais,* ritually unclean, but also the Greek word for "common." Aside from simply be-

ing the word for ritually unclean, the word hints at the issue of status, suggesting the Pharisees are a group that holds itself aloof from the masses. Mark
reinforces it with the image of the marketplace in vv. 3–4, the ultimate public space, where the masses gather. Just *anyone* and everyone could be there,
slaves, freedmen and women, merchants. So when the Pharisees return from
this public space they must purify themselves.[2] We hear no more from them.
They do not have much of a part, but provide an opportunity for a diatribe
against "the tradition of the elders," probably a proto-version of what the
rabbis would later call "the oral law."[3]

Mark has already prepared us not to expect much from the Pharisees.
Acting as a single character, they are consistently obstructionist straw men,
displaying misunderstanding and opposition to Jesus. This portrayal is
founded in Mark's polemic, not in history. A huge literature exists on who
and what the Pharisees were, but that is secondary to our interests here.[4]

But we might expect the Pharisees and scribes to be the first to understand Jesus. They are the most learned in the Torah and concerned with its
interpretation. According to Josephus, and, by implication, Luke-Acts, they
enjoy legitimacy with the people. They were the only Jewish group, aside from
believers in Jesus, to survive the catastrophe of 70. So in one way, we might
expect the most understanding from them, but, Mark tells us, they deliver
the least.

In v. 17, the second group arrives on stage: the disciples, who act as a
single character. We might expect more from them. Although they lack the
Pharisees' learning, they have been given the secret of the kingdom of God
(4:11) and, as Peter reminds Jesus, they have given up everything to follow
him. They do not *begin* to apprehend Jesus' meaning. They do not even have
a speaking part. In v. 18, Jesus chides them, "Are you as dull as the rest?" This
is one of many scenes in Mark where Jesus chides the disciples. They blun-
der along in amazement and awe at Jesus (1:22,27; 4:10,38,41; 6:2; 10:24,26),
and he shows increasing frustration at their inability to understand him, in-
terspersing his remarks with commands to "Hear," "Listen," and "Understand." The disciples surely do not understand Jesus either, and provoke another speech.[5]

The third actor arrives in v. 25, the so-called Syro-Phoenician "Greek"
woman. We have no reason to expect any understanding from her. Some
point to her—a Gentile, a foreigner, and a woman—as "triply marginalized."[6] She asks an exorcism from Jesus for her daughter, one of hundreds
he performs in this gospel.

Jesus rebuffs her and speaks sharply to her, as he did to the Pharisees
and the disciples. This saying, "Let the children first be fed, for it is not right

to take the children's bread and throw it to the dogs," refers to an exclusive mission to Jews. Unlike the other two characters, the Pharisees and the disciples, she persists. She engages in some repartee. Her rejoinder, "Lord,[7] even the dogs under the table eat the children's crumbs" convinces him. He is forced to agree. This is the only occasion in the gospels where Jesus is bested in an argument by anyone. The usual form of pronouncement story ends with the pithy saying of the teacher silencing all opposition (2:17; 2:27). But here he declares her deeper understanding. She is sent on her way and her daughter healed, not for her faith (as in Matthew), but as Joanna Dewey points out, because of the *content* of her words,[8] her "logos" (*dia touton ton logon hupage*). "Logos," word, has weighty associations: in Stoicism with the divine reason that fuels the universe, also with personified Wisdom, and with Hebrew Scripture, where the world is created through the divine word. It is not far-fetched to translate it here as "teaching": "for your teaching go your way."

So the apparent odd couple here is the Syro-Phoenician woman versus the disciples.[9] She is juxtaposed with the disciples because she acts out in fact what Jesus has just been trying to teach the disciples in words in v. 15, "It is not what goes into a man that defiles him, but what comes out of him." We assume that as a Gentile foreigner she does not worry about what goes into her, neither the kashrut nor the ritual purity of the food she ingests. But what comes out of her, her "logos," or teaching, identifies her as one who really understands Jesus.

She is also linked to the disciples because of the issue of confusion over literal and metaphorical statements of Jesus about food. When he talks about what goes into and what comes out of a person, the disciples show no sign of understanding that "what goes in" means food literally, but "what comes out" means actions and personal qualities, a nonliteral meaning. Whereas when Jesus talks to her about bread, "it is not right to take the children's bread and feed it to the dogs," she knows *exactly* what he means, that it is about his mission to Jews, not Gentiles. She comes back with a quick retort, on exactly the same level, "Lord, but even the dogs get the children's crumbs."

She understands. The triple outsider, the one we might expect the least from, is the one who understands Jesus' message and even, as Elisabeth Schüssler Fiorenza suggests, teaches Jesus by his own example against his saying.[10] This sends a powerful message of inclusion, for Gentiles, women, outsiders. The categories of worldly standards of nationality, ethnicity, and gender have been reversed, putting into motion Mark's principle that "many that are first will be last, and the last first (10:31)."

This passage has evoked a number of similar feminist readings. Most of them, including my own just now, base themselves on surprise. We assume that Mark means us to find something remarkable and unexpected about the foreign Gentile woman who understands Jesus and see this as rejecting an exclusivist system. Let us consider some of these interpretations.

In 1978, Antoinette Clark Wire explained this in literary terms as a form of the literary type of "demand story," where the seeker overcomes opposition before her wish is granted.[11] In some cases, as here, the obstacle is from the miracle-worker himself. The suspense draws in the reader, she says, "calls the hearer to break out of a closed world." Here is "a marvelous breakthrough . . . an extraordinary rift in a given, closed system."[12]

In 1984, Elizabeth Schüssler Fiorenza took a historical approach, saying this is a pre-Marcan scrap of material that points to Galilean women as important to the early Gentile mission. Women are paradigms of faithful followers. But she assumes it is pre-Marcan and at odds with Mark, but has somehow made its way into the gospel.[13]

In 1992, in *The Women's Bible Commentary*, Mary Ann Tolbert sees the woman as also overturning expectations, teaching Jesus that social conventions do not matter.[14] All three of these commentators also include the idea that the Syro-Phoenician woman's contact with Jesus and her wisdom in understanding him are surprising.

John 3–4: Nicodemus and the Samaritan Woman

One of the most attractive and nuanced pairs in the NT is Nicodemus and the Samaritan woman in John 3 and 4. As with the previous odd couple, they also appear in a set of three people who encounter Jesus, including the royal official (4:46) who asks for healing of his son.[15] The clear contrast, however, is between the two characters who talk with Jesus about different kinds of water, spirit, and who he is, Nicodemus and the Samaritan woman.

To my mind Nicodemus is not a negative character. Some have taken his coming to Jesus at night to suggest he stands for the "secret Christians" to whom John alludes, people afraid to openly declare their faith in Jesus,[16] or have seen him as exemplifying the disbelieving world, represented by "the Jews."[17] Yet both interpretations founder when the three appearances of Nicodemus are taken together and it becomes clear that Nicodemus moves toward public identification with Jesus. Nicodemus is better understood as a symbol of someone who tries to grasp Jesus in a totally intellectual way. Clearly he has pedigree, like the Pharisees in Mark 7. He is a Pharisee and an *archon,* a ruler of the Jews, some sort of official, and Jesus calls him a teacher of Israel (*didaskalos*); Jesus expects Nicodemus to understand him. He does have some faith in Jesus, but it is a faith based on "signs" or miracles (v. 2), something about which John is very ambivalent.

Nicodemus is well meaning, but he does not understand Jesus. His first misunderstanding stems from the two meanings of the Greek word *anothen,* "from above" and "again." Jesus, the man from heaven in this gospel, means "unless one is born from above he cannot see the kingdom of God," while Nicodemus understands it as "born again." From this awkward beginning the confusion multiplies. In vv. 4 and 9 Nicodemus asks "how" three times, trying to get at Jesus' meaning, but he does not progress. His status and pedigree as a teacher of Israel lead us to expect understanding. Jesus even says, "You a teacher of Israel, and you do not know these things?" But he does not.

This is the last of Nicodemus in this passage. Ultimately he moves along in the gospel, appearing twice more, when he argues for a fair hearing for Jesus (7:50–51), and finally, asking for Jesus' body (19:39). Wayne Meeks is correct that John often communicates through successive repetition, a progressive spiral. But I part company with Meeks in his negative assessment of Nicodemus's role. Nicodemus is not like the Jews in 8:31, who begin by believing in Jesus, then turn murderous. Rather, in his three appearances he moves from words to deed, from a private setting with Jesus, to a semipublic proceeding with the chief priests and Pharisees, to a public setting where he helps Joseph of Arimathea take Jesus' body to bury him. John reminds us that he had first come at night (15:39) to underscore that now he has come out into the open, just as he tells us that Joseph had been a secret disciple (v. 38) who is now out in the open. So Nicodemus does eventually "come out" in the gospel as a disciple of Jesus. But for the moment in chapter 3 he drops out, and we are left in suspense as to whether or not he will understand Jesus.

Immediately following Nicodemus, Jesus encounters the Samaritan woman in chapter 4. Her pedigree is lower; as a descendant of the mixed northern kingdom, Samaritans were of mixed religious status—not Jews, but not exactly Gentiles either. Her sexual history is mixed: she has had five husbands, and now is with someone to whom she is not married. She could also be said to be triply marginalized, as a Samaritan, a woman, and someone with a questionable sexual history. She too is nameless, like the Syro-Phoenician woman. So our expectations that she will understand Jesus are quite low. If the learned Pharisee, teacher, and leader Nicodemus stumbles, how will she, an unlettered Samaritan woman of dubious status, possibly cope with the mysterious man from heaven?

Unlike Nicodemus, who comes to Jesus at night, perhaps out of fear, the Samaritan woman meets Jesus at noon, in broad daylight.[18] Like Nicode-

mus, she asks a reasonable question, which sends Jesus into a theological exposition that she will not understand. Another play on words brings confusion. He says "living water," meaning life-giving water, whereas she seems
to understand it as "flowing water," obviously preferable to standing water.
Like Nicodemus, both are talking about water and spirit, "born of water and
the spirit" in the one and "living water" in the other.

Many have pointed out the image of meeting at the well evokes scenes
of betrothal in the Hebrew Bible (Gen. 24:10–61, Rebecca and Abraham's servant; Gen. 29:1–20, Jacob and Rachel; Exod. 2:16–22, Moses and the Midi-
anite women).[19] Sandra Schneiders suggests that Jesus is presented as the
true Bridegroom in John (2:9–10; 3:27–30). Also, I think the Samaritan
woman can be understood as having a flirtatious, perhaps teasing, quality
in v. 9, something along the lines of "I didn't think you Jews talked to the
likes of us."

The theological exposition and the play on words had left Nicodemus
struggling and perplexed. She does not understand Jesus either, but continues to *try* to understand. She asks questions, talks back, and moves ahead.
She seems to grope her way forward as the dialogue unfolds, willing to live
with confusion. Her response in v. 15 is surprising: "Sir, give me this water."
She cannot have understood Jesus' words, and so she took him literally. But
she is willing to go along, as if to say "all right, give me some of this water."

In vv. 16–18, Jesus reveals her sexual history, and she declares him a
prophet. She has moved forward another step in understanding. In v. 25 she
looks forward, is open to revelation. She does not yet grasp Jesus' meaning,
but she *will*. In some intuitive way she is ready to understand. By v. 28, we
still have not heard how much she understands, but her actions show she
has grasped Jesus' identity, at least in part. By v. 39, she has said the equivalent of, "Well, I don't know, but he told me everything I did." She has become the first preacher to the Samaritans (v. 39). The earliest group of Samaritans believe because of her "logos," or teachings, the same label applied to
the Syro-Phoenician woman's words to Jesus. Here many believe first because of the Samaritan woman's "logos," then more because of Jesus' "logos" in v. 41. She is a female John the Baptist, preparing the way for people
to believe in Jesus. She also symbolizes one who grasps things instinctively,
experientially, who lives with partial knowing and partial understanding and
it is enough. She moves forward in faith, even if she does not get it all. Nicodemus, by contrast, tries to grasp Jesus' words intellectually, and is undone by
his demand for total clarity. John is saying that is not how one comes to faith.
This fits with John's other thoughts on faith. Faith based on signs (miracles)
is pure empiricism, and John is clearly uneasy with it.

The male disciples do not grasp Jesus' meaning either. Because they marvel at him talking with a woman in v. 27, one may assume they are male. Jesus mentions spiritual food in v. 32, and they take him literally, saying "did someone bring him food?" Ironically, while Jesus is charging them to go out and preach, to gather in the ripe harvest in vv. 35–38, the Samaritan woman is already on her way, preaching successfully among her own people. Like the Syro-Phoenician woman, she is already acting out what he is trying to teach them in words. Both Raymond Brown and Elisabeth Schüssler Fiorenza suggest this is part of a traditional legend that recalls the first mission to the Samaritans.[20]

Both ethnicity and gender are pointed to explicitly in this passage. In v. 9, the woman needles Jesus, "You a Jew, talking to me a Samaritan," echoing Jesus' words to Nicodemus, "You a teacher of Israel, and you do not understand these things?" Both questions come out of expectations based on ethnic identity, expectations that are dashed. John turns convention inside out. Moreover, vv. 21–23 predict the erasing of boundaries between Jews and Samaritans. Similarly, gender is an apparent category because the disciples are said to be murmuring about Jesus speaking to a woman. But, as scholars such as Gail O'Day and Sandra Schneiders say, the conversation with Jesus and the Samaritan woman and her exemplary role imply that the boundaries between men and women are in the process of being erased.[21] Many commentators say this passage, like the story of the Syro-Phoenician woman, promotes the breaking down of all conventional boundaries—between Jew and Samaritan, men and women. Schneiders calls it a world of "shocking inclusiveness."

While we might have expected little of the Samaritan woman relative to the learned teacher of Israel, Nicodemus, she is gradually led along into faith. She comes to understanding not through rational argument, empirical proof, or demands for complete clarity but in an intuitive, experiential way, illustrating Pascal's famous insight, "The heart has reasons, which Reason knows nothing of" (*Pensées* 143). John is not positing a simple heart-versus-head opposition, but throughout the gospel reflects on different ways of "seeing" or understanding, and puts belief based on proof in last place.

John 20: Peter, the Beloved Disciple, Thomas, and Mary Magdalene

Another apostolic woman appears in John 20. Mary Magdalene discovers the empty tomb, encounters the risen Jesus, and is sent off to tell the disciples she has seen Jesus. Like the Samaritan woman, she also meets him sometime during the day (vv. 1 and 19). Here she is part of two pairings. She is contrasted with Peter and the Beloved Disciple on one side, then Thomas on the other, all three men being part of the Twelve, the inner circle around Jesus. We might have low expectations for her because she is not one of the Twelve, and because she has not appeared at all in this gospel until the scene at the cross in 19:25, which reflects the strong tradition of her witness to Jesus' death, burial, and the empty tomb.

Initially in 20:1–9 there is a struggle between firsts. Who is the first to discover the empty tomb? The complex choreography is probably as a result of mixed traditions over who is the first to realize the resurrection. Clearly a strong tradition exists that Peter is first to see the risen Jesus, as reflected in 1 Corinthians 15:4–8. Yet in this gospel, the hero is the Beloved Disciple, so he also has to be first. The text compromises. The Beloved Disciple outruns Peter to the tomb, gets there first, peeks in and sees the linen wrapping, sees it is empty, but does not go in. Peter actually goes into the tomb, doing a more thorough search; then the Beloved Disciple goes in, sees and believes. Both could be argued to be first. But all this is based on the report of Mary Magdalene, who is the first to find the tomb empty when she finds the stone has been moved. Whether she goes in or not is unstated, but she clearly knows Jesus' body is not there because she reports it missing (v. 13).

Mary is the first to encounter the risen Jesus. In a poignant scene, infused with emotion, she is initially confused, but recognizes Jesus when he says her name. One could debate about who found the empty tomb first, but in this gospel *no one* can doubt who is first to see and recognize the risen Jesus. Both Peter and the Beloved Disciple go home without reporting the tomb empty. She remains, trumping both Peter and the Beloved Disciple with the scene in the garden where she is first to encounter the risen Lord. Mary is the first to say "I have seen the Lord." Her declaration is echoed by the male disciples in v. 25. She is the first apostle of the risen Jesus, sent off to declare him in v. 17, "go, tell my brothers," before he sends off the others in v. 21.

The second couple that appears in contrast are Mary Magdalene and Thomas. The declaration "we have seen the Lord" is not enough for Thomas, also one of the Twelve. He requires empirical proof: "unless I see in his hands the print of the nails, and place my finger in the mark of the nails, and place my hand in his side, I will not believe" (v. 25). But so too do the other disciples; only after he shows them his hands and side do they recognize Jesus (v. 20). Mary, however, has a dramatic, revelatory moment when Jesus says her name.[22] She does not demand proof, or signs, as the male disciples seem to. John, throughout the gospel, understands that signs are effective to bring faith, but it is an immature faith, inferior to those who believe without demanding signs. Mary Magdalene is exemplary in that she believes without signs, declaring she has seen the Lord. As O'Day argues, she is the most human, showing grief, confusion, then recognition. She "bore witness to the tomb even in her confusion; Peter and the Beloved Disciple kept silent."[23]

The scene with Mary Magdalene is a hinge, contrasting with Peter and the Beloved Disciple on the one hand, and Thomas on the other. Two pairs are contrasted, rather than a threesome or a successive unfolding. Peter, the Beloved Disciple, and Thomas share some characteristics, since they all are part of the Twelve. Furthermore, all the men rely on some physical proof, so the examples show no progress in faith. Some politics is probably at work here, since all the men can readily represent communities. Mary is sandwiched between Peter, who represents what later became orthodox Christianity, the Beloved Disciple, who represents the Johannine community, and Thomas, who according to at least one scholar, represents a Gnostic community.[24] Whether Mary represents a particular community or not, she is a favorite with those who present an alternative vision of Christian origins. She is the hero of various Gnostic documents, at times teaching and reassuring the male disciples.[25]

Similarities

These three passages show some similarities. The dialogue unfolds in stages, bringing the characters and the readers along in understanding. Confusion trips up some characters and impedes understanding. The women move forward in faith in spite of partial understanding. An intuitive groping forward moves them along. They do not insist on empirical proof or total reassurance. The Syro-Phoenician woman simply assumes he can save the daughter. The Samaritan woman goes off to preach only with the assurance "he told me everything I did." Mary Magdalene recognizes him when he speaks to her and does not require physical proof.

Jesus often speaks on a different level than his characters. A cerebral, rationalist grasping at his words does not bring one to faith. Neither the questions of the Pharisees and the disciples in Mark, nor Nicodemus's how-what questions in John bring clarity. The demand for empirical proof falls equally short, both Thomas's challenge "show me some proof" and Peter's and the Beloved Disciple's elbowing each other out of the way to get to the tomb first, looking around for physical evidence of Jesus' absence.

We rightly greet with suspicion interpretations that associate women with intuition and men with rationalism. Yet these women are clearly more perceptive than those seeking rational proofs or empirical evidence. More significant is their place within a strain in early Christianity that rejects some kinds of intellectualism respected in the Greco-Roman world in favor of other kinds of understandings that apprehend the mystery and hidden secrets of God. Witness Matthew's revision of a Q saying, "I thank you, Father, Lord of heaven and earth, for hiding these things from the wise and understanding, and revealing them to babies" (11:25).[26] Paul too attacks worldly wisdom, particularly philosophy, in 1 Corinthians 1:19–25, "the folly of God is wiser than human wisdom."

At some point, in all these stories, the women are declared to have understood. The Syro-Phoenician woman is told "for this teaching you may go your way" in Mark 7:29. In John 4:39 the Samaritan woman's effect is underscored: "many believed because of her 'logos.'" In John 20:17 Mary has sufficiently grasped the reality of Jesus' presence that she is charged to spread the word: "Go and tell my brothers, 'I am ascending to my Father and your Father, to my God and your God." We are advised that these women all "get it." These excellent women all appear in groups of three and are exemplary witnesses. All three women are apostolic, going out and declaring Jesus in the Johannine scenes, providing a rationale for Gentile mission in Mark.

All three passages show a surprising overturning of expectations, an upending of the pyramid of power and patronage in ancient society. Women, the least likely ones to grasp the message, are the ones first to understand and to bear witness even in confusion and partial understanding. They illustrate the inclusiveness of the kingdom, expressed in Mark as the last shall be first, or that a follower of Jesus must become a servant of all. John, for his part, tells us that the kingdom is not like this world, and rejects worldly categories and expectations. In the kingdom, issues of gender, class, and ethnicity are erased.

We could stop here, and all feel very good about the gospel and its liberating message. These interpretations, I hope, have much to recommend them. But now I would like to engage in some creative betrayal. Having given with one hand I am (partially) going to take away with the other. I would like to nuance our interpretations by looking at some of the assumptions behind these interpretations.

Some Questionable Assumptions

All of these interpretations, including my own, revolve around surprise, the assumption that these women represent negative or disadvantaged categories to the authors and readers. Mary Rose D'Angelo's recent article on women in Mark and John challenges us to reconsider these assumptions.[27]

Retracing Our Steps: Mark 7

My own initial interpretation about the middle group, the dull disciples who precede the appearance of the Syro-Phoenician woman, assumed that they were all male. David Rhoads and Donald Michie in *Mark as Story* say that the disciples act as one character, and are the same as the Twelve, the inner circle of twelve men around Jesus. The Twelve *are* all male, but that group in Mark 4:10 given the secret of the kingdom is larger than the Twelve: "And when he was alone, those who were about him *with the twelve* asked him concerning the parables. And he said to them, 'to you has been given the secret of the kingdom of God.'" The women at the cross in Mark 15:41 are called "those who *followed* him and ministered to him when he was in Galilee." "Follow" is a technical term in Mark for discipleship ("Take up his cross and follow me"). So we should not assume that the author assumes the disciples are a group of men.[28] The male/female categories here begin to crumble.

Second, many of these interpretations of surprise make assumptions about Jewish life and treatment of women and Gentiles that are unfounded. The idea that a Gentile would be completely "other" or unable to have conversation with a Jew is doubtful. Luke-Acts refers to Gentile women in the synagogue; inscriptions refer to Gentile donors to synagogues; there are the famous "god-fearers" in the synagogue at Aphrodisias, people who are not full converts to Judaism, but seem to be part of the synagogue. Similarly, the idea that women in Judaism were inevitably inferior is belied by inscriptions calling them *archisynagogos,* "ruler of the synagogue," and "*mater synagogae*" "mother of the synagogue," some kinds of honorific.[29] All these pieces of evidence are from the diaspora. But the ancient synagogues in Galilee do not show any sense of an exclusion of women, such as a separate women's section. At times there has been an attempt to paint Judaism as uniformly repressive in its treatment of women in order to depict Jesus and his movement as the great liberator of women, offering relief from these strictures.[30] But I would ask, what religion was Jesus, and what religion did these women profess? Is not the presence of women in the Jesus movement rather proof that Judaism did show evidence of women's autonomy?

I recalled the theory that the Gentile foreign woman suffers inferior status in three ways, and is therefore "triply marginalized." D'Angelo makes a provocative suggestion that if Mark's gospel was written in Syria, as some people suggest, the Syro-Phoenician woman may be a triple insider to *Mark and his readers.*[31] Most agree his readership is largely Gentile. Crowds from Tyre and Sidon, Mark tells us, come to see Jesus (3:7). Women do rather well in Mark. It may be that his readers greet the arrival of the Syro-Phoenician woman onstage not with surprise and low expectations but with knowing nods of recognition, thinking, "it's about time—someone is finally going to understand him." They would enjoy the repartee with Jesus, and his final affirmation that her "logos" or teaching is correct.

Recently some question whether the Syro-Phoenician woman is such a daring heroine. D'Angelo argues that her answer is quite submissive, and of course is on behalf of her daughter. She is playing the role of the good mother.[32] Ross Kraemer questions whether a Gentile woman is chosen to receive this harsh saying to soften it, make it less offensive.[33] I disagree with both. First, I do not think she is submissive. This is a convention, an inferior talking to a superior, like the page talking to the king, Joseph before Pharaoh, or the first gravedigger in Hamlet, teaching him about life and death, where the superior is convinced by the brilliance of the argument, not by overturning of roles. It would ruin the effect if the lower-status person stepped out of the conventional role, spoke rudely or flouted convention. It is the content, her "logos," that saves the day. Second, regarding Kraemer's suggestion, to whom would a brutal remark to a Gentile woman be less offensive? Mark's readers are Gentiles and probably many women. Jesus is equally harsh with the Jewish (male?) disciples in this gospel. Kraemer assumes the Syro-Phoenician woman is a powerless woman and outsider. She may still represent a type or group, but expanding on D'Angelo's suggestion, I suggest that her gender may not be remarkable to Mark and his readers as we first thought, but to us in our imagining of the ancient world.

Retracing our Steps: John 4 and John 20

First, many assume the Samaritan woman's sexual history is significant. The commentaries are so universal in their assumption of her supposedly negative sexual history that Schneiders calls it "a textbook case of the trivialization, marginalization, and even sexual demonization of biblical women."[34] Why is a woman with five husbands assumed to be loose? Kraemer has suggested that at least for the few aristocratic Jewish women we know of, it was common for young women to marry older men, be widowed young, and marry again to bear another set of children (*Origins* 58). Could that not be the case here? Could she, suggests O'Day,[35] like the biblical Tamar, have not had a string of terrible luck? Even more significant is that *the text* does not paint her in a negative way because of her five husbands and current paramour. Jesus does not chide her, tell her to sin no more, or anything of the kind. The point of the exchange about her husbands is to prove Jesus' prophetic power and move her along in recognizing who he is. Similarly, her response to Jesus is laudable: "I see that you are a prophet." One commentator sees her as "mincing and coy." The same commentator sees the blind man in chapter 9, who also talks back and moves along in understanding, as "one of the most attractive figures of the gospels."[36]

Are our low expectations because of the same assumptions made in the story of the Syro-Phoenician woman? This gospel itself has not really set us up to expect little of women. Jesus' mother in chapter 2, Mary and Martha, Mary Magdalene in 20, all seem to be people who show exemplary discipleship and come to understand Jesus. Gender and ethnicity are mentioned in this narrative as in Mark 7. But should we imagine John's readers surprised, or once more nodding in recognition?

In John 20 gender is not pointed to explicitly. I would make the same point as before. If our expectations are low for Mary Magdalene in this gospel, it is not because she is a woman. On the contrary she fits in with the mother of Jesus, the Samaritan woman, Mary and Martha, all of whom show some misunderstanding of Jesus that does not interfere with their coming to faith and model discipleship.

I have been speaking in terms of dichotomies. If two characters are juxtaposed and different, we often assume they negate and compare unfavorably with one another. There must be a "winner." Is that what the gospel authors mean, or is that our modern either-or mentality? Perhaps they mean us to start in one place and move to another, along a spectrum of responses. Perhaps in the case of Nicodemus and the Samaritan woman, John is arguing that there are different ways to faith. Nicodemus, after all, does eventually go public as a disciple of Jesus. Perhaps Peter, the Beloved Disciple, Mary Magdalene, and Thomas are all examples of people who grope for understanding in clumsy ways, but finally come to faith.

We often assume that if gender is a visible category, it is crucial to the author. It is not clear that it is a category important to John or Mark. I have already suggested the problem with assuming the thickheaded disciples in Mark are all male. Is it the first generation of disciples that is being brought down a notch by Mark's characterization, as some have suggested, perhaps to remove some sense of inferiority for Mark's readers who were not eyewitnesses to Jesus' life and ministry? If so, gender is irrelevant. Consider a newspaper report today of a dramatic event that interviews a series of witnesses. The gender of those witnesses is normally insignificant. For John's gospel, gender is not clearly a conscious category either. Women appear very positively in John, but so do some men: the Beloved Disciple (I assume to be male because of 19:26, "Woman behold your son"), John the Baptist, and Nathaniel, the true Israelite.

Are the gospel authors emphasizing sameness or difference in portraying men and women? Are our pairs more alike or unlike? Judith Hallett has written an illuminating article that notes how frequently the theme of sameness of male and female appears in Greek and Latin literature, in descriptions both of divinities and of elite women. In the Iliad and Odyssey, for example, gods and goddesses excel in war, athletics, and sea faring.[37] Many instances of upper-class women in Greco-Roman literature emphasize their similarity to the men in their families. She cites the example of the younger Pliny, eulogizing the thirteen-year-old Minucia Marcella, noting that she was "the exact living image of her father in her appearance and ways," including his love of books and learning (*Letters* 5.26).[38] For lower-class people fewer texts exist, but Hallett notes inscriptions of married couples that stress their shared professions (*brattieria* and *bratierius,* gold-workers, and *vestiarii,* tailors). She cites numerous texts along these lines, attempting to fill out the picture and balance the many studies that have revolved around ancient texts that emphasize female difference. Both models, of sameness and difference, existed side by side in the ancient Mediterranean, and were inherited by earliest Christianity.

Commentators often assume that if a text is pro-woman, it is not from the gospel author. If these stories are positive toward women, many argue, they are at odds with the gospel author's view and therefore are earlier fragments of material, whether pointing to Galilean mission in Mark, Samaritan mission in John 4, or the memory of Mary Magdalene's discovery of the empty tomb in John 20. It may *be* earlier material. But why assume it is not what the author thinks? How often do we bring in material that contradicts our message?

A troubling assumption that Jewish culture is unfriendly to women lies behind some interpretations. Dewey, for example, tells us the Syro-Phoenician woman is "doubly oppressed because of her gender and her race" and goes against the "ancient Mediterranean ideal stereotype of the silent and obedient woman."[39] Kraemer notes that sweeping assessments of negative Jewish treatment of women are often based on uncritical use of rabbinic statements from a later period.[40] Even without the problem of late dating, we do not know what percentage of ancient Jewish society was rabbinic. The ancient synagogues excavated in Galilee go against rabbinic prohibitions about images, suggesting the rabbis were not in control of society.[41] It has often served Christian interests to portray Judaism as putting women in a kind of purdah.[42] Yet positive portrayals of women as disciples in the gospels are usually Jewish women. The people around Jesus, including the women, illustrate the mores of a Jewish renewal movement, not early Christianity. Kraemer discusses the personal documents of the woman Babatha, found among the Bar Kochba letters, which suggest someone who used the courts, appeared in the public arena, and possessed some business sense.[43]

One of the broadest assumptions we often hear, especially in the classroom, is that in regard to women, the farther back we go in history, the worse things were. The Jesus movement is seen as more enlightened than the Judaism from which it emerged, and both were hopelessly repressive compared to our own time. Many visualize steady progress as we move forward in time. But history moves in waves. Mark Twain is often cited as saying, "history doesn't repeat, it rhymes." Kathleen Corley has shown that the Jesus movement fits into a progressive Jewish framework in the first century, but that egalitarian ethic erodes in the next centuries as part of an overall reversal of attitudes toward women in Greco-Roman society in the first to the mid third century.[44] Since the New Testament canon is not stabilized until the fourth century, the documents of a progressive first-century movement are culled and fixed in a very different atmosphere. Deirdre Good has suggested they are a fourth-century ideal of what the first century should have looked like.[45] Are we more like or unlike the people of the first century? They were not feminists in any sense that we use the word. We do not repeat them. But perhaps we rhyme with them in taking women's spirituality for granted. These authors may not be consciously promoting women as virtuosi of the spirit, but presupposing that they are or could be. Women as spiritual leaders and faithful followers is not an idea invented in our time.

NOTES

1. These are hardly the only examples of women and men presented in pairs. Mary Rose D'Angelo notes Luke's tendency to pair women and men for purposes of catechesis, "Women in Luke-Acts: A Redactional View," *JBL* 109 (1990): 441–61.

2. Mark says "all the Jews" practice this purification, which was not the case. Joel Marcus points out that Mark's aim is to implicate the whole people, preparing them for the citation of Isa. 29:13, *Mark 1–8* (AB: New York: Doubleday, 2000), 440–41, n. 3.

3. See Albert Baumgarten, "The Pharisaic Paradosis," *HTR* 80 (1987): 63–77.

4. See Anthony Saldarini, *Pharisees, Scribes, and Sadducees in Palestinian Society* (1988; reprint, Grand Rapids, Mich.: Eerdmans, 2001); Albert Baumgarten, *The Flourishing of Sects in the Maccabean Era: An Interpretation* (Leiden: Brill, 1997); Gunther Stemberger, *Jewish Contemporaries of Jesus: Pharisees, Sadducees, Essenes* (Min-

neapolis: Fortress, 1995); Jacob Neusner, *From Politics to Piety* (New York: Ktav, 1979); ibid., *The Pharisees: Rabbinic Perspectives* (Leiden: Brill, 1973).

5. A grand literature also surrounds this question of the portrayal of the disciples in Mark and its purpose. Historical criticism suggests it is a slap at the first generation. Reader-response criticism argues that it means to evoke the reader's desire to witness to Jesus, to succeed where the disciples fail. Feminist criticism argues whether only the male disciples fail and the women are the true followers, or both the men and women show themselves to be "fallible followers." See Ernest Best, "'Concerning the Loaves:' Comprehending Incomprehension in Mark 6:45–52," *JSNT* 83 (2001): 3–26; idem, *Disciples and Discipleship: Studies in the Gospel according to Mark* (Edinburgh: T and T Clark, 1986); Bastiaan van Iersel, "Failed Followers in Mark: Mark 13:12 as a Key for the Identification of the Intended Readers," *CBQ* 58 (1996): 244–63; Elizabeth Struthers Malbon, "Texts and Contexts: Interpreting the Disciples in Mark," *Semeia* 62 (1993): 81–102; idem, "Fallible Followers: Women and Men in the Gospel of Mark," *Semeia* 28 (1983): 29–48; C. Clifton Black, *The Disciples according to Mark: Markan Redaction in Current Debate* (Sheffield: Sheffield Academic Press, 1989); Winsome Munro, "Women Disciples in Mark," *CBQ* 44 (1982): 225–41.

6. Elisabeth Schüssler Fiorenza, *But She Said: Feminist Practices of Biblical Interpretation* (Boston: Beacon, 1992), 12.

7. Some manuscripts have "Yes, Lord," probably an assimilation from Matt 15:27. See Marcus, 475.

8. Joanna Dewey, "The Gospel of Mark," in *Searching the Scriptures*, vol. 2: *A Feminist Commentary*, ed. Elisabeth Schüssler Fiorenza (New York: Crossroad, 1994).

9. Mary Rose D'Angelo suggested to me that she must also be understood in juxtaposition with the woman with a hemorrhage in 5:21–43, who is also ritually unclean and encounters Jesus before a daughter's healing. Joel Marcus notes that these two women's stories surround another, more negative mother-daughter pair, Herodias and her daughter.

10. Elisabeth Schüssler Fiorenza, *In Memory of Her: A Feminist Theological Reconstruction of Christian Origins* (New York: Crossroad, 1984), 137.

11. Antoinette Clark Wire, "The Structure of the Gospel Miracle Stories and Their Tellers," *Semeia* 11 (1978): 83–113.

12. Wire, 109.

13. Schüssler Fiorenza, *Memory*, 137–38.

14. Mary Ann Tolbert, "Mark," in *Women's Bible Commentary* (Louisville: Westminster John Knox, 1998), 356.

15. If the royal official is a Gentile, this would make for a neat transition from skepticism to unquestioning faith, from Jew (Nicodemus) to someone connected to the traditions of Israel (Samaritan woman) to Gentile (royal official). Unfortunately we cannot assume the official is Gentile, and as a servant of Herod he might well be a Jew.

16. These "crypto-Christians" are described by Raymond E. Brown in *The Community of the Beloved Disciple* (New York: Paulist, 1979), 71–72. Brown, however, does not consider Nicodemus a secret Christian.

17. Wayne Meeks's famous essay explains the passage by way of the social location of the Johannine community. He argues that the descending/ascending redeemer myth is employed by John in the service of a developing other-worldly Christology that matches the increasing alienation of the Johannine community from the local Jewish community, "The Man from Heaven in Johannine Sectarianism," *JBL* 91 (1972): 44–72.

18. Adele Reinhartz, "The Gospel of John," in *Searching the Scriptures*, vol. 2, ed. Elisabeth Schüssler Fiorenza (New York: Crossroad, 1994), 572.

19. See for example Sandra Schneiders, *The Revelatory Text* (San Francisco: Harper San Francisco, 1991), 187; P. Joseph Cahill, "Narrative Art in John IV," *RSB* 2.2 (1982): 44–47.

20. E. Schüssler Fiorenza, *Memory*, 327; Raymond E. Brown, *The Gospel according to John*, AB (Garden City, N.Y.: Doubleday, 1966), vol. 1, 176.

21. O'Day, "John," in *Women's Bible Commentary*, 384; S. Schneiders, *Revelatory Text*, 196.

22. Jesus tells her not to touch him (v. 17) because he has not yet ascended to his father. D'Angelo suggests that he is in a transitional state, not fully in his body. Drawing on a similar idea in the Apoc. Moses 31,3–4, she suggests that if Jesus surrendered his body to the Father at death, he receives it back in stages. While Origen says that this symbolizes the incompleteness of her gospel, it just as easily suggests her uniqueness. She recognizes Jesus even in an incomplete transformation, while the male disciples demand proof even of the fully restored Jesus. See "A Critical Note: John 20:17 and Apocalypse of Moses 31," *JTS* n.s. 41 (1990): 529–36.

23. O'Day, 389.

24. Gregory Riley argues that Thomas represents a Gnostic community that denied the physical reality of the resurrection, asserting a spiritual resurrection, in *Resurrection Reconsidered: Thomas and John in Controversy* (Minneapolis: Fortress, 1995). The author of John is needling that community by taking their hero and having him do something particularly fleshy and distasteful.

25. See Stephen Shoemaker's discussion of the *Gospel of Mary* in this volume, as well as Deirdre Good's discussion of Mary as a composite figure of several women spiritual leaders, including Mary of Bethany in the New Testament and Miriam in the Hebrew Bible. See also D. Good, "Pistis Sophia," in *Searching the Scriptures*, vol. 2, ed. Elisabeth Schüssler Fiorenza, 678–707.

26. See discussion by Celia Deutsch, *Hidden Wisdom and the Easy Yoke: Wisdom, Torah and Discipleship in Matthew 11:25–30*, JSNTSS 18 (Sheffield: Sheffield Academic Press, 1987).

27. Mary Rose D'Angelo, "(Re)presentations of Women in the Gospels: John and Mark," in *Women and Christian Origins*, ed. Ross Kraemer and Mary Rose D'Angelo (New York: Oxford, 1999), 129–49.

28. I am guilty of a bit of disingenuousness here, since this point is quite familiar to readers of feminist work on Mark, such as Malbon, Schüssler Fiorenza, Munro, and others. I always invite students to plug in men's names to the scene at the cross in Mark 15:40, to show no one would doubt for a moment that they were disciples.

29. See Bernadette Brooten's classic work on this, *Women Leaders in the Ancient Synagogue,* Brown Judaic Series 36 (Chico, Calif.: Scholar's, 1982).

30. This point has been made by a number of scholars, including Judith Plaskow, Katarina von Kellenbach, Amy-Jill Levine, and Kathleen Corley. See the recent articles by Ross Kraemer in *Women and Christian Origins,* "Jewish Women and Christian Origins: Some Caveats," 35–49, and "Jewish Women and Women's Judaism(s) at the Beginning of Christianity," 50–79.

31. D'Angelo, "(Re)presentations of Women," 139.

32. Ibid., 140.

33. Ross Kraemer, *Her Share of the Blessings: Women's Religions among the Pagans, Jews, and Christians in the Greco-Roman World* (Oxford: Oxford University Press, 1992), 133.

34. Schneiders, *Revelatory Text,* 188.

35. O'Day, "John," 384.

36. R. E. Brown, *The Gospel according to John,* vol. 1, 175, 377.

37. Judith Hallett, "Women's Lives in the Ancient Mediterranean," in *Women and Christian Origins,* 13–34.

38. Ibid., 125.

39. Dewey, 484–86.

40. Kraemer, "Some Caveats," 37–39.

41. See Seth Schwartz, *Imperialism and Jewish Society* (Princeton, N.J.: Princeton University Press, 2001), 162–76.

42. See note 30.

43. Kraemer, "Jewish Women," 54–56.

44. Kathleen Corley, "Feminist Myths of Christian Origins," in *Re-imagining Christian Origins: Essays in Honor of Burton Mack,* ed. Elizabeth Castelli and Hal Taussig (Valley Forge, Pa.: Trinity, 1996), 60–61.

45. Good, "Pistis Sophia," 678.

The Miriamic Vision

6

࿇

"I have seen the Lord": Mary Magdalen as Visionary, Early Christian Prophecy, and the Context of John 20:14–18

MARY ROSE D'ANGELO

He comes to us as one
unknown. . . . [1]

She comes to us as one
unknown? . . .

*I*n contemplating this essay, I envisioned myself opening it with these famous words from Albert Schweitzer's Quest for the Historical Jesus, but with the pregnant pronouns transposed from masculine to feminine— "She comes to us as one unknown." Schweitzer's critique had placed a caesura to all the liberal lives and reconstructions of Jesus from the eighteenth and nineteenth centuries, offering in their place an alien, apocalyptic visionary who died in disillusion. Recalling this warning as I began a quest for the historical Mary Magdalen seemed particularly apt. After all, I reasoned, even less can be said of the "historical" Mary than of the "historical" Jesus. Far less is said of her in the gospels, and of that little, virtually none can be placed in the pre-crucifixion memories of the movement.

A quick check of Schweitzer's text required me to reconsider:

He comes to us as one unknown as of old, by the lakeside, he came to those men who knew him not. He speaks to us the same word: "Follow thou me!" and sets us to the tasks which he has to fulfil for our time. He commands. And to those who obey him whether they be wise or simple, he will reveal himself in the toils, the conflicts, the sufferings which they shall pass through in his fellowship, and as an ineffable mystery, they shall learn in their own experience who he is.[2]

What seemed to speak to me so strongly, I had misremembered, perhaps fictionalized, both in wording and in context. What Schweitzer had actually written left me with a new set of problems and questions. Schweitzer's peroration turned out to be both much less applicable to my investigation of Mary Magdalen and much more illuminating of it than had been my expectation.

This portion of Schweitzer's work does not dwell upon the mysterious and alien character of the Jesus of history, but rather turns from the unknown Jesus of the past to the risen Jesus encountered in the spirit, by those who *do* know him—as he acts among and in them now. Mary does indeed "come to us as one unknown," but my goal is not to contemplate a Mary Magdalen who is known today in the spirit, as distinct from the unknown Mary of history. My feminist sensitivities balked at proclaiming of Mary Magdalen, "She commands. And to those who obey her, whether they be wise or simple, she will reveal herself." Instead I will argue for the recognition of Mary Magdalen as the unknown knower, the visionary whose encounter with Jesus in the spirit became the avenue of revelation through which later Christians could "learn in their own experience who he is."

Distant and hidden as she is, a "Mary Magdalen of history" is in some sense the avenue for Christian and, insofar as is possible, of historical access to the Christ of faith. For, insofar as history can recover her, she was a witness to and interpreter of the death and resurrection of Jesus. In this essay, I shall argue that the visionary experience of Mary, particularly the vision report in John 20:14–18, deserves a special scrutiny from scholars of early Christianity, from theological thinkers, and from women and men who want to read the beginnings of Christianity in the light of a fuller and more inclusive understanding of what it means to be human.

Mary's vision offers an entrée to the character of the resurrection appearances and of early Christian prophecy in general. The insight it offers into this experience is an important lens through which to rethink the context of Jesus and the gospels as a source for the "teaching of Jesus." This essay is not an argument for the historicity of the scene depicted in John 20:14–18. By definition, this narrative is "post-resurrection material," a category normally opposed to "historical" traditions. Rather, I shall delineate the features of the narrative that suggest its antiquity and point to analogous narratives that can illuminate its formal characteristics and impact a reading of its function.

The Search for Mary Magdalen:
Mary in the Tradition as One and Many

Ever since Koester's treatment of early gospel types under the rubric "one Jesus, four primitive gospels," NT scholars have been more explicit in celebrating the multiplicity and diversity of images of Jesus in the texts that pass on the traditions about him.[3] Despite the slenderness of the material about Mary Magdalen in the canonical and most of the noncanonical texts, it is also possible to delineate both multiple Marys and central threads in the early Christian gospels.[4] Scholars of Christian origins, especially feminist scholars, have worked through the varying gospel traditions in the effort to dislodge the early Christian Mary from the long history of Mary the repentant harlot.[5] Mary the penitent has been revealed as a figure patched together out of a variety of biblical women in later Christian antiquity amid a spiritual fashion for tales of the conversions of famous and famously beautiful whores.[6] And contemporary theology and piety have widely revived Mary's ancient title *apostola apostolorum*—apostle to the apostles, or perhaps greatest of the apostles.[7]

The multiple Marys of the early sources warrant a brief review.[8] Here I shall focus on the four canonical gospels, and the appendix to the Gospel of Mark (the "longer ending," long printed as Mark 16:9–20), briefly considering the Gospel of Peter and four works from Nag Hammadi: the Gospel of Thomas, a sayings collection, and two dialogue gospels, the Gospel of Mary and the Dialogue of the Savior, and the Gospel of Philip, a sort of florilegium of Valentinian aphorisms. Except for the Gospel of Philip (and perhaps the Gospel of Peter), all of these texts are likely to have been composed between 70 and 170.[9]

Mark's gospel is generally understood to be the earliest of the gospels, and lays down the basic lines of the picture of Mary in the three synoptic gospels. Mary appears in three scenes of the gospel: at the cross, at the burial of Jesus, and at the empty tomb (Mark 15:40–41, 15:47–16:8). At the cross, she is one of three named women disciples; the other two are Salome and Mary of Jacob (or James) and Joses.[10] The names of these three women are given because of their status as witnesses: they perform the essential task of tying together the death of Jesus, his burial place, and its discovery.[11] All three are characterized as both disciples (they "followed" Jesus— ἠκολούθουν) and *diakonoi* (they ministered to, διηκόνουν him; 15:40–41)— the latter term may reflect their roles in later Christian mission.[12] At the cross, they stand "far off" among many women who are said to have come up from Galilee to Jerusalem with Jesus (41).[13] This brief reference implies that the author has taken for granted the presence of a substantial number of women in the circle and on the travels of Jesus.[14] Mary is named first, and is the only woman who clearly reappears in Mark's interpreters. She thus seems to be the foremost among the women disciples and ministers. Mary "of Joses" goes with her to see the place where Jesus is laid (47). And both Salome and Mary "of Jacob," go with her to anoint the body of Jesus (16:1–4).[15] They receive a vision (16:5) and an oracular message that interprets the emptiness of the tomb in terms of the death of Jesus and of their memories and expectations (16:6–7). The fear in which they flee and their silence (16:8) has been subjected to extensive and disputatious analysis.[16] But at the very least it associates their vision with the numinous and terrifying character of other such revelations. Thus Mark identifies Mary as disciple and *diakonos,* chief witness that the one who died was the one who was raised.

In Matthew also, Mary is re/presented at the death, burial, and resurrection of Jesus (Matt. 27:55–56, 61; 28:1–8, 9–10). While these accounts are based heavily on Mark, subtle changes in the narrative introduce Matthean theological concerns and depict a particularly intrepid and fearless Mary. Mary's companions change. Salome is replaced at the cross by the mother of the Zebedees. This figure's role seems to be to see and so to underline the fulfillment of Jesus' pronouncement that the places at his right hand and left are assigned; they go to the two thieves crucified on either side of him (Matt. 20:21–23, see 27:38).[17] She then disappears from the narrative. "Mary the mother of Jacob and Joseph" (probably the same figure as in Mark) also appears at the cross; as "the other Mary," she accompanies Mary Magdalen to the burial of Jesus, thus providing the second witness required by the biblical prescription (see Matt. 18:16, citing Deut 19:15). In Matthew, Joseph of Arimathea is described not as a pious Jew also awaiting God's reign but as a disciple, so the two Marys are able to sit openly opposite the tomb (27:61). Their courage is manifested by their willingness to visit the tomb, despite the Roman soldiers set to guard the tomb in this gospel (27:62–66). The focus of this scene is the dramatic, indeed earthshaking, vision of an angel descending from heaven, described in terms that evoke the transfiguration, and the prophetic visions of Daniel (28:2–4; see 17:2, Dan. 7:9, 10:6 Theodotion). While the Roman guards are overcome by their terror (Matt. 28:4), the women receive the angel's greeting, commission ("go tell the disciples"), and message (5–7) with joy and a fear that is clearly holy awe, running to fulfill it by telling the disciples (28:8). They then experience a second vision: they are met by Jesus, who repeats the angel's commission in very slightly different words ("go tell my brothers") and an abbreviated message (28:9–10).

Matt. 28:16 makes clear that the women have fulfilled their task and have been heeded by the eleven.

The Gospel of Luke also revises Mark's version of Mary's role and that of the other women. Early in the narrative Luke 8:1–3 introduces a list of women disciples, apparently to parallel the male disciple list in 6:13–16. Unlike the men's, the women's discipleship is explained as gratitude for being cured from "evil spirits and diseases" and as consisting of financial support for the men's mission.[18] Mary is named first, and described as one from whom seven devils had gone out (cf. 11:24–26). Mary Magdalen thus is established as the client of Jesus and a patron of the male apostles, a cured demoniac. Two "new" women are mentioned, Susanna and Johanna, wife of Chuza, Herod's steward. At the cross, no women are named; "all his acquaintances and female fellow travelers" see Jesus' death (23:49). All the women who had come from Galilee follow behind the burial and see where the grave is, then go to prepare ointments. On the Sabbath they rest to observe the law (23:55–56). In the morning they bring the ointments and find the empty tomb (24:1–3), where they see "two men in shining garments" who interpret the empty tomb in terms of the passion predictions (24:4–7).[19] Without a commission, they report this to the eleven (8–9); only then are the women identified as "Mary Magdalen, Johanna and Mary of Jacob and the rest with them" (24:10). "The apostles" are said to disbelieve the women, because their message seemed nonsensical. Their skepticism is hardly to the discredit of the women; rather it lays the ground for the dramatic irony when the two disciples tell the "stranger" that the women claim to have seen "a vision of angels, who say that he is alive" (24:23–24). Acts alone narrates the ascension scene, which closes the appearances forty days after the resurrection. At the end of this scene, the eleven male disciples are listed again; they are said to take up a vigil in the upper room "with women, Mary the mother of Jesus and his brothers" (Acts 1:14).[20] The names of the famous women disciples do not recur in Acts, though the narrative suggests that they too experience the descent of the spirit.

The Gospel of John seems to have undergone a long development independent of Mark, Matthew, and Luke, but also to have had some contact either with these gospels or with their sources at the cross (19:25–26). As in the synoptic gospels, Mary appears at the empty tomb (20:1–18), though not at the burial. At the cross, Mary is named only after "the mother of Jesus and her sister, Mary of Clopas" (19:25). Because Jesus is then said to see his mother and "the disciple whom he loved standing at hand," this mysterious disciple has occasionally been identified as Mary, despite becoming the substitute son of Jesus' mother (19:26).[21] At the tomb, Mary appears alone, and then goes to find Peter and this disciple (20:1–2), who inspect the tomb, finding it empty except for the grave clothes (20:3–7).[22] While the disciple "believes," he and Peter depart with no resolution to the scene (8–10). Mary, who stays at the tomb weeping, first sees two angels (11–13), then encounters Jesus first and alone in a scene of great intimacy (14–18). This vision will be the focus of the main part of this essay, so I will postpone discussion of it.

In most manuscripts of the Gospel of Mark dating from the fifth century or later, the gospel closes with an appendix that supplies the appearances of the risen Jesus that are so conspicuously missing from the gospel.[23] Until recently, this appendix was printed without interruption as 16:9–20. Verses 9–11 recount a first appearance (ἐφάνη) to Mary Magdalen, "out of whom he had cast seven devils." She then reports the vision to "those who had been with him" but is disbelieved. Verses 12–13 relate a second appearance (ἐφανερώθη) to "two of them going to the country." They too are disbelieved. All three are vindicated by Jesus' reproaches when he appears (ἐφανερώθη) to the eleven (14). The reference to an appearance to Mary alone is reminiscent of the gospel of John, but the rest of the summary seems to be based on Luke and the beginning of Acts (cf. Luke 24:14–36, 37–51, 10:17–20; Acts 1:1–11, 2:38).

Another text of an uncertain date, Gospel of Peter, appears to be a revision of traditions that appear in the canonical gospels.[24] In this gospel Mary Magdalen, identified as a disciple, braves the anger of the Jews, gathers her friends, and goes to perform mourning rites at the tomb. There they are granted the vision of a "young man," who explains the empty tomb by announcing the resurrection (13–14). Mary does not appear at the cross or burial, and the women are not commissioned to tell anyone else.[25]

As in the narrative gospels, in the sayings collection called the Gospel of Thomas (late first or early second century), Mary and her companion Salome are disciples; Thomas in fact makes Mary a spokesperson for the disciples; she turns the table on Jesus, requesting from him an analogy for the disciples (21) as he asked them for an analogy for himself (13). In the last saying of the gospel, Peter's demand that she be dismissed "because women are not worthy of life" makes her the representative of women disciples in general—and of all the women who struggled to claim their role in the context of Thomas (114).

The Gospel of Mary, a fragmentary dialogue gospel, opens with a vision in which the "savior" converses with the disciples; when he departs, they are at a loss and turn to Mary for the special revelation she has received. At the request of Peter, she recounts a vision whose content is rejected first by

Andrew and then by Peter; Levi comes to her defense. The gospel thus uses her to put forward the issues of women as communal leaders/prophets and of the legitimacy of prophecy itself—of visions and revelations.[26]

Like Gospel of Mary, the Dialogue of the Savior is in form a dialogue in which Jesus instructs the disciples by answering their questions. Mary seems to be the most intrepid and most insightful of the interlocutors (see esp. 53, 60, 64, 69). At one point, Jesus brings Judas, Matthew, and Mary to the edge of heaven and earth, where they see a vision (36). If post-resurrection, the dialogue is in itself a vision.

The Gospel of Philip does not fit the gospel genre as it is now defined; it is an anthology of aphoristic meditations on the Christian message in its Valentinian form; it appears to have been culled from earlier works and, in its present form, to date from the later part of the third century.[27] In it Mary is twice described as the κοινωνος, companion or partner, of Jesus: "there were three who always walked with the Lord: his mother and his mother's sister, and the Magdalen, who is called his companion. His mother and his sister and his companion were each called Mary" (59,6–10). The second passage may identify Mary the κοινωνος with the (divine) Wisdom who is mother of the angels; it further relates that Jesus loved Mary and kissed her often.[28] The (other) disciples complain and ask why Jesus loved her more than them; Jesus gives a double answer. First is a rhetorical question, "Why do I not love you like her?" Thus he turns their question back to them, inviting them to emulate her. He then tells a parable: "When a blind man and one who see are both together in darkness, they are no different from one another. When the light comes, then he who sees will see the light, and who is blind will remain in darkness" (63,30–64,12).[29] The parable in some way suggests that Mary is enlightened in ways that the other disciples are not, or are not yet enlightened. The reference to seeing may imply or commemorate her visionary status.

In all these versions of Mary, she is a disciple among the disciples. In the gospels of Thomas, Mary, and Philip, her gender plays an explicit role in the representation of her discipleship; that she appears at the tomb with other women may suggest that her gender is also significant in the synoptic gospels and Peter. In all the narratives she is a witness to the resurrection. Most, perhaps all, of these early texts depict her as a visionary. The gospels of John, Matthew, and Mary, the appendix to Mark, and perhaps Dialogue of the Savior celebrate Mary's vision of the risen Lord. All the canonical gospels and Peter credit her with a vision of angels, and Dialogue of the Savior with an apocalyptic vision. Only the gospels of Philip and Thomas do not directly engage with this picture, though both texts may assume it. Thus

Mary/Mariam, the early Christian visionary, is a sister of Miriam the Hebrew prophet.

Recovering the "Resurrection Experience"

Locating the significance of Mary as visionary and prophet both for the earliest stages of Christianity and for Christian feminists evokes significant questions about the event usually referred to as the resurrection of Jesus. Approaching it from a historical perspective raises particular difficulties, for as an event its very claim is to transcend and therefore to escape history—the early texts never treat the fate of Jesus as return to life (like that of Lazarus in John 11:1–44 or of the daughter of Jairus in Mark 5:21–43), but always describe it as a transformation of the world.

New Testament scholarship has generally divided the reports about the fate of Jesus into (1) brief reports of appearances of the risen Jesus, such as 1 Cor. 15:5–8 and 9:1; (2) stories about the empty tomb, that is, Mark 16:1–8, the revisions of this story in Matthew and Luke, and John 20:1–11; and (3) longer narratives that describe appearances of Jesus, for instance, the story of the two disciples on the road to Emmaus or the appearance to the eleven in Matthew 28:16–20 and to the assembled disciples in Luke 24:36–51. The brief reports in the letters of Paul are significantly earlier than the other texts and contain no hint of the empty tomb. At the same time, there are no substantive correspondences among the appearance narratives. These observations have contributed to an opinion on the part of many (but by no means all) scholars that the earliest source of belief in the resurrection was experiences of meeting Jesus alive from the dead. These experiences were interpreted through the emerging Jewish doctrine of resurrection of the dead. The story of the empty tomb was ultimately created as a dramatization of this interpretation. The first reports of meeting Jesus were elaborated by various theological motifs that explained his fate or enabled the community to continue, and so developed into the variety of appearance stories in the gospels.[30] This picture is complicated by other questions, in particular by ancient and modern conflicts over the physical or spiritual character of the resurrection and by reflection on the difference between imaging the fate of Jesus as resurrection (awakening or standing up) or as exaltation (ascending or being lifted up).[31]

"Second-wave" feminist interpretation of the New Testament quickly fastened upon the role of women in the resurrection traditions, in part as an antidote to the claim that since only men were apostles, only men could be ministers or priests.[32] But the list of witnesses in 1 Corinthians 15:5–8 mentioned no women: its "first witness" is Cephas, usually, though not always, identified with Peter.[33] This posed a problem, for not only is 1 Corinthians earlier than the gospels, the list is probably earlier than 1 Corinthians. The conflict between the list and the traditions about an appearance to Mary could mean that this early list ignored or rejected the appearances to women or that the traditions about the appearances to women are later.

Elisabeth Schüssler Fiorenza stands over against the relatively widespread consensus that the experience of meeting Jesus alive from the dead (in visionary experiences) preceded the creation of the empty-tomb narratives. Arguing that it is difficult to determine whether the empty tomb narrative or the vision reports are earlier, she rejects the historical positivism inherent in the question, or at least in attempts to answer it. Her concern is different: analyzing the material according to gender as male and female traditions, she calls into question the significance of appearance reports for feminist readings of the resurrection of Jesus, seeing them as created by and authorizing men. The empty tomb, on the other hand, she takes to be a "women's tradition."[34] Schüssler Fiorenza argues for "privileging the empty tomb" as the originating space. This does not mean that the empty tomb narratives were earlier and closer to "what really happened." Rather she proposes locating the empty tomb narratives as the basis of a feminist constructive theology of future hope that does not spiritualize suffering.[35]

In her view, "the texts of the empty tomb tradition take suffering and death seriously but do not allow them to have the 'last word' or a religious-theological value in themselves." They "leave open what happened to the body of Jesus. Their narrative valorizes a compassionate practice of honoring those unjustly killed."[36] In contrast to the traditions of the empty tomb, Schüssler Fiorenza sees "visionary experience" not only as claiming "individual male religious experience as authorizing experience" but also as transforming Jesus' death so that it is "no longer an execution, but a 'sacrificial atonement,' no longer a violent dehumanization, but an obedient self-immolation, no longer an encounter with brutal force, but a willingly accepted victimization."[37]

This evaluation of the visionary narratives appears to focus heavily on 1 Corinthians 15:3–8, which certainly sees visionary experience as creating apostles (cf. 9:1–2). The forgiveness of sins is attached to the death (not the resurrection) of Jesus in 1 Corinthians 15:3. While most of the visionary narratives include some authorization of the visionaries, the motif of atonement and sacrifice is virtually absent from the appearance narratives in the canonical gospels. The only texts from which such a theology might be deduced are the expositions of the way Jesus' death and resurrection are said to fulfill the passion predictions in the empty tomb scene in Luke 24:6–7, and the scripture in Luke 24:25–27 and 46–47. But even in these texts, atonement and sacrifice function only by elaborate comparison with other texts from Luke.

In contrast to Schüssler Fiorenza's, Kathleen Corley's investigation of the roles of women in the narratives of the crucifixion and the empty tomb focus on the question of historicity and context. She sets the texts among ancient practices and views of mourning and burial, contextualizing their depictions of women in light of female roles in these practices and the ancient *topoi* and conflicts around them, and she argues that the empty tomb narratives were created as a "female tradition" precisely in order to obfuscate or denigrate the association of women with the visions of the risen Jesus: "The empty tomb and physical appearance stories in the gospels disavow visionary experience as a possible origin for Christian belief and practice by replacing it with resurrection theology."[38] These stories were "developed to correct the assumption that Jesus' resurrection 'on the third day' was a simple matter of women (or other family members) going to the gravesite to commune with the spirit of the deceased as women had done for thousands of years."[39] Thus, in Corley's view, the empty tomb stories are both historically secondary and subtly denigrating of the women disciples.[40]

A yet more recent treatment of that issue appears in Jane Schaberg's *Resurrection of Mary Magdalene*. While she recognizes the complexities of historical inquiry, Schaberg attempts a reconstruction of the events behind the texts. She argues for a historical basis for both the tradition that Mary and other women discovered the tomb empty (and for the women's presence at the cross and burial of Jesus)[41] and the tradition that the first resurrection appearance was to Mary Magdalen. Schaberg locates this vision in the experience of prophecy in the movement before Jesus' death (as I do). She further suggests that the discovery of the empty tomb was the catalyst for that first vision, which she reconstructs on the basis of John 20:11–18 and Matthew 28:9–10. It was inspired by receiving the empty tomb into a corporate understanding of the son of man ("Human One") in Daniel 7 and 12 and the narrative of Elijah's ascent in 2 Kings 2. Thus, as the witness of Jesus "ascending to my father and your father, to my God and your God," Mary emerges as the successor of Jesus as Elisha became the successor to Elijah. Schaberg does not allot this status to Mary alone, but sees it as shared among the visionaries.[42]

The attempt to identify either vision reports or empty tomb narratives with the memory of only male or only female disciples seems to me mistaken. The persistence with which Mary is identified as a visionary demonstrates that the visionary accounts cannot be classified as a "masculine tradition." Further, the empty tomb accounts, beginning with Mark, all treat the women as visionaries: a vision of angels is still a vision. Nor is the empty tomb exclusively associated with women. Found by Mary in John 20:1–2, it is also explored by Peter and the beloved disciple in John 20:3–10, although they do not see angels there.[43] Luke, or one of the correctors of Luke, also appears to know either John's account or this tradition (see 24:12). Thus it is far from clear either that the purpose of the empty tomb narrative was to denigrate the women's witness or that visionary reports were a tradition for and from men.

While certainty is unattainable, I am inclined to accept the view that the visionary experiences were the earliest source of faith in the resurrection and to locate these experiences within the context of the movement's prophetic character. In another context, I argued that the reign-of-God movement might have been led by a trinity of prophets: Jesus, Mary, and Peter, like the prophetic trinity of Moses, Miriam, and Aaron that Trible proposed for the exodus.[44] Whatever the extent of prophetic activity in the movement before the death of Jesus, the visionary experience of "meeting Jesus alive from the dead" was widely shared. That much is clear from the list of 1 Corinthians 15:5–8, however its gendered character and chronology are to be interpreted. The question of "first" appearance cannot be resolved. It seems best to simply acknowledge multiple traditions: the tradition known to Paul, which identifies Cephas as the first to see Jesus, the tradition reflected in John 20:14–18 and Matthew 28:9–10, which claims (or assumes) Mary, and perhaps also a third tradition, which claims Simon, who may or may not be [Simon] Peter, reflected in Luke 24:34. Alternatively, Luke may be presenting Cleophas and his companion "on the way" to Emmaus as the first visionaries; they hear of Simon's vision only after they return to Jerusalem, and the text gives no indication whether Simon's vision took place before, after, or simultaneously with theirs.

The Prophetic Visions of Mary and John the Prophet of Revelation

Among the canonical gospels, John 20:1–18 gives the fullest account of Mary Magdalen as visionary; here she is credited with a very brief vision of angels and a more substantial account of a vision of the risen Jesus. John 20:14–18, which recounts her vision of Jesus, gets surprisingly little attention from interpreters of the resurrection, who tend to be more taken with the problems and interests of the appearances to the assembled disciples in John

20:19–29, or with the narratives in the other gospels.[45] Indeed the very first commentator, the author of the appendix to John, seems to exclude Mary's vision from the count of three appearances to the disciples (John 21:14).

Yet this narrative shows far fewer of the motifs identified as secondary than do the other narrative reports of visions. John 20:14–17 manifests little direct concern for authorizing Mary Magdalen and no emphasis on physical proof, in contrast to the other appearance narratives in John, Matthew, and Luke-Acts, all of which are dominated by motifs seen as secondary: the authorization of the disciples, provision for the continuance of the community, and anti-docetic concerns.[46] The brief summary report in 20:18 compares well with Paul's reports of his visions. Apologetic concerns do play a role in the empty tomb account; Mary herself three times articulates the obvious interpretation of the tomb: grave-robbing. "They have taken him away," she says (20:2,13,15). Thus she makes clear that Jesus' disciples and successors did not leap credulously to a superstitious interpretation of a perfectly normal phenomenon.

Juxtaposing Mary Magdalen's vision of Jesus in John 20:14–18 to the programmatic vision of the prophet John in Revelation 1:10–19 manifests the location of both these visions in the context of early Christian prophecy. John 20:18 deserves attention as a brief summary report in itself, while John 20:14–17 and Revelation 1:10–19 share four formal features, which emerge in the parallels shown in table 6.1. Both the vision of Mary in John and the opening vision of Revelation are reports of the visions of the risen Lord, but later interpretation has contextualized them very differently. In part their likenesses have been obscured by the plot of Luke-Acts, which created a caesura between the appearances of the risen Lord in the first forty days after his resurrection and visions of a later time. But this distinction is an artificial one, unknown to the other texts of earliest Christianity and in particular to Paul, who considers the vision of the risen Lord that made him an apostle to be continuous with and in no way inferior to that of the very earliest witness.

The first of the four formal features these two visions share is an odd repetition. In John 20:14, when Mary finished speaking to two angels inside the tomb "she turned back (ἐστράφη εἰς τὰ ὀπίσω) and saw Jesus." He then speaks, asking "woman, why do you weep?" as if she were a stranger. She replies also as to a stranger; then, the text tells us, "Jesus said to her: 'Mary!' turning (στραφεῖσα) she said to him in Hebrew: 'Rabbouni!'" (16). An attempt to stage this scene comes up against the difficulty of that second "turn." According to 14, Mary has already turned to face Jesus before he speaks to her; turning again, she ought to be facing away from him. The opening of the first vision in Revelation gives a clue to the significance of this strange

Table 6.1

John 20:14–18	Rev. 1:10–19
1. turning to the vision 14 Having said these things, she turned **behind** (ἐστράφη εἰς τὰ ὀπίσω) and saw Jesus standing there and she did not know that it was Jesus. Jesus said to her, "woman, why are you crying? whom do you seek?" (cf. John 1:38) 15 supposing it was the gardener, she said to him, sir, if you have taken him away, tell me where you laid him, and I will take him. (cf. John 20:2,13) He said to her, "Mary!" 16 **Having turned** (στραφεῖσα), she said to him in Hebrew, "Rabbouni!" (Which means teacher)	10 in the spirit. .. I heard **behind me** (ὀπίσω μοῦ) a great voice like a trumpet saying . . . 12 and **I turned** (ἐπέστρεψα)
17 Jesus said to her,	**and having turned** (ἐπιστρέψας) I saw . . .
2. admonition **do not touch me** (Apoc. Mos. 31: "let **no one touch me**") for I have not yet ascended to the father.	17 "**do not fear** (cf. 19:10, 22:9: "look! don't!")
3. commission but **go and tell my brothers** [and sisters?], (cf. Matt 28:10: **go, announce to my brothers** [and sisters?])	19 **write** therefore what you have seen and what things are and what will happen after this" (cf. 1:11 **write . . . and send**)
4. oracle 'I ascend to my father and your father, to my God and your God.'" 18. Mary went and proclaimed to the disciples, "**I have seen the Lord**," (cf. 1 Cor. 9:1: "**have I not seen our Lord Jesus?**" John 20:25: "**we have seen the Lord**") And that these things he said to her.	17–18 "I am the first and last, and the living one, and I was dead, and lo I am living forever and ever and I have the keys of death and hell"

description. John declares that while he was "in the spirit . . . I heard behind me (ὀπίσω μου) a great voice like a trumpet saying, 'Write . . .' and I turned (ἐπέστρεψα) to see the voice that was speaking to me, and having turned (ἐπιστρέψας), I saw seven lampstands" (1:10, 12). Taken together, the two passages suggest that "turning behind" signals a change of state, functioning as a cue that introduces the vision report.[47] In both cases, the repetition functions to emphasize the change.[48]

The second shared feature emerges in a second problem in the text of John: the mysterious command, "Do not touch me!" (μή μου ἅπτου) that opens Jesus' speech in John 20:17. This command is probably the single feature of this vision that has inspired the most commentary; debate about its implications overshadows every other aspect of the vision report. Comparing the text to Revelation casts into relief an aspect that is usually ignored: that it is formally and functionally similar to negative commands that tell a visionary how to receive the vision. The command "Do not fear" (μὴ φοβοῦ) opens Jesus' speech in Revelation 1:17; some version of it appears in many other visionary speeches, including the message of the angel at the empty tomb in Mark and Matthew (Mark 16:6; Matt. 28:5), Jesus' appearance to the disciples walking on the water in Mark, John, and Matthew (Mark 6:50; John 6:20; Matt. 14:27); the annunciation scenes in Matthew and Luke (Matt. 1:20; Luke 1:13,30, 2:10) and the oracles to Paul in Acts 18:9, 27:24. A closer parallel to the command "don't touch me!" is found in the monition in Revelation 19:10 and 22:9, where the angel who mediates the revelation fends off the prophet's obeisance with the words "Look! don't!" ("Mind you don't!" ὅρα μή) and the explanation "I am your coslave and that of your brothers. Worship God."

The command "don't touch" has overly preoccupied commentaries on John 20:17, but, in my view, without offering much enlightenment. Recent interpretation has generally preferred to translate it as "do not cling to me" or "do not hold on to me." This translation absolves the text of distaste for the touch of a woman or perhaps even of the flesh, and at the same time manages to reconcile the tensions between the vision of Mary and the later vision in which Thomas is invited to touch, allowing the gospel to have a consistent position on the question of whether the resurrection appearances were palpable, or in the terms of Luke, have flesh and bones.[49] But this translation is shaped not only by Luke's rendering of the resurrection, but also by a more contemporary form of sexism: Mary is portrayed in a favorite of more recent misogynist stereotypes: as the woman whose clinging love holds a man back from his true destiny (whereas Thomas's desire to touch can be seen as the misplaced, but in contemporary terms laudable, desire for experiential knowledge).

That "don't touch" is the better reading is suggested by a parallel from an ancient life of Adam and Eve. The Apocalypse of Moses offers a prophetic scene that casts different light on this warning. When Adam predicts his death and burial to Eve, he instructs her, "When I die, leave me and let no one touch me until an angel says something about me. For God will not forget his vessel that he formed." Similarly in John 20:17, Jesus explains the warning as a temporary measure. The command not to touch signals the liminal and temporary state of the not-yet-ascended Jesus as Apocalypse of Moses 31 does that of the not-yet-buried Adam.[50]

The third common feature of the visions of Mary and John is a commission. In John 20:17 Mary is told: "go tell my brothers [and sisters?]."[51] These "brothers [and sisters?]" appear to be equated by the narrator with the disciples. This equation is an anomaly in the gospel; the references to the "brothers of Jesus" in the gospel refer literally to his family rather than metaphorically to his disciples (2:1, 7:2–10). Interestingly enough, the very brief message the risen Jesus delivers to the women disciples in Matthew seems to be no more than an abbreviation of the message the angel gave them. But where the angel sent them to the disciples, Jesus' word sends them to "my brothers [and sisters?]." In Matthew's gospel there are a few references to believers as "brothers [and sisters?]" of Jesus (12:46–50, 25:40) and several references to the community as each other's' siblings, so that the phrase is less anomalous than in John. Even so, the likeness between Matthew and John may suggest a tradition that is older than either.[52]

John the prophet also receives a commission to deliver a message: the words "write what you see," bracket the vision in Revelation, preceding it in 1:11 and repeated after the first oracle in 1:19. The audience of this message is the churches of Asia Minor—send it to the seven churches, the voice says. But Revelation also may offer a clue to the significance of "brothers" for the visionary context. In Revelation, this term refers to the author's fellow prophets (22:9 cf. 1:9, 6:11, 12:10, 19:10). In light of this, the identification of Miriam the prophet as "sister" of Moses or Aaron raises a particularly significant echo with the portrayal of Mary: Might not this commission envisage Jesus, Mary, and the others of their circle as a "brotherhood" of prophets?

The fourth common feature is an oracle that explains both the vision itself and the fate of Jesus. The message is entrusted to Mary in John 20:17: "I ascend to my father and your father, to my God and your God." Unlike the message the angel commits to the women in the empty tomb scene in Mark 16:7 and Matthew 28:7, this message is not a prediction of future appearances; it neither implies nor requires them. Rather it explains Jesus' departure (both his death and his new life) as an ascent, a going up to God, his origin and source. The parallel phrases "my father and your father, to my God and your God" remind their audience that they share the origin and destiny of Jesus. Although the gospel elsewhere explains Jesus' fate through the doctrine of resurrection (2:19,20,22; perhaps 7:52; see also the appendix 21:14), this oracle does not refer to or even imply that explanation, but rather uses the metaphor of ascension, one that is important in, but by no means exclusive to, the gospel (using ἀναβαίνω in 3:13, 6:62, perhaps 7:8; using ὑψόω, 3:14, 8:28, 12:32,34). The word "I go up/ascend" (ἀναβαίνω) in this oracle is an important factor in Schaberg's suggestion that the visions are formed by reflection on the ascension of Elijah.[53] With or without other appearances, this message can in itself serve as the foundational proclamation for the new community.[54]

At first reading this message appears to be couched in entirely Johannine language. While it fits well with John's insistence that Jesus knew that he came from God and returns to God (13:1–3), subtle variations from the usual Johannine diction suggest that this message may not be the creation of the author or community behind the fourth gospel, but a remnant of the inherited material on which their theology was based. Nowhere else in John are "my father" and "my God" so explicitly identified. This is not because these terms are not synonymous for the gospel, but because they are so synonymous that the point need never be made. Right from the beginning of the gospel, everyone knows who "the father" is. Nor does this gospel speak of God as "your father" as the other gospels do. Some interpreters have suggested that the verse marks a turning point for this gospel: Before the resurrection, God is exclusively the father of Jesus, and becomes the disciples' father only at this point.[55] But this is a misreading; this gospel prefers the absolute "the father," which refers to the deity as the father of the disciples, all Jews, probably even all human and heavenly beings.[56]

What then of the oracle delivered in Revelation 1:17–18? This oracle has as its first function identifying the giver of the revelation, the alien and awesome figure who speaks to the prophet. But it makes that identification not by naming Jesus (as does the closing vision 22:16) but by describing Jesus' fate: "I am the first and the last and the living one and I was dead and lo I am alive forever and ever." Like the oracle in John 20:17, this description does not resort explicitly to the explanation "resurrection." Also like the oracle in John 20:17, this message declares its meaning for the revelation's recipients: "and I have the keys of death and hell" (Rev. 1:17–18).

These four shared features—the "turn" that signifies a change of consciousness, the admonition, the commission, and the oracle—all suggest that the vision of Mary in John 20:14–18 and the vision of John in Revelation 1:9–19 share a prophetic context. Beyond these four features I wish to point to two other features of the passage in light of prophetic literature from Christian and Jewish antiquity.

The first of these features is the exchange in which Jesus calls Mary by name and she responds with a greeting that demonstrates her recognition of him, perhaps her acquiescence to the visitation. There is no parallel to this exchange in Revelation; none of the revelatory figures address the author by name. But visions in Acts and in the Hebrew Bible frequently feature such an exchange of addresses: "Saul" is addressed by name at the beginning of the vision in Acts 9:4–5, as are Ananias in 9:10, Cornelius in 10:4, and Peter in 10:13–14. All of these figures respond with the address "Lord." Probably the exchanges of Acts are modeled on the call of Samuel (1 Sam. 3:2–10, but see also Gen. 22:1).

The second is the final verse of this narrative. John 20:18 is a vision report in miniature. It identifies Mary with her full name, Mariam Magdalēnē, and describes her as coming and announcing, making a proclamation, to the disciples. That proclamation consists of two parts: The first is delivered in direct discourse and in the first person: She says, "I have seen the Lord (ἑώρακα τὸν κύριον)." The language is virtually identical to the formula Paul uses to put forth his vision of the Lord in support of his apostolic claim: "Have I not seen our lord Jesus?" (οὐχὶ Ἰησοῦν τὸν κύριον ἡμῶν ἑόρακα;). These same words report the assembled disciples' vision to Thomas in John 20:25: "we have seen the Lord" (ἑωράκαμεν τὸν κύριον). The second part is in indirect discourse. When the text says, "these things she said to them," it conveys a picture of Mary delivering the oracle that Jesus had communicated to her. One might imagine her proclaiming it among the assembled companions of Jesus, beginning with the oracle formula: "thus says the Lord: 'I ascend to my father and your father, to my God and your God.'" Similarly when the mediator of John's vision dictates oracles that John must write and send to the seven churches of Asia, the threats and promises of the oracles are articulated in the first person, and the speaker is not John, but the figure who appears in 1:9–19. The same is true of the lengthy and complex oracles of Isaiah 40–55 as well as other prophetic material from the Hebrew Bible.

The very brief vision report in John 20:18 summarizes the claim of Mary to the title *apostola apostolorum*, for it depicts her as fulfilling Paul's criteria for apostleship: She has had a vision of the risen Lord (1 Cor. 9:1), her mission is to proclaim (1:17), and her message is the foundation for a new community (9:1). Unlike Paul, she can claim also her memories of Jesus from the time between the baptism of John and the "ascension" (cf. Acts 1:22).

Making a Difference

What difference does my argument make? How does it change the picture of Mary to suggest, as I have done, that the vision described in John 20:14–17 is closer in form to the vision of John that opens Revelation than to the other resurrection narratives, and that the report in John 20:18 is parallel in function to Paul's reports? How does it change the picture of varieties of early Christianity and of the career of Jesus behind them? And does it, as Margaret Farley has asked of the message of the women returning from the tomb, mean "good news for women?"[57]

First, recognizing Mary's experience as similar to the prophet John's makes clear that there is a closer continuity between Mary of the fourth gospel and Mary of the Gospel of Mary than is usually recognized. Both depict Mary as prophet and originator of the mission. This is a picture of Mary that is likely to have been widely known within and to some extent outside the Christian movements. In the later years of the second century, a critic of Christianity named Celsus seems to have seen her role as evidence of the credulous and superstitious character of Christians. He charged that the Christians believed in the resurrection of Jesus on the basis of secret meetings, a single woman, and a few insiders (*C. Cels.* 2,70).[58]

> But who saw this? A hysterical woman, as you say, and perhaps some other one of those who were deluded by the same sorcery, who either dreamt in a certain state of mind, or had a hallucination due to some mistaken notion.[59]

This passage is the starting point of Margaret MacDonald's study of Greek and Roman writers' views on early Christian women.[60] These references, as she shows, are almost certainly to Mary Magdalen. MacDonald chooses to retain the word "hysterical" in order to convey the misogynist stereotype the charge draws upon, and gives her book the subtitle *The Power of the Hysterical Woman*. But πάροιστρος, the word behind it, actually means frenzied or frantic (as she points out), and Celsus also appears to have used it to characterize the Christian prophets of his time (*C. Cels.* 7,9–10). While Celsus's use of πάροιστρος was always pejorative, the application of the word to prophets is not inherently negative, for frenzy, madness, ecstasy were used by the Greek philosophical tradition to designate the state in which the prophet, the poet, and ultimately the philosopher bring forth their inspired work. The references to dreams and sorcery also evoke prophetic practices cast in a pejorative light. Elsewhere, Celsus accuses some early Christians of being "Sybillists"—that is, followers of Greek women prophets called the Sybils. In fact, as MacDonald points out, the early Christian prophet Hermas first identifies his vision of a female figure who represents the church as an encounter with the Sybil.[61] Christians of the early (and later) centuries were in fact much taken with the long poems called the *Sibylline Oracles,* which purported to be the work of ancient women prophets. Thus in the late second century, and by an enemy of Christianity, Mary was still understood as a prophet, as a witness and interpreter of the resurrection and an originator of the Christian message, and Christians were seen as followers of women prophets.

This leads to a second observation. Attention to commonalities between Mary's vision and that of the prophet John (which presents itself as having taken place between 70 and 90 CE) helps to eradicate the division created by Luke's overly rationalized picture of the origins of Christianity. It reminds later interpreters that Luke's theory that resurrection appearances stopped or perhaps changed in definitive ways after forty days is not shared by the other early Christian witnesses. For most, perhaps all, early Christians, the spirit was not only the advocate who supplied Jesus' absence, but also the medium of his presence; appearances of Jesus were not sealed in the past but a continuing source of power and wisdom. Locating Mary's vision in this context also makes clear that these experiences should not be explained as projections or hallucinations arising from grief, guilt, or wishful thinking and extrapolated from current theories of the psyche. Rather, they were the product of modes of prophetic experience and the practices that made that experience accessible. These practices are not fully recoverable, although they undoubtedly involve meditation upon the products and traditions of earlier prophets. Jane Schaberg has suggested that these meditations focused especially upon Daniel and the ascent of Elijah.[62] Such texts as Revelation, the later chapters of Acts, the *Shepherd of Hermas,* the visionary reports of Priscilla/Quintilla, Maximilla, Montanus, and the other prophets of the New Prophecy, the Gospel of Mary, and Thecla's vision of the Lord as Paul in *Acts of Paul and Thecla* reflect literary versions and remnants of these practices.

Third, putting the visions of a prophetic Mary at the center of attempts to interpret the resurrection traditions can help to produce important shifts in the interpretation of the phenomenon now widely called the Jesus movement. Scholarly interpretation of the career of Jesus has long interpreted him as a prophet, but his prophetic role has generally been imagined along the lines of a persona created by and for the texts of Amos and the narratives about Moses and Joshua—that is, as a heroic and lonely figure standing in opposition to kings and priests, and with followers, perhaps, but no equals. This picture is at best anachronistic. Even for the texts of the Hebrew Bible, this picture is less than accurate, as the traditions about Miriam the prophet show. And it is also highly problematic for current theological thinking, especially for Christology. It focuses attention on a single male leader and at the same time places Jesus in opposition to the Judaism of his time, fostering anti-Jewish versions of Christology.

More recently scholarship has attempted to turn from the focus on retrieving Jesus' individual mission and intent to locating him in the context of a movement. Some versions of the movement, largely inspired by Elisabeth Schüssler Fiorenza, have at least raised questions of women's participation. This shift ought in theory to have produced a remedy for both of these problems by placing Jesus into the context of collaborative experience and of Jewish expectation. On the whole it has been less than successful in doing either of these, but instead has inspired a new and unnervingly self-confident quest for the historical Jesus. To some extent, speaking of the "Jesus movement" inevitably reinscribes the heroic isolation of Jesus within the tradition. I prefer to speak of the reign-of-God movement on the grounds of the older critical insight that insisted that Jesus preached not himself, but God's reign, and to see God's reign as a movement of Jewish spiritual resistance to the violent and idolatrous reign of Caesar.

The analysis that produced the concept "Jesus movement" also described that movement as prophetic and charismatic, that is, spirit-driven, with no distinction between the career of Jesus and the years that succeeded his death.[63] A Mary Magdalen whose experience is seen as continuous with that of John the prophet of Revelation and the New Prophets can help to illuminate the character of that experience. Mary saw the risen Lord because like Jesus and their companions in the movement she too was a prophet, accustomed to the voice of the spirit. The resurrection marked a transformative point in her prophetic experience, but that transformation did not consist of receiving the spirit for the first time, but of knowing the spirit in a new way. Once Jesus became the martyr of the movement, the visions that she saw were of him, the spirit in which she prophesied was his, the "word of the Lord" she spoke, the word of the lord Jesus.[64]

Recognizing the prophetic character of the movement and the first communities should have an effect on understanding both of the movement and of the creation of the gospels. Scholarship has long suggested that at least some of the sayings of Jesus in the gospels originated as sayings of the risen Lord who spoke through the early prophets—to resolve communal problems, to comfort and encourage the growing community, to explain when they needed enlightenment. To imagine what this means, one might add Mary into the category of those prophets: Recall my suggestion that John 20 depicts Mary as delivering an oracle with the words: "thus says the Lord, 'I ascend to my father and your father, to my God and your God.'" She speaks, but the "I" in the saying is the "I" of the Lord or of the spirit. This practice survived into the second century, and is attested in the sayings of a prophetic movement originated by another "trinity": two women, one named either Priscilla or Quintilla and one named Maximilla, and a man named Montanus; the movement called itself the new prophets, but was characterized by its enemies as Montanists (from the name of the man). Most of the few oracles that survive from the New Prophecy are reported by their enemies. Even so, it is clear that the spirit spoke through them in the first person. To Montanus is attributed an oracle that proclaims, "Lo, the human being is like a lyre, and I fly over like a plectron (pick); the human sleeps, while I wake." This oracle deploys a standard ancient metaphor that explains the working of prophetic inspiration. Its continuation defends prophetic experience by identifying its source: "The one who displaces the heart of human beings and gives human beings a heart is Lord."[65] Similarly an oracle attributed to Maximilla expresses the experience of rejection by other groups of Christians: "I am hunted like a wolf from the sheep: I am not a wolf; I am word, and spirit and power."[66] This "I" is the "I" of the Holy Spirit, probably complaining of the condemnation of the prophets by their opponents, who claim to defend orthodoxy as they sponsor the institutionalization of church offices. Consider the Johannine sayings "I am the good shepherd" (10:11,14) or "I am the living bread." Might they not have originated in the prophetic inspiration of Mary or one of her women or men companions? In response to the terror and disarray of the days after the crucifixion, the prophet speaks in the spirit of the risen Lord, who explains his death and promises his guidance and sustaining power with the words: "I am the good shepherd, I lay down my life for my sheep"; "I am the living bread come down from heaven. The one who comes to me will never hunger, the one who believes in me will never thirst" (John 6:35,32). Thus, when the voice of Jesus speaks in the gospels, it may have come into the gospel texts through the inspiration of Mary the prophet or some other of her inspired companions.

Like Schweitzer's *Quest for the Historical Jesus,* my quest for a Mary of history comes to rest in the experience of the spirit. I do not suggest that Mary comes to us in the spirit, or that she commands and we obey. Rather I wish to suggest that women and men seekers in the spirit and the memory of Jesus take a place as companion to Mary, moving forward to meet God's reign. But I also want to close with a caution, by recalling that Mary the repentant harlot was created in and by Christianity's early and increasing difficulties reconciling the spirit and the flesh. *Noli me tangere* echoes through the ages in attitudes toward the female body and sexuality in general that have done women no good. The memories of the prophets Miriam and Mariam can be liberated to speak "good news for women" only insofar as the heirs of those memories can learn to love the flesh in which the spirit dwells. And finally, I suggest that the person of Mary the prophet, the visionary, the witness, was never as fully lost as it sometimes seems.

Mary the visionary survived in the tradition, even after she acquired a past from which she was required to repent. If the liturgy for the Western feast of Mary Magdalene focused on her career as repentant harlot, in the Easter celebrations of the West she emerged as witness, visionary, and apostle. *Victimae Paschale Laudes,* one of five sequences that survived the Tridentine reforms of the Roman Catholic liturgy, is in part a dialogue in which Mary is invited, by the congregation or perhaps by the other disciples, to recount her experience:

> Dic nobis, Maria, quid vidistis in via?
> Tell us Mary what you saw on the way? (Luke 24:35)

Like the appendix to Mark, Mary's reply is a compendium of vision narratives—she proclaims her own witness to the empty tomb, her vision of the risen Jesus, the angels she saw. But she also claims to have seen the mute evidence that the beloved disciple and Peter are said to have seen in John 20:5–7. She takes over the tradition of a vision "on the way" from Luke 24:35, and she delivers the message that does not get delivered in Mark 16:7–8:

> *Sepulchrum Christi viventis et gloriam vidi resurgentis*
> The tomb of the living Christ I saw, and the glory of the rising one
> (John 20:1–18)

> *Angelicos testes, sudarium et vestes*
> the angelic witnesses, the handkerchief and grave clothes (John
> 20:11–13, 5–7)

> *Surrexit Christus spes mea praecedit suos in Galilea!*
> Christ my hope is risen; he goes before his own into Galilee! (Mark
> 16:7)

Although the sequence was written well after the creation of the repentant Magdalen, no trace of her appears in this dialogue: only Mary the sublime apostle, who here delivers the message of her visions to audiences who hear and proclaim their belief:

Scimus Christum surrexisse a mortuis vere! Tu nobis victor rex, miserere
We know Christ has arisen from the dead, truly! Have mercy on us. O victor king!

NOTES

1. Albert Schweitzer, *The Quest of the Historical Jesus* (London: A. and C. Black, 1910), 403.

2. Ibid.

3. Helmut Koester, "One Jesus and Four Primitive Gospels," *HTR* 61 (1968): 203–47.

4. I attempted to represent the complexities in my earlier essay "Reconstructing 'Real' Women from Gospel Literature: The Case of Mary Magdalene," in *Women in Christian Origins*, ed. Ross Shepard Kraemer and Mary Rose D'Angelo (New York: Oxford University Press, 1999), 105–28.

5. See especially now Jane Schaberg, *The Resurrection of Mary Magdalene: Legends, Apocrypha, and the Christian Testament* (New York: Continuum, 2002). This essay was substantially completed before the publication of Schaberg's work, and I have not been able to integrate it fully into the argument. The scholarly effort to distinguish Mary Magdalen, Mary of Bethany (John 12:1–8), and the sinful women of Luke 7:36–50 goes back to Lefevre d'Etaples, and has been accepted by the major Western churches. The distinction had in fact been maintained in the Orthodox churches.

6. Mary was identified with both Mary the sister of Martha who anoints Jesus' feet in John 12:1–8 and the unnamed woman penitent who anoints Jesus' feet in Luke 7:36–50. For a collection of the romances, see Benedicta Ward, *Harlots of the Desert: A Study of Repentance in Early Monastic Sources* (Kalamazoo, Mich.: Cistercian Publications, 1987). For more critical texts and introductions for some of these figures, see Sebastian P. Brock and Susan Ashbrook Harvey, *Holy Women of the Syrian Orient* (Berkeley: University of California Press, 1987).

7. For an early revival of the title, see Raymond E. Brown, "Roles of Women in the Gospel of John," *Theological Studies* 36 (1975): 688–99, reprinted in *The Community of the Beloved Disciple: The Life, Loves and Hates of an Individual Church in New Testament Times* (New York: Paulist Press, 1979), 183–89.

8. See also D'Angelo, "Reconstructing Real Women," 108–19.

9. For overviews, see Antti Marjanen, *The Woman Jesus Loved: Mary Magdalene in the Nag Hammadi Library and Related Documents,* Nag Hammadi and Manichaean Studies 40 (Leiden: Brill, 1996); Anne McGuire, "Women, Gender and Gnosis in Gnostic Texts and Traditions," in *Women and Christian Origins,* 257–99.

10. In the NRSV and most other translations, the relation of Mary to Jacob and Joses is specified: She is called "the mother" of James (Jacob) and Joses.

11. Kathleen E. Corley's study of these narratives in light of women's mourning practices suggests the probability of the women's presence at the cross, while arguing for a strong compositional hand in Mark's narrative; see *Women and the Historical Jesus: Feminist Myths of Christian Origins* (Santa Rosa, Calif.: Polebridge Press, 2002), also "Women and the Crucifixion and Burial of Jesus," *Forum* n.s. 1 (1998): 181–217. In particular she disputes that any of the companions of Jesus could have known where he was buried and rejects the empty tomb stories (*Women and the Historical Jesus*, 134–38).

12. See W. D. Davies, *The Setting of the Sermon on the Mount* (Cambridge: Cambridge University Press, 1966), 422–23, for the significance of the word; he actually sees the term as reflecting a relation between the disciples, including these women, and Jesus, based upon the pattern of the relation between Moses and Joshua. They thus become his successors.

13. The phrase ἀπὸ μακροθεν appears to be influenced by Ps. 38:11 (37:12LXX), but it also reflects the political realities for associates of someone being executed for sedition.

14. Winsome Munro, and following her Kathleen Corley, suggests that Mark has suppressed the presence of women in the movement to this point. Munro, "Women Disciples in Mark?" *CBQ* 44 (1982): 225–41; Corley, *Women and the Historical Jesus*, 136.

15. R. Bultmann suggested that the variation of the second Mary's names results from the joining of different traditions; *History of the Synoptic Tradition;* trans. John Marsh (New York: Harper and Row, 1963), 276. But the variation may also be a means of avoiding a tedious repetition, or it may simply testify to the author's lack of interest in this woman.

16. For a treatment and some of the literature, see Joan Mitchell, *Beyond Fear and Silence: A Feminist-Literary Reading of Mark* (New York: Continuum, 2001), 66–75; Hisako Kinukawa, "Women Disciples of Jesus (15:40–41;15:47;16:1)," in *A Feminist Companion to Mark*, ed. Amy-Jill Levine with Marianne Blickenstaff (Sheffield: Sheffield Academic Press, 2001), 171–90; in the same volume, Victoria Phillips, "The Failure of the Women Who Followed Jesus in the Gospel of Mark."

17. D'Angelo, "(Re)Presentations of Women in the Gospels: Matthew and Luke-Acts," in *Women in Christian Origins*, 174.

18. Ibid., 184–85; also "Women in Luke-Acts: A Redactional View," *JBL* 109 (1990): 441–61. Esther de Boer suggests that this cure may raise them from the sickly status of women to manliness; "The Lukan Mary Magdalen and the Other Women Following Jesus," in *A Feminist Companion to Luke,* ed. Amy-Jill Levine with Marianne Blickenstaff (Sheffield: Sheffield Academic Press, 2002), 140–60, esp. 146–49.

19. For a broader interpretation of this passage, see Maria-Luisa Rigato, "'"Remember" . . . Then They Remembered': Luke 24:6–8," in *A Feminist Companion to Luke,* 269–80.

20. Rigato takes this position; see esp. 279–80; see alternatively de Boer, 157–58, who suggests that the Galilean women are restricted to Jesus' lifetime.

21. Sandra Schneiders has absorbed and redirected this idea into a reading of the beloved disciple as a corporate personality; *Written That You May Believe: Encountering Jesus in the Fourth Gospel* (New York: Crossroad, 1999), 211–32. See also the discussion in Schaberg, 344–45.

22. Corley sees no evidence that John used an independent source for the crucifixion, empty tomb, and appearances, and suggests that Peter and the beloved disciples were secondarily introduced specifically to lessen the importance of the women; 134.

23. The appendix is missing in the great fourth-century Codices Sinaiticus and Vaticanus and from some ancient Syriac, Sahidic, and Armenian texts. Clement, Origen, Eusebius, and Jerome also know texts from which it is absent. But it appears in the old Latin tradition cited in Irenaeus' *Adversus Haereses* 3,11,5 (extant only in Latin). This suggests that it was composed during the later half of the second century, probably in the West.

24. It has been suggested that this text incorporates sources that were contemporaneous with the formation of the passion narrative. See John Dominic Crossan, *The Cross That Spoke* (San Francisco: HarperCollins, 1988); for a summary of this theory, see Paul Allan Mirecki, "Peter, Gospel of," in *Anchor Bible Dictionary*, vol. 5, 278–81.

25. For a fuller analysis of this text and a review of the other accounts of the empty tomb, see Carolyn Osiek, "The Women at the Tomb: What Are They Doing There?" in *A Feminist Companion to Matthew*, ed. Amy-Jill Levine with Marianne Blickenstaff (Sheffield: Sheffield Academic Press, 2001), 212–20.

26. See Karen King, "The Gospel of Mary Magdalene," in *Searching the Scriptures*, vol. 2: *A Feminist Commentary*, ed. Elisabeth Schüssler Fiorenza (New York: Crossroad, 1994), 601–34; also "Why All the Controversy? Mary in the Gospel of Mary," in *Which Mary? The Marys of Early Christian Tradition*, ed. F. Stanley Jones, SBL Symposium Series, 19 (Atlanta: Society of Biblical Literature, 2002), 53–74.

27. Wesley Isenberg assigns the Gospel of Philip to the later part of the third century.

28. See Antti Marjanen, in this volume, who explains the kiss as communicating secret knowledge.

29. Trans. Wesley Isenberg from *Nag Hammadi Codex II, 2–7 together with XIII,2*, Brit. Lib. Or.4926(1), and P.Oxy. 1, 654, 655*. Vol. 1: *Gospel according to Thomas, Gospel according to Philip, Hypostasis of the Archons, and Indexes*, ed. Bentley Layton, NHS 20 (Leiden: Brill, 1989), 169.

30. For fuller accounts of this process, see D'Angelo, "Re-Reading Resurrection," in *Crossroads in Christology: Essays in Honor of Ellen M. Leonard*, ed. Anne Anderson and Mary Rose D'Angelo, *TJT* 16 (2000): 108–29; the summary in the primer on the historical Jesus produced by Gerd Theissen and Annette Merz, *The Historical Jesus: A Comprehensive Guide*, trans. John Bowden; bibliographies revised

and updated by Robert Morgan (Minneapolis: Fortress, 1998), 478–85; Gerd Lüdemann, *What Really Happened to Jesus?* trans. John Bowden (Louisville: Westminster
John Knox, 1995), esp. 93–94, 132.

31. See D'Angelo, "Re-Reading Resurrection," 111–12.

32. See, e.g., Elisabeth Schüssler Fiorenza, "The Apostleship of Women in Early
Christianity," in *Women Priests: A Catholic Commentary on the Vatican Declaration,*
ed. Leonard Swidler and Arlene Swidler (New York: Paulist, 1977), 135–40; Margaret
A. Farley, "Feminist Consciousness and the Interpretation of Scripture," in *Feminist Interpretation of the Bible,* ed. Letty Russell (Philadelphia: Westminster, 1985),
41–51.

33. Gerd Lüdemann has moved from this conclusion to the further hypothesis
that this vision was produced by Peter's guilt and grief; 93–94, 132. Bart Ehrman, on
the other hand, argues against identifying the Cephas of 1 Cor. 15:5 with Peter; see
"Cephas and Peter," *JBL* 109.3 (1990): 463–74.

34. Elisabeth Schüssler Fiorenza, *Jesus, Miriam's Child, Sophia's Prophet: Critical Issues in Feminist Christology* (New York: Continuum, 1994), 124.

35. Ibid., 127–28.

36. Ibid., 125.

37. Ibid., 126.

38. Corley, *Women and the Historical Jesus,* 138.

39. Ibid., 139.

40. Ibid., 203–209.

41. As does Osiek, 212–19.

42. This is a summary of a lengthy and complex argument put forward in two
chapters of the book; 254–356.

43. Corley sees this as a further attempt to marginalize the role of women; see
Women and the Historical Jesus.

44. D'Angelo, "Re-membering Jesus: Women, Prophecy and Resistance in the
Memory of the Early Churches," *Horizons: Journal of the College Theology Society* 19
(1992): 199–218; see also Phyllis Trible, "Bringing Miriam Out of the Shadows," *Bible
Review* 5 (1989): 14–25, 34.

45. See, e.g., Gregory J. Riley, *Resurrection Reconsidered: Thomas and John in
Controversy* (Minneapolis: Fortress, 1995), who relegates it to a brief mention (94)
and a long footnote (98, n. 86) and harmonizes this passage's treatment of Jesus' body
with the Thomas story. The exceptions are feminist; see Harold W. Attridge, "Don't
Be Touching Me: Recent Feminist Scholarship on Mary Magdalene," in *A Feminist
Companion to John,* vol. 2, ed. Amy-Jill Levine, Feminist Companion to the New Testament and Early Christian Writings Series 5 (New York: Sheffield Academic Press,
2003), 140–66. Attridge's study was published too recently to be integrated into this
essay.

46. John 20:18 may make an authoritative claim for Mary, though hardly an explicit one.

47. Other interpretations of the repetition suggest a source; see Ernst Haenchen,

A Commentary on the Gospel of John, vol. 2: *Chapters 7–21,* trans. Robert W. Funk, Hermeneia (Philadelphia: Fortress, 1980), 209; he postulates scribal error; a variety of explanations are collected by Raymond Brown, *The Gospel according to John,* vol. 2, Anchor Bible 29A (Garden City, N.Y.: Doubleday, 1970), 991; Schaberg collects moralizing interpretations, often inferring from it some defect on the part of Mary; 329–30 and nn. 168–69.

48. This is true even if one postulates a source.

49. See, e.g., Riley, 98, n. 86.

50. Mary Rose D'Angelo, "A Critical Note: John 20:17 and Apocalypse of Moses 31," *Journal of Theological Studies,* n.s. 41 (1990): 529–36.

51. The Greek words for sister and brother, ἀδελφός and ἀδελφή, are distinguished only by an ending (like the Spanish, *hermano* and *hermana*), so the generic plural, which is masculine in form and usually translated "brothers," is less exclusive than the English plural "brothers." Thus the NRSV has in most cases chosen to translate it as "brothers and sisters."

52. See also Schaberg's reconstruction of a common source behind John 20:1–18 and Matthew 28:1–10; 294–99.

53. Schaberg, 304–19.

54. It may best fit the category of an oracle of assurance; see David Aune's description of this category in *Early Christian Prophecy in its Ancient Mediterranean Context* (Grand Rapids, Mich.: Eerdmans, 1983), 117–18; I do not, however, wish to limit the use of the word "oracle" to his categories; I am using the word to describe the content of any prophetic communication.

55. Brown, vol. 2, 1016–17, and the literature cited there.

56. D'Angelo, "Intimating Deity in the Gospel of John: Theological Language and 'Father' in 'Prayers of Jesus,'" in *God the Father in the Gospel of John,* ed. Adele Reinhartz, *Semeia* 85 (1999): 59–82.

57. "Feminist Consciousness and the Interpretation of Scripture," in *Feminist Interpretation of the Bible,* ed. Letty Russell (Philadelphia: Westminster, 1985), 41.

58. Celsus's work, *The True Word,* is known only through Origen's response in a treatise called *Against Celsus.* The objections to the resurrection were apparently attributed by Celsus to an unnamed Jewish critic. This particular charge is from *C. Cels.* 2,70.

59. *C. Cels.* 2,55. The passage continues with an implication of fraud. Trans. Henry Chadwick, *Origen: Contra Celsum* (Cambridge: Cambridge University Press, 1953), 109.

60. *Early Christian Women and Pagan Opinion: The Power of the Hysterical Woman* (Cambridge: Cambridge University Press, 1996), 1–5, 102–26.

61. See 4–5, 104–109.

62. 254–75, 304–19.

63. Gerd Theissen, *Sociology of Early Palestinian Christianity,* translated from the German work *Soziologie de Jesusbewegungs* by John Bowden (Philadelphia: Fortress, 1978).

64. D'Angelo, "Reconstructing 'Real' Women from Gospel Literature: The Case of Mary Magdalene," in *Women in Christian Origins*, 124–25; also "Gender in the Origins of Christianity: Jewish Hopes and Imperial Exigencies," in *Equal at the Creation: Sexism, Society and the Christian Tradition*, ed. Joseph Martos and Pierre Hégy (Toronto: University of Toronto, 1998), 36–39; and "Re-membering Jesus: Women, Prophecy and Resistance in the Memory of the Early Churches," *Horizons: Journal of the College Theology Society* 19 (1992): 211–18.

65. Epiphanius, *Medicine Box against All Heresies*, 48,4.

66. Eusebius, *Ecclesiastical History*, 5.16,17.

7

On the Visual and the Vision: The Magdalene in Early Christian and Byzantine Art and Culture

DIANE APOSTOLOS-CAPPADONA

We have had a very long and circuitous relationship—*she* and I. *She* appears, disappears, and reappears, as is her wont. Sometimes I have released *her* from my thinking, research, and visual investigations; other times, I have re-invited her into my life. Absence and presence, denial and affirmation, textual inquiry and the visual, these are our forms of communication. My first memory of *her* is clear and powerful. *She* came into my life formally for the first time when I was seven or eight years old. The detail of my exact age is a blur, as age should be for a woman. However, the event itself remains so vivid that I can *see* myself and my mother so clearly and describe not simply what we were wearing and where we were sitting but every emotion on both our faces as we talked that weekday afternoon. My regular Sunday School teacher had been absent that previous Sunday, and her replacement had terrorized, perhaps unknowingly, my entire class with her exacting descriptions not simply of hell but of all the punishments sinners received according to their sins—the tongues of liars nailed to the burning roofs of tall buildings, the mouths of those who swore stuffed constantly with hot coals, and so forth. Perhaps Dantesque, perhaps not, nonetheless terrifying for a group of young children who silently met their parents at the end of the Divine Liturgy. It was several days before I could even possibly begin to voice my fears to my mother, for the teacher, substitute or no, was very firm: there was no salvation for those who had sinned. My greatest terror was that my father—who was a sports fanatic—would be condemned to hell for all those "words" he exchanged in a monologue with various prize fighters, baseball players, football players, coaches, and referees. "What exactly," I asked my mother, "was the point of being in heaven, if all the people you loved were in hell?" My mother's facial expression exuded simultaneously compassion and wisdom as she replied, "Do you know the story of the great sinner?" I replied with all the sagacity and erudition of any seven- or eight-year-old, "Ah, yes, Mary Magdalene."

My mother asked me to recount the story of Mary Magdalene and I did—of course, unaware of the exact meaning of the "great sin" and of the scriptural inaccuracies I had learned. Once I had finished, my mother's face shone with relief and maternal solace as she then asked me, "If God through Jesus forgave Mary Magdalene her great sin, why wouldn't God through Jesus forgive your father for his unfortunate use of language?" Totally relieved by my mother's theological expertise and recognizing that it was rooted in her own faith in God, I expressed great relief and began a lifelong relationship with *her*—the "great sinner" who that fateful afternoon represented my father's salvation and the restoration of my own confidence.

My reason for recounting this autobiographical episode is its direct connection to the relationship between story and image, or vision and the visual, as mediated through the feminine figure I identify as Mary Magdalene with her many personae and meanings. *She* disappeared from my research for an extended period, only to return with vigor, or should I write "with vengeance," in the spring of 2001. Our conversations have taken many turns these last few years and attained a new height at the symposium entitled "Mary Magdalen: Prophet and Apostle in the Miriamic Tradition." As I listened to the insightful presentations by my colleagues from the fields of scripture study, church history, art history, and gender studies, I was overwhelmed not simply by the multiplicity of Magdalenes who inhabit our scholarly domains but by the interconnections between the concepts of her as prophet, visionary, and apostle. My own thinking about the Magdalene's place in the early Christian and Byzantine art of the third through the seventh centuries was transformed without the proverbial "flash of lightning" or "thunderbolt" of conversion.

This essay is the result of my own reexamination of many of the images I have looked at for more years than I wish to confess in print. Yet, my *seeing* of them has been colored not simply by my own years of research but by the questions the work of my colleagues such as Mary Rose D'Angelo, Karen King, Susan Haskins, and Katherine Ludwig Jansen has raised for me. As part of my process of rethinking, I returned to earlier mentors, including that magisterial group of art historians: André Grabar, Ernst Kitzinger, and Kurt Weitzmann. This essay, then, is not simply an investigation of the place of the Magdalene in early Christian and Byzantine art and culture, but a revisiting of my understanding of the role of the visual in early Christianity. The clear but not often discussed distinction between the verbal and the visual is crucial to my methodology of *seeing*.[1] Since the Enlightenment, if not the Reformation, Western culture can be characterized as logocentric in nature. As such, the authority of word is primary, and a text—as the compilation of words—is understood to be factual, clear, and not subject to a myriad of interpretations. Words are unequivocal carriers of meaning and value, and clear presenters of ideas and teaching. The image, however, was consigned to a diminished class of testimony, given its multivalent and aesthetic constitution. Not simply "open to interpretation" but evocative of individualized reception, the image was deemed untrustworthy—image as opposed to word was not fixed.

With the advent of what I identify as the scholarship of "the marginalized,"[2] there has been recognition of the multiple modes of reading a text and of the distinctions between the individual act of reading of a text, the reading of a text for group consumption, and the hearing of a text. Further, the interest in the multiplicity, if not primal ambiguity, of the visual was reassessed and revalued with the introduction of "response theory,"[3] and the issue not simply of the production but the reception of an image emerged as indispensable to scholarly analysis. How an image is seen and experienced by differing classes, races, and genders is as critical to an investigation such as this one as what one comes to know about its creation, iconography, and patronage. Fundamental to this inquiry into Mary Magdalene in early Christian and Byzantine art and culture is the dual recognition that the vestiges of pre-Christian cultures and cultural attitudes were deeply embedded into the early Christian and Byzantine worlds and that from its beginnings, Christianity was neither clear, uniform, or unitary in fact or in referent but was rather a complex, varied, and localized phenomenon.

The Beginnings of Christian Art and the "Image" of Mary Magdalene

During its first four centuries, Christianity developed a complex system of a theology: rites of initiation and celebration, administration, communication, pastoral care, and an initial written canon. The general perception was that Christianity, especially in the West, was a religion of the book, a logocentric tradition if you will. Its originating worldview was one without art, premised upon a combination of the Mosaic proscription, denial of an imminent Parousia, persecution, and the economic argument for a religion of "the lowest classes." The reality, however, was that from its beginnings, Christianity recognized the primary role of the visual modality.

Scriptural references such as Luke 11:34–36 combined with the understanding of Jesus Christ as the "illuminator," that is, the one who brings the light to those who are spiritually or physically blind, display an early Christian fascination with the sense of sight and the role of *seeing* as a form of religious communication. The knowledge gleaned from twentieth-century archaeological excavations has proved the existence of "Christian art" that was largely indistinguishable from the art of the larger Greco-Roman culture prior to the third century. Thus, this religion of the book was simultaneously a religion of the image: Christians had *seen* their God in the Incarnation.

The earliest Christian imagery, which preceded a clearly defined Christian art, was premised upon the subtle ties between language and image, conceptualization and visualization. The preliminary employment of signs and symbols integrated within the visual vocabulary of classical Greco-Roman art was a form of "indirect" communication that by the third century evolved into a clearly Christian visual vocabulary in a fashion similar to the development of Christian theology and liturgy.[4] As André Grabar advises, "Iconography is, after all, the aspect of the image that informs."[5] This "informing" was evident from the third century forward with the transformation from Christian imagery to Christian art.

The fundamental discourses of early Christian imagery were the signs and symbols related to salvation: the Good Shepherd, the *refrigeria*, Hebrew scriptural figures in situations of peril, Christian scriptural figures in situations of peril, and the ubiquitous *orans* (praying female figure standing with outstretched arms).[6] The evolution into early Christian art begins organically with what Ernst Kitzinger identified as the "tentative beginnings" in the process of coming to terms with the representational style of "signitive" visual ciphers proclaiming deliverance and redemption through divine power in the third and early fourth centuries.[7] Within that eventful fourth century, as Christianity moved from a persecuted cult to the official religion of the Empire under Constantine through the reign of Justinian, Christian art underwent what Kitzinger characterized as "the great age of expansion" as the themes of peril and salvation were replaced with motifs of Christ's power and grandeur.[8] The third and final moment of early Christian iconography extends from the middle of the sixth to the beginning of the eighth century, and is categorized by Kitzinger as the "era of potentiation." He was careful in his employment of the otherwise unfamiliar word "potentiation" as the appropriate term to describe the nature of the visual, which provides "for a more direct and intimate communication with the heavenly world."[9]

This historical scheme of identifiable stages in the establishment of Christian iconography provides an objective frame for the evolution of the Magdalene's imagery in early Christian and Byzantine art. The historic boundaries for my analysis begin in the formative third century and end in the early eighth century with the advent of the Iconoclastic Controversies. I begin every iconographic study with "the evidence of my eyes," that is, seeking out and "reading" the images.[10] For me, the visual is primary documentation for the understanding of theology and culture.[11]

Curiously, as I gathered together and began to categorize these visual images, I discovered that three iconographic motifs related to Mary Magdalene emerged that paralleled chronologically Kitzinger's three stages. More stunning, perhaps, was the fact that the visual evidence argued for a reading closer to the feminist retrieval of Mary Magdalene both as first witness of the Resurrection and as apostle.[12] My own re-*seeing* of these images forced me to consider the irony of history that the historical individual responsible for the transformation of Western Christian art from "potentiate" icon, to paraphrase Kitzinger, to literal narrative changed in tandem the Western Christian perception of Mary Magdalene from witness and apostle to repentant sinner. The issue is not the malicious or misogynist cause(s) of these transformations but rather the possible connections between Pope Gregory the Great's proclamations that defined both Mary Magdalene and Christian art.[13]

Traditionally, art and church historians have identified the motif of the "Women at the Tomb" as the initial iconography of Mary Magdalene. The frescoed fragment of three women on the lower register of the west wall of the Christian baptistery at Dura-Europos (ca. 230) is identified as the earliest documented representation of this scriptural episode.[14] I have seen photographs and drawings of this damaged fresco many times, as well as the reconstruction displayed at Yale University Art Gallery. However, when I reviewed my study photograph for this essay, I was struck by a new possibility.

The fragmentary depictions of at least three women, perhaps five, on the west wall are paralleled by five sets of "feminine" feet on the lower register of the east wall. The symbolism of the numbers entered into my thinking: What if the lit torches and unguent jars visible in the hands of the women on the western wall were not matched by what had been in the hands of those on the eastern wall? What if these were not the "Three Marys"—and how could they be when they suddenly numbered two groups of five women, or ten Marys—but rather an early rendering of the parable of the Wise and Foolish Virgins?[15] How, I asked myself, could I justify this new reading? What visual elements were suddenly evident to lead me to a new way of *seeing* this otherwise well-known image?

Figure 7.1. *Women at the Tomb.* Mural from the Christian Baptistery,
Dura-Europos (ca. 230). **Courtesy of Dura Europos Collection,
Yale University Art Gallery, Z68.**

The mode of dress, the rendering of the body, and the attributes of torch
and clear (glass) jar: These were the visual connectors that caused me to reconsider the identification of the female processions on the walls of the Christian baptistery at Dura-Europos.[16] More significantly, these visual connectors represented a clearly defined classical Western iconography for virgins
and virginity.[17] I recognized that my search for Mary Magdalene in early
Christian and Byzantine art and culture had taken a significant directional
turn.

Classical and Christian Iconography of Virgin/ Virginity and the "Image" of Mary Magdalene[18]

Although we may live in the twenty-first century, we are the children of
the nineteenth century, especially with regard to social and cultural definitions relating to categories of sexual behavior. There was a "sea change" in
the language and demeanor related to sexual conventions in the nineteenth
century; for example, "virgin" and "virginity" came to denote a state of physical ignorance of the opposite sex.[19] However, the etymological roots indi-

cate the condition of not being married, a reality separate from sexual activity or gender identity.[20] The Latin word *virgo,* translated commonly as "virgin," intends "a woman without a man," while the Greek *parthenos* signifies "belonging-to-no-man."

In the classical pre-Christian Western world, the category of virgin/virginity was neither sex-specific nor a permanent "state-of-being-in-the-world." Rather it was a transitional stage in which the virgin was neither male nor female but rather an intermediary between the human and the sacred.[21] Virginity could be temporary and purposive, as in the state of sexual renunciation necessary for spiritual cleansing and/or ritual purity, or the stage of life that began with the death of the spouse. Whether the virgin had sexual experience or not, the state of virginity was understood to be one of ambiguity, one between childhood and adulthood.

There existed two categories of sacred virgins in classical culture: virgin goddesses and their priestesses. Virgin goddesses could renew their "virginity" by ritual baths in sacred waters, signifying the powerful forces of regeneration that mirrored the cycles of nature. Artistic depictions, whether painted or sculpted, incorporated iconographic elements such as costume, hairstyle, and attributes, which came to identify not simply the goddesses but also their priestesses as virginal. The common visual characteristics associated with virginity in classical art were long, loose, flowing hair; loose, unrestrained white garments; heroic androgynous body;[22] and any of the following attributes: crescent moon, white flowers, clear glass jar/bottle, and a companion animal, most often a little dog. A cursory viewing of the priestess and her female devotee depicted on the Diptych of the Symmachi (388–401: Victoria and Albert Museum, London) affirms the employment of this "classical" iconography even as Christianity came to dominate the Imperium.

This Classical attitude influenced the concept and iconography of virginity in early Christian and Byzantine art and culture. Early church fathers advocated that commitment to the virginal life lessened a Christian woman's special penalties, such as pain in childbirth, from "the Fall." Similarly, it was understood that a virgin's physical body was a mirror of her spiritual body, so that the image of "wholeness," as in *virgo intacta,* took on a new meaning. Early Christian female virgins were characterized as holy women who sought to be "like men" at least in the heroic androgynous image of their bodies. Early Christian theology described Jesus Christ as the vehicle, and his male body as the vessel, of salvation. Thereby, to be saved was defined as being male; to be male was to be saved.[23]

Renderings of holy women in early Christian and Byzantine art were premised upon the image of the male body, excluding genitalia, so one could argue that the visual evidence of Classical depictions of the virgin goddesses and their priestesses were heroic and androgynous, if not male. Artists were fully capable of depicting the reality of the female "bodiliness" as evidenced by the image of Athena on a bronze casket plaque (third/fourth century: Staatliche Museen, Berlin); the renderings of the Maenad (Ariadne?) and Tyche-Fortuna on an ivory box (fourth/fifth century: Dumbarton Oaks, Washington, D.C.); and the depiction of Aphrodite on a silver situla (early seventh century: Kunsthistoriches Museen, Wien).[24] Therefore, I can conclude that the decision to render the bodies of virgins—divine or human— distinctively heroic and androgynous was intentional and purposeful.

Patristic documents fused, and confused, devotional and pious legends of the early Christian female virgin martyrs with modes of behavior and dress for women. These "holy women" became an ideal that could be achieved through strict ascetic discipline, physical suffering, and proper activities: teaching catechisms, assisting as deaconesses, and covering their heads. I refer regularly to the fourth century as pivotal to Christianity—religiously, culturally, artistically, and spiritually; however, it is the pivotal century in the Christian understanding of virgin/virginity, which was reshaped by Constantinian edicts, conciliar decrees, and patristic texts.

Constantine assisted unwittingly in the formation of the Christian interpretation of virginity as a life of self-denial and ascetic renunciation of the flesh as a mode of overcoming a woman's fundamentally decadent and depraved nature, inherited from Eve. The imperial ban on crucifixion as a form of punishment for being a Christian resulted in a new category of Christian martyrdom. The "red" martyrdom of human blood waned as the "white" martyrdom of female virginity and male celibacy became normative in the Christian community. To be a virgin/virginal was to be ascetic, self-denying, dedicated to God, heroic, and a martyr!

The fourth-century Church Fathers, including Ambrose of Milan, Augustine, and Jerome, wrote letters and treatises that provided detailed instructions to "virgins" as to the appropriate modes of dress and hairstyles, the impropriety of makeup and jewelry, the proper texts to read, and spiritual meditation as a method of sexual renunciation.[25] These documents supported a Christian cultural ethos in which virginity as a state of physical perfection was achieved by sexual innocence and chastity. A virgin's body was pristine and whole; it was imaged as heroic, androgynous, and nonsexual.

When the Council of Nicaea (325) declared, "If therefore a girl wants to be called a virgin, she should resemble Mary," it established the spiritual and devotional definitions, and the iconography of Mary's virginity as both ideal and model for Christian women. A century later, the decree of the Council of Ephesus (431), which pronounced Mary as *Theotokos* (God-bearer), promulgated the appropriate modes of veneration and iconography for this new definition. Visual images of Christian female virgin saints and martyrs followed the pattern of Mary's "disembodied" bodiliness as both an ideal and an advance over the heroic androgyny of third- and fourth-century Christian iconography. Loose, unrestrained garments provided ephemerality and denied physicality as sentimentalized facial expressions and long, flowing hair became stereotypic.

The Classical iconography of the renewal of the goddess's virginity through ritual bathing found a Christian counterpart in the sacrament of baptism as "a new life in Christ." Women, like Mary of Egypt, who had experienced lives of sexual activity as wives, courtesans, and prostitutes, were restored to virginal perfection by the waters of baptism. Early Christian and Byzantine artists emphasized this "new" life through the long, flowing hair and heroic androgynous bodies that characterized these women.

Mary Magdalene represented a special case, for her ecclesiastical identification as the repentant sinner was not pronounced by Pope Gregory until the end of the sixth century. Within the next two centuries, the iconographic motif of her copious tears—shed in sorrow and repentance—restored her as the ritual bathing had restored Hera and Aphrodite and the baptismal waters had restored Mary of Egypt. Nonetheless, Mary Magdalene was identified by the honorific "virgin" in ecclesiastical texts, hymns, and prayers regularly from the fourth century. Perhaps, however, this title is only an "honorific" when we look backward with twenty-first-century eyes, for the iconography of Mary Magdalene in early Christian and Byzantine art from the third through the seventh centuries, as for example in the fragmentary fresco in the Christian baptistery at Dura-Europos, affirms her status as a "virgin."

Images of Mary Magdalene in Early Christian and Byzantine Art

I return to the depiction from Dura-Europos identified as that of the "Women at the Tomb" (fig. 7.1) with the caution that in early Christian and Byzantine art, the Resurrection of Christ was never explicitly depicted but rather was signified initially by the empty tomb and the female witnesses, and in the later Byzantine period by the *Anastasis*, or Descent into Hell. As this building at Dura-Europos is identified as a Christian baptistery, Thomas F. Mathews's connecting of these female images to the scriptural passage of the Wise and Foolish Virgins and the procession of the neophytes at baptism, is more than appropriate. André Grabar had earlier made the associations between the neophyte procession at baptism and the Greco-Roman custom of the *paternalia,* or family visits to tombs, while also emphasizing that the tomb is closed, signifying that the depicted event represents "the moment before the Resurrection."[26] Carl H. Kraeling premised his original identification of these five female figures as the "Women at the Tomb" on his reading of Tatian's *Diatessaron.*[27]

The fragments of the women on the western wall provide several iconographic elements by which I can identify them as virgins: heroic androgynous bodies; flowing hair covered with a veil; loose, unrestrained, and predominately white garments; and a clear (glass?) container. Each also holds a lighted candle or torch. Whoever they are, the following is obvious even in their fragmentary condition: They form a ritual procession, they are moving from the back of the room forward toward the "soon-to-be-empty tomb" and the baptismal font, and the presence of the lighted candles and the stars indicates that it is night.

I want to suggest that what we have here at Dura-Europos is neither one scriptural episode nor one liturgical ceremony being represented, nor a conflation caused by confusion. Rather, I believe we have here a symbolic, thereby multivalent, vision that incorporates the rituals of baptism and burial, the parable of the Wise and Foolish Virgins as the witnesses to both a baptism and the Resurrection, and the discovery of the Resurrection by the "holy women." Can I single out one of the female figures and identify her as Mary Magdalene? No, I can't. However, I can justify iconographically a "sight" reading of this fresco as visual evidence for the active role of women in Christian rites and practice, and for the assimilation of classical conventions associated with sacred virgins into the newly emergent third-century Christian iconography.

Two fifth-century ivory objects—"Holy Women at the Tomb of Christ" (early fifth century, ca. 400: Castello Sforzesco, Milano) (fig. 7.2) and the Passion Scene plaques (ca. 420–30: The British Museum, London)—attest to a more careful presentation of this scriptural event. Without doubt, we witness here the two women's arrival at the tomb and their recognition of the event of the Resurrection. Both renderings place the empty tomb center stage. As opposed to the depiction of the tomb in the Dura-Europos fresco, this tomb is empty, as signified by both the open doors and the images carved on the doors, which include the Raising of Lazarus. The major difference between these two presentations is that the women on the Passion Scene plaque sit behind the sleeping soldiers, and position their heads, hands, and arms in the classical postures of dignified but deep grief. The two women

Figure 7.2. *Holy Women at the Tomb of Christ* (early fifth century:
Castello Sforzesco, Milano). Ivory panel. **Courtesy of Foto Marburg/Art
Resource, N.Y.**

on the ivory panel take on the positions of adoration as the one bows and the other grasps the feet of the seated angel, who ostensibly announces the Resurrection (Matt. 28:1–6).

Again in both of these depictions, the female figures can be identified as virgins by their androgynous bodies, loose, unrestrained garments, veiled heads, and appropriate postures. Obviously, it would be difficult to identify one of the two women definitively as Mary Magdalene on the Passion Scene Plaque; however, the action of the woman who grasps the feet of the angel in the ivory panel offers the iconographic possibility of identification as Mary Magdalene, as the gesture foretells visually her reaching forth in the iconography of the *Noli Me Tangere* motif.

The narrative cycle of the life of Christ found in the mosaics of the mid-sixth-century royal basilica of San Apollinare Nuovo, Ravenna (ca. 548) (fig. 7.3) includes an innovation in the Resurrection iconography. Once again we find the empty tomb with the open door placed center stage, a seated angel gesturing greeting at stage left, and the two Marys gesturing acceptance at stage right. Grabar identifies this representation as the first clear presentation of the conversation of the Resurrection between the angel and Mary.[28] Following the convention of "reading" Western Christian art from left to right, I can suggest that this mosaic provides us with a "story," which begins with the possibility of God's presence on earth through his angelic messenger, the dispensing of the message by the messenger, whose hands gesture toward the empty tomb; the empty tomb itself with a door ajar is the heart of the story; and the climax of this story is the acceptance of this powerful event by the two female witnesses, for whom "seeing is believing." The viewer's attention is focused on the empty tomb by the "visual game" of the angel's hands, palm side down, which tilt upward on a 45–degree angle and parallel the slanted tomb door and the right hands of the two women, which tilt downward, palm side up, on another 45-degree angle.

Once again, the two female figures are indistinguishable from each other with the exception of the colors of their garments—one wearing soft gold, the other bluish purple. Both continue to have heroic androgynous forms, loose, flowing garments, and veiled heads. Neither woman carries any other identifying attribute. Based solely on the distinctions of color symbolism, I would suggest the woman garbed in bluish purple might be Mary Magdalene.

Almost contemporary with the Ravenna mosaic is the Rabbula Gospels (586: Biblioteca Laurenziana, Firenze) (fig. 7.4). On the same illustrated page are found the Crucifixion, the guards overthrown, the Marys at the Tomb, and the iconographic motif identified by Kurt Weitzmann as the *Chairete*. In this illustration I can clearly identify Mary Magdalene, who stands,

Figure 7.3. *Women at the Tomb* (548: San Apollinare Nuovo,
Ravenna). Mosaic. **Courtesy of Alinari/Art Resource, N.Y.**

among the three holy women, closest to the Crucified Christ, while the Virgin Mary is depicted on the opposite side of the scene, leaning on the Beloved Disciple. The Magdalene, again depicted with her now ubiquitous androgynous body, loose, unrestrained garments, and veiled head, holds her veiled hands upward toward her face in the conventional posture of grief and despair.

On the lower register, she is represented twice with the Virgin Mary (who is distinguished by her purple garments and golden halo). They receive the "good news" from the seated angel in the first episode of the lower register's depictions; then center stage is the now familiar empty tomb signified by the open door; and the final episode is the *Chairete*, which I believe is the Eastern Christian, that is, Byzantine, visual formula for what becomes the *Noli Me Tangere* in Western Christian art. From the Greek for "Hail," the *Chairete* identifies the iconography of Christ's greeting to the two Marys after his Resurrection (Matt. 28:9). The Virgin Mary and the Magdalene are rendered in the Rabbula Gospels as kneeling before the risen Christ. His right hand is extended toward them in a gesture of greeting, while they both reach out to

Figure 7.4. *Crucifixion and The Women at the Tomb*, from the Rabbula Gospels, Ms. Plut. I, 56, fol. 13r. (586: Biblioteca Laurenziana, Firenze). Vellum. **Courtesy Scala/Art Resource, N.Y.**

him in a posture and gesture prophetic of the sixteenth- and seventeenth-century depiction of the *Noli Me Tangere*.

During the sixth and seventh centuries, Christian pilgrims to the Holy Land acquired small "souvenir" objects such as ampullae, jewelry, and reliquaries, and liturgical items such as censers, pyxides, and chalices as evidence of their spiritual journeys. Given the extant number of existing little lead flasks, I must conclude that these ampullae were mass produced and were a most popular "spiritual souvenir." Each ampulla would have been filled with oil taken from the lamps at Christianity's most sacred sites, such as the Holy Sepulcher. Each of these "souvenir" items was decorated in that early Christian and Byzantine manner of signification in which the images identified the visited sacred site or the relic contained therein.

So for example, the representation of the women at the tomb on a sixth-century pyxis (Metropolitan Museum of Art, New York City) advances this iconographic survey of Mary Magdalene in early Christian art as the scriptural narrative emerges with the concept of both Christian pilgrimage and liturgy. Once again, the two women, that is, the two Marys, are indistinguishable from each other, garbed in loosely flowing robes and veils and gesturing grief with their upraised left hands upon their respective chins. However, these women capture our visual attention because of the activity they perform with their right hands: each holds a censer and approaches the altar, which substitutes for the empty tomb at the familiar center stage position. The altar is elevated upon a platform and protected by a domed three-arch structure, which with the curtains performs the liturgical function of separation, later done by the *iconostasis* of the Byzantine tradition. Weitzmann suggested, "By substituting an altar for the actual tomb, the artist illustrated the popular belief in the symbolic identification of the Holy Sepulcher with the altar, an association that grew out of the Eastern belief in the presence of the crucified Christ on the altar during the celebration of the Eucharist."[29]

The intriguing question that Weitzmann, beyond his speculation that this pyxis may have originally been intended as a ciborium, and other art historians have left unanswered, if not unasked, is "What does it mean for a woman to be portrayed in the act of censing an altar in a sixth-century work of Christian art?" No matter how physically small this specific pyxis may be, the reality of its mass-produced nature and the innovative iconography piques my interest, especially if I accept Karen Jo Torjesen's interpretation of the *orans* as "an artistic representation of women's liturgical prayer and prophecy," and more specifically as visual evidence for women preaching in the early church,[30] for the imagery of two *orans* is found on the remainder of this pyxis. I ask myself, "Am I seeing here visual evidence for the scriptural identification of Mary Magdalene as not simply the first witness of the Resurrection but as apostle to the apostles and further as preacher/ teacher/celebrant?"

Two sixth-century ampullae continue the popular interest in this iconographic fusion of the "tomb" with the "altar" in relation to Mary Magdalene, and, I suggest, with her identification as a leader in the early Christian community. My guess is that these two ampullae are not singular in iconographic motifs but rather normative for this late-sixth- through early-seventh-century period as mass-produced pilgrimage souvenirs. One ampulla is decorated with seven images depicting scenes from the life of Jesus Christ (Cathedral Treasury, Monza), while the other is covered with a depiction of the Crucifixion on one side and with the Women at the Tomb (Dumbarton Oaks Collection, Washington, D.C.) on the other. In both instances, tomb/altar is placed center stage, with the two Marys approaching from stage right and the gesturing angel seated on stage left.

Although once again both women are garbed in the now familiar loose, unrestrained garments, with their heads covered by veils, I would venture to identify the leading, or first, woman as Mary Magdalene not because she is first but because she carries a censer in her right hand. My intellectual reading here is that the censer substitutes for, or foretells, her scripturally appropriate attribute of the unguent jar; while my intuitive response is that this early Christian imagery is the visual evidence for the participation of women in active roles in the early church.[31]

Another popular early Christian pilgrimage souvenir was a censer, which could be used in liturgical services in either an ecclesiastical edifice or a home. The connection between the life of Christ and the liturgy is continued with the depictions of five scenes—Annunciation, Nativity, Baptism, Crucifixion, and the Women at the Tomb—on a seventh-century bronze censer (Virginia Museum of Fine Arts, Richmond). Once again, the Resurrection is not envisioned as a "historical event" but is made known by its initial result—the empty tomb. Once again the seated angel holds a staff with one hand and gestures with the other toward the "center stage" tomb as the now familiarly garbed and veiled female figure stands on stage left: an iconographic innovation of immense proportion in such a small space!

There is only one woman at this tomb. In this visual survey, the number of "women" has decreased from the possible ten found on the frescoed walls of the Christian Baptistery at Dura-Europos to the one witness on this seventh-century censer. The number of female witnesses present at the tomb vacillates in the Christian Scriptures from Luke's unspecified "group" of women to Mark's identified three and Matthew's two; the normative understanding has been that there had to have been at least two witnesses to attest to the veracity of an event under Jewish law.[32] This iconographic innovation of only one Mary accords with John's gospel, and by emphasizing one female witness elevates her authority and position.

Although not "normative" from the seventh century, the presence of only one female witness to the Resurrection begins to garner artistic affirmation at least as seen on such popular objects as the pilgrimage souvenirs and jewelry. For example, the scenes of the life of Christ inscribed on a seventh-century gold marriage ring (Dumbarton Oaks Collection, Washington, D.C.) conclude with that of the Woman at the Tomb to signify once again the Resurrection. Works of Christian art such as these pilgrimage souvenirs and jewelry serve several functions within the believer's daily experience, from proof of spiritual quest and religious devotion to the merging of personal prayer with the realm of amulets. This daily and personalized *seeing* of the Christian narratives permitted the individual believer the reality of participation in her faith as the past fused with the present, as the liturgical reenactment became actualized on a personal level.

Simultaneously, a visual definition was encoded in Byzantine iconography for the Resurrection and for Mary Magdalene as the "equal to the apostles." The fourth through the sixth century development of Byzantine iconography corresponded to the Christological and Mariological formulations of the Ecumenical Councils from Nicaea through Ephesus. According to Byzantine iconic traditions, one of the first depictions to appear was that of the *Myrrophores,* or Myrrh-Bearing Women, which illuminated the otherwise ineffable event of the Resurrection. Byzantine liturgy and spirituality incorporate and are shaped by the sacramental aesthetics of the icon for "that which enters through our sight penetrates to the uttermost depths of our being and directly influences our spiritual life."[33] As the liturgies related to the Holy Week and *Pascha* evolved, the two icons of the *Anastasis* and the *Myrrophores* came to presence the two aspects of a single reality, the meaning of the Resurrection event.

However, by the seventh century, the icon identified as the *Chairete* is confirmed as the visualization of the apostolic charge to Mary Magdalene (ca. seventh century: Old Library, Monastery of Mount St. Catherine, Sinai) (fig. 7.5). This is the scriptural first encounter between the risen Christ and the two Marys, following the arrival at and discovery of the empty tomb, the announcement of the Resurrection by the angel, and the dispersal of the male apostles at the empty tomb. In this icon, the risen Christ holds a scroll in his left hand pressed against his abdomen, perhaps to highlight his side wound, as he raises his right hand in a gesture of greeting to the two women

Figure 7.5. *Chairete* (ca. seventh century: Old Library, Monastery of Mount Saint Catherine, Sinai). Icon. Published through the courtesy of the Michigan-Princeton-Alexandria Expedition to Mount Sinai.

that the Byzantine tradition identifies as his mother, the *Theotokos,* or the God-bearer, and Mary Magdalene.

As in the earlier images discussed in this essay, the two women are indistinguishable from their dress—both wearing long-sleeved red tunics and purplish-red paenulae (cloaks), both veiled and haloed, and both bodily androgynous. The two women's postures are telling. The standing female figure is obviously the *Theotokos,* who is identified not simply by her regal posture or her double-handed gesture of worship, but by the monogrammatic inscription that appears to be simply the monogram *MP* but that should be read as *H ΑΓΙΑ ΜΑΡΙΑ*.[34] The figure I would have identified as Mary Magdalene is in the foreground, bending or crouching down to touch the left foot of the risen Christ with her left hand as she raises her right hand upward toward him in a gesture of worship.

As mentioned in my discussion of the initial *Chairete* motif in the Rabbula Gospel page, the postures, gestures, and relationship between the risen Christ and Mary Magdalene are the visual antecedents of the *Noli Me Tangere.* However, the Byzantine identification of *Chairete,* or the greeting "Hail!" is significant because the emphasis in Eastern Christianity, which has never accepted the composite Magdalene of the Gregorian decree, is on the Mary Magdalene who is the first witness of the Resurrection and the "apostle to the apostles." Although noncanonical, the presence of the *Theotokos* is significant as both a visual and a spiritual connector to liturgical music and her "signitive" visual gesture toward the Magdalene's apostolate. For in this icon, it is the Magdalene who mediates between the church and the sacrament, between the mother and the son, between the believer and the meaning of the Resurrection.

Preliminary Conclusions

As a form of conclusions to this investigation of the visual evidence of Mary Magdalene in early Christian and Byzantine art, I will suggest, first, some proposals relating specifically to the documentation of the first witness and, second, avenues for further research. I have been reminded in my own re-*seeing* of these well-known images of women that they provide correlation with textual materials while offering simultaneously an alternative to the written canon. The image and the word are not separate realities that operate either only in distinct opposition to each other or in tandem with each other; rather they are varied elements of the same reality, just as the Magdalene's vision of the risen Christ and his message to her formulated her act of "telling," which constituted the essence of the faith pronouncement for early

Christianity that "I have seen the Lord." The critical interpretive questions are the issue of whether the word and the image are for the same or different audiences and whether the mode of reception for the word and the image were similar or distinctive in early Christian and Byzantine culture.

My survey of the early Christian and Byzantine images of Mary Magdalene has evidenced a progression from the "anonymous" group of women found in the early third-century frescoes in Dura-Europos to the emerging of an identifiable Mary Magdalene within the context of the Women at the Tomb in the fifth-century ivory Diptych Leaf, the mosaics of San Apollinare Nuovo, and the Rabbula Gospel, to the visual singularity of her as witness and apostle in the seventh-century pilgrimage souvenirs and the Byzantine iconography of the *Chairete.* I can relate this evolution of Magdalene motifs to Kitzinger's three-part chronology for Christian iconography from its "tentative beginnings" in moving from Christian imagery to Christian art, toward the "great age of expansion" with its emphasis on scriptural narrative, and ultimately toward the "potentiation" that results in a participative intimacy between vision and viewer. I can suggest further that this individuation of the "anonymous" woman into Mary Magdalene as witness and apostle parallels the evolution of Christian interests from the urgent concerns of an imminent Parousia toward the formal establishment of the Christian tradition. A tradition garners authenticity from the *reality* of its story of origins and the authority of its founders. Similar visual journeys from anonymity to individuation were encountered by Jesus as the Christ and Mary as *Theotokos,* who were identified in early Christian imagery by their actions and later by distinctive physiognomies.

For me the visual relationships between the depictions of Mary Magdalene, whether as "anonymous" or named, and the classical iconography of virgin/virginity was revelatory not simply as to how the early Christian community *saw* her but as to the connectors to sacred authority. Imaging her in this manner—androgynous body garbed in loose, unrestrained garments, flowing hair covered with a veil, and accompanying attribute of a clear glass jar—reaffirmed her role as intermediary, a messenger if you will, between the sacred and the human. As I have indicated, the meaning of virgin/virginity from an ungendered spiritual state-of-being-in-the-world was reformed by the fourth-century Church Fathers to an engendered state of physical perfection achieved by sexual innocence and chastity. Similarly, the "power" of virgin/virginity was transformed from that of sacral intermediary to that of martyr. Curiously, the visual and verbal representations of Mary Magdalene into the eighth century continue the associations of both the Classical and the Christian understandings of virgin/virginity, and of the etymology of the English word "martyr," which comes from the Greek *martyr-, martys,* for witness.[35]

In my re-*seeing* of these otherwise familiar early Christian and Byzantine images of Mary Magdalene, I found two significant motifs that deserve further investigations. The first is the visual and theological connectors between the Byzantine iconography of the *Chairete* and the later Western Christian iconography of the *Noli Me Tangere.* I would suggest that a careful study of these two motifs, including the liturgical and spiritual influences upon their iconographic development, will reveal direct connections between Byzantine and late medieval/early Renaissance Western Christianity.[36] Such an iconological analysis should bear witness to the meaning of the *Noli Me Tangere* not simply as a visual motif but as a theological concept.

My second motif is that found on the pilgrimage souvenirs in which Mary Magdalene performs liturgical actions such as censing the altar or preaching. My own previous experiences of investigations into the iconology of women in Christian art argue for the reality that such studies are based rarely on field research by the current investigator but rather on previously published studies.[37] When challenged by a much-respected colleague that there was no major Christian interest in the Jewish heroine Judith except during the Renaissance, I proceeded to search for Judith throughout research travels in France, Germany, and Italy. The results of my field research amazed me as to the numbers, media, and stylistic variations of the image of Judith in Western Christian art.[38] Further, my own research relating the influence of the visual on societal and cultural values has persuaded me of the critical importance of those works of art I might have earlier dismissed as folk art, low art, popular culture, or material culture.[39] Therefore, I am convinced not only of the crucial significance of the imaging of Mary Magdalene on the "pilgrimage souvenirs" for the devotional/religious life of the Christian collective but of the evidence that this second motif found its way into works of art for more public or liturgical purposes.

I want to suggest a two-part investigation that seeks out and examines early Christian and Byzantine images from all media and of all sizes and qualities, of (1) Mary Magdalene and (2) women in postures, positions, and actions of ecclesial authority. Building upon the stimulating proposals of Torjesen and Jansen, and the fieldwork analyses of Linda Sue Galate, the results of these new field studies will need to be correlated with primary textual materials, including liturgical music and poetry. My proposed new investigation(s) should provide historically appropriate documentation of women's participation in the early Christian and Byzantine church activities and traditions.

I cannot yet answer the questions posed by, but continue to be intrigued by, the connections between Pope Gregory the Great's pronouncements defining the proper use of Christian art and the identity of Mary Magdalene. The significance of these Gregorian decrees has been formative for Western Christian attitudes toward the visual and this female saint. My intuitive response, not yet factually firm enough to be a conclusion, is that the connection lies within the effectivity and affectivity of the act of *seeing*. Our modern English word *aesthetic* is derived from the Greek *aesthetikos* (from the root *aisthanesthai*), which means to perceive, as in to come to know, through the senses. Simply enough, when one partakes of an anesthetic, one has no feelings. So perhaps Gregory's decrees were premised upon the unspoken, unconscious dangers that connect women and the visual: paraphrasing Kitzinger's term "potentiation" to signify that intimacy created between vision and viewer. Perhaps Gregory needed to re-form Mary Magdalene not because her "apostolate" threatened that of the male apostles but rather because it was premised upon her trust in and retelling of what she had *seen*.[40]

NOTES

I am grateful to Professor Deirdre Good, who, as organizer of the conference "Mary Magdalen: Prophet and Apostle in the Miriamic Tradition," invited my participation and engaged me in helpful conversations; and who as editor of this present volume encouraged my contribution of this essay.

1. For an in-depth analysis of the relationship between word and image in logocentric cultures and its influences on the formation of female imagery, see my "Discerning the Hand of Fatima: An Iconological Investigation of the Role of Gender in Religious Art?" in *A History of Our Own: Muslim Women and the DeConstruction of Patriarchy*, ed. Amira El-Azhary Sonbol (Syracuse: Syracuse University Press, 2004).

2. By "the marginalized," I intend those varied groups, from ethnic and racial identities to women and the middle class, who had previously been dismissed, if not ignored, by traditional scholarship. For example, the advent of Black Studies coincided with that of Regional Studies and Women's Studies during the late 1960s and early 1970s. The methods and materials included in those new areas of research and teaching opened the eyes of many to material culture and eventually a reappraisal of the visual. The more recent scholarly interests in Popular Culture and Visual Culture are the expansions of that early "new" scholarship.

3. The first significant book on "response theory" was David Freedberg, *The Power of Images: Studies in the History and Theory of Response* (Chicago: University of Chicago Press, 1982).

4. However, as with Christian liturgy and theology, those connectors between Christianity and classical culture were identified as Christian in form and origin as the pre-Christian classical world was denied. The classic texts on the origins of Christian art, such as André Grabar, *Christian Iconography: A Study of Its Origins* (1968; reprint, Princeton, N.J.: Princeton University Press, 1980), acknowledged the traditional litany that this initial relationship was identified as a "baptism" or assimilation of the classical into the Christian as a natural progression of events, and thereby a denial of the classical roots of the imagery and iconography. However, several recent texts, most importantly Thomas F. Mathews, *The Clash of the Gods: A Reinterpretation of Early Christian Art* (Princeton, N.J.: Princeton University Press, 1993), question the "reality" of the denial and consider the survival and ramifications of the pre-Christian classical motifs and images even into the Byzantine period.

5. Grabar, xlv.

6. For a general discussion of the salvific themes of early Christian art, see for example, Grabar; Walter Lowrie, *Art in the Early Church* (1947; reprint, New York: W. W. Norton, 1969); and Neil MacGregor and Erika Langmuir, *Seeing Salvation: Images of Christ in Art* (London: BBC Worldwide, 2000). For two alternative but intriguing discussions on the meaning of the *orans,* see Linda Sue Galate, "Evangelium: An Iconographic Investigation of an Ante Pacem Image" (Ph.D. dissertation, Drew University, 1997) and Karen Jo Torjesen, "The Early Christian *Orans:* An Artistic Representation of Women's Liturgical Prayer and Prophecy," in *Women Preachers and Prophets through Two Millennia of Christianity,* ed. Beverly Mayne Kienzle and Pamela J. Walker (Berkeley: University of California Press, 1998), 42–56.

7. Ernst Kitzinger, "Christian Imagery: Growth and Impact," in *Age of Spirituality: A Symposium,* ed. Kurt Weitzmann (New York: Metropolitan Museum of Art, 1980), 141.

8. Ibid.

9. Ibid., 148.

10. Throughout this essay, I am employing the term "reading" in relation to the experiencing and interpreting of an image as if the process were the same as for a text. I would like to argue for the concept of *seeing*—hence my italicizing of this word—as more appropriate for the mode of analysis of an image.

11. I have advocated that the image is equitable in weight and cultural value to a text as primary evidence in evaluating historical or theological claims, or in understanding cultural history. Both a text and an image are open to interpretation, censorship, editing, and misrepresentation. In the best of all possible methodological and interpretative analyses the primary texts and original images might be found to work in tandem with each other. However, the "truth" of human history may be that text and image may illumine, contradict, or refine each other and, most probably, that they were created for different audiences, and thereby, different classes. The latter situation—an appeal to different audiences and classes—is what I believe to have been the case of the earliest Christian centuries, when the majority of the

populace was verbally illiterate. By the time of Pope Gregory the Great, Christian art may have been normalized as the *biblia pauperum,* or "bible of the poor"; however, this definition was no affirmation for the earlier period.

12. After my careful re-*seeing* of these visual materials, I have come to agree with Mary Rose D'Angelo's reflection: "Among the most striking and successful results of feminist reinterpretation has been the remaking of Mary Magdalene." See her essay "Reconstructing 'Real' Women from Gospel Literature: The Case of Mary Magdalene," in *Women and Christian Origins,* ed. Ross Shephard Kraemer and Mary Rose D'Angelo (New York: Oxford University Press, 1999), 105.

13. Pope Gregory the Great preached a homily on the gospel pericope of Luke 7:36–50 in the Basilica of San Clemente, Rome, on 21 September 591. In this text, he "defined" Mary Magdalene as a composite of varied named and anonymous women from the Christian Scriptures. His "composite" Magdalene became normative for Western Christianity. In his famed early-seventh-century Letter to Serenus, Bishop of Marseille, Pope Gregory the Great defined the role of visual art as the "bible of the poor," that is, as a mode of teaching the faith to those who were unable to read or incapable of reading the Bible. This understanding of art as visual Christian narrative became normative for Western Christianity.

14. Carl H. Kraeling, *The Christian Building: The Excavations at Dura-Europos,* Final Report 8, pt. 2 (New Haven, Conn.: Yale University Press, 1967). See also Kurt Weitzmann, ed., *Age of Spirituality: Late Antique and Early Christian Art, Third to Seventh Century* (New York: Metropolitan Museum of Art in association with Princeton University Press, 1977), exhibition catalogue, especially 404–405.

15. Matthew 25:1–13. After this idea "flashed" in my mind, I found affirmation of "my" new reading of these female processions in Mathews, 152–53. However, Mathews continues to refer, as would I if I advocated a complete re-reading from the Three Marys, to the wise and foolish virgins, to the women as "they walk in procession toward the tomb of the risen Christ."

16. Throughout this essay, I am employing the term "visual connector" to signify not simply the more traditional concepts of sign and symbol but also what I believe to have been the unconscious process of identification between the pre-Christian classical culture and early Christianity. In my opinion this process operated in a fashion similar to that which I identified as "visual analogy" in my study of the significance, relationship, and enculturation of the masterpieces of Christian art into twentieth-century cinema, especially biblical epics; see my "The Art of *Seeing:* Classical Paintings and *Ben-Hur,*" in *Image and Likeness: Religious Visions in American Film Classics,* ed. John R. May (New York: Paulist Press, 1992), 104–15, 190–91.

17. Diane Apostolos-Cappadona, "Virgin/Virginity," in *Encyclopedia of Comparative Iconography: Themes Depicted in Works of Art,* ed. Helene E. Roberts, vol. 2 (Chicago: Fitzroy Dearborn, 1998), 899–906. The reader is especially urged to consult the "List of Works" that accompanies this entry and its bibliography. Additionally, the reader is referred to Kenneth Clark, *The Nude: A Study in Ideal Form*

(New York: Pantheon, 1956), for a now classic understanding of the relationship between classical and Christian imaging of the human body.

18. The following interpretation of the imaging of the heroic androgynous body and the emerging principle of Christian virginity is established from a variety of sources, including my textual and visual research for the "Virgin/Virginity" entry in the *Encyclopedia of Comparative Iconography* (see the detailed bibliography and list of works); a comparative *seeing* of the rendering of the human body in both its male and female formulae in classical and early Christian art; and textual analyses of both primary and secondary sources as indicated throughout the notes and bibliography of this essay. One alternative interpretation of what I see as a fusion of the classical and the Christian visual figurations is found in Margaret R. Miles, *Carnal Knowing: Female Nakedness and Religious Meaning in the Christian West* (Boston: Beacon Press, 1989), as she "reads" the goal to become neither virginal nor androgynous but fully male in order to achieve salvation. Another reading of the early Christian attitudes toward virginity and the female body is as a triumph of religious commitment that incites a failure to penetrate the otherwise highly gendered and penetrable female figure; for example, see Elizabeth A. Clark, *Ascetic Piety and Women's Faith* (Lewiston, N.Y.: Edwin Mellen, 1986); idem, *Women in the Early Church* (Collegeville, Minn.: Liturgical Press, 1983); and Susanna Elm, *"Virgins of God": The Making of Asceticism in Late Antiquity* (Oxford: Clarendon Press, 1994). However, my analysis is, I believe, the first attempt to correlate the visual with the textual from both a comparative methodology and a commitment to the visual as a primary vehicle of historical documentation.

19. Note that the nineteenth-century conventions would publicly recognize heterosexuality as normative. A more appropriate late-twentieth/early-twenty-first-century phrasing would read "a state of physical ignorance of a sexual partner."

20. Throughout this essay, I make a cautious distinction between the terms "gender" and "sex." Sex is the physical, or biological, reality identified by specific bodily, predominantly genital, parts, and may or may not be related to sexual preference. Gender is the socially conditioned forms of behavior, dress, and speech, and may or may not be related to sexual identity or preference.

21. I intend here an existential but transitional state between the traditional categories of male and female. Throughout this essay, I am employing the careful descriptor "heroic androgyny" or "heroic androgynous" as opposed to the condition of being a hermaphrodite, which is a state of being simultaneously male and female in consciousness, demeanor, action, and bodily sex. The figurations of both the classical and Christian female virgins, including Mary Magdalene, are depicted as being female; my interpretative interest is, "What is the nature of their femaleness? Is this femaleness depicted as normative to our traditional visual understandings or does it transcend traditional visual boundaries?"

22. Throughout this essay, I propose the descriptor "heroic androgynous" in reference to the figurations of the bodies of the virgin goddesses and priestesses of classical culture, and of the virgin saints and martyrs of Christian culture. My prin-

ciple here is the nature of the imaging of the body that is premised upon religious and/or theological tenets, and the classical motif of the hero—one who is tested and perseveres the challenge—as a visual connector to the then emerging Christian concepts of saint and martyr. A perusal of Clark's *The Nude* will provide the reader with recognition of the visual and cultural category of the hero, which is the foundation of my descriptive phrase "heroic androgynous body."

23. For an alternate reading of the meaning and process of salvation for the male body, see Miles.

24. All of these classical comparisons have been carefully selected to correspond chronologically to the periods of early Christian and Byzantine art. An in-depth viewing of these works results in a visual recognition of the challenge to the then traditional cultural perception of the female body, which was soft and curvaceous, with distinctive breasts, narrowed waist, and wide hips. The rendering of the bodies of virgins in classical art, with the exception of Aphrodite, displays an ephemeral yet solid form projecting sturdiness, power, and resolve in the flattened breasts and a thickened waist that almost dissolves into the hips. While such a rendering may be identified as being more "masculine" than "feminine" or as representing the physical characteristics of menopausal women, I would argue that the message being projected visually was that the fundamental nature of these women was as "the hero," ergo their heroic and androgynous nature.

25. Most famous among these patristic texts were Ambrose's *Instructions of a Virgin* and Jerome's *Letter to Eustochium.* These documents are the precursors of the medieval and nineteenth-century advice manuals for young Christian women.

26. Grabar, 124.

27. Kraeling, 86–88.

28. Grabar, 124.

29. Weitzman, *Age of Spirituality,* 581.

30. Torjesen, 42–56.

31. I have found few secondary, or interpretative, materials examining early Christian art, i.e., catacomb frescoes, sarcophagi, ampullae, et al., for the image of woman as celebrant, preacher, or teacher. Based upon a series of conversations with my mentor in the Patristics, Johannes Quasten, I would expect that much could be gained in understanding the role of women in early Christianity by a careful study of the visual evidence as primary documentation, not as textual illustrations. Dorothy Irvin's brief study raises some preliminary and intriguing questions relating to a series of tomb inscriptions, a singular (?) mosaic portraying the Episcopa Theodora in the ninth-century Basilica of St. Praxedis, and the same first-century fresco of the *fractio panis* from the Catacombs of Priscilla discussed by Torjesen. See Dorothy Irvin, "The Ministry of Women in the Early Church," *Duke Divinity School Review* 2 (1980): 76–86; and Torjesen.

32. The flaw in this reasoning is that the testimony of women was not valid under Jewish law; nevertheless it has been a guide for analyses of Mary Magdalene's

identity by art historians, Christian iconographers, church historians, theologians, and Scripture scholars for centuries.

33. Michel Quenot, *The Resurrection and the Icon,* trans. Michael Breck (New York: St. Vladimir's Theological Press, 1977), 9.

34. See Kurt Weitzmann, *The Monastery of Saint Catherine at Mount Sinai: The Icons,* vol. 1: *From the Sixth to the Tenth Century* (Princeton, N.J.: Princeton University Press, 1976), 50.

35. For a preliminary discussion of this relationship, that is, the visual tradition of Mary Magdalene as witness, see my *In Search of Mary Magdalene: Images and Traditions* (New York: American Bible Society, 2002), especially 49–53.

36. For an example of this style of analysis relating Byzantine and Western Christian theology and attitudes toward women from visual connectors, see my essay "Picturing Devotion: Rogier's *St. Luke Drawing the Virgin,*" in *Rogier van der Weyden "St. Luke Drawing the Virgin": Selected Essays in Context,* ed. Carol J. Purtle (Turnhout: Brepols, 1997), 5–14.

37. See the introduction to my *Dictionary of Women in Religious Art* (1996; reprint, New York: Oxford University Press, 1998), ix–xvii.

38. The preliminary results of my research on Judith were incorporated into my essay "'The Lord has struck him down by the hand of a woman!' Images of Judith," in *Art as Religious Studies,* ed. Doug Adams and Diane Apostolos-Cappadona (1987; reprint, Eugene: Wipf and Stock, 2001), 81–97.

39. For example, see either my essay "*A Daughter's Own Book:* Cultural Reflections on Women's Literacy in Nineteenth-Century American Culture," *AAQ* 19.4 (Fall 2002): 8–13, or my *In Search of Mary Magdalene.*

40. On my emerging interpretation of the Gregorian documents, especially on the importance of the vision and revelation to Mary Magdalene and her place as a woman leader in the early Christian community, see D'Angelo, "Reconstructing 'Real' Women," especially 111–12, 125. I am grateful to Professor D'Angelo, who in a correspondence following the 2002 conference advised me to read this particular essay of hers, suggesting correctly that it would prove helpful to my research.

The Miriamic Tradition

8

Jesus' Gnostic Mom: Mary of Nazareth and the "Gnostic Mary" Traditions

STEPHEN J. SHOEMAKER

A brief personal anecdote can perhaps best situate the nature of my contribution to this volume. At the annual meeting of the Society of Biblical Literature in 2000 I presented a paper on the "Gnostic Mary" traditions in a session on Mary in apocryphal literature. After the session, Deirdre Good very kindly invited me to participate in an upcoming conference on "Mary" in early Christianity, an invitation that I enthusiastically accepted on the spot. I immediately began looking forward to this future conference on the *Virgin* Mary. When I later on received a more formal invitation to this conference (whose presentations lie behind the essays collected in this volume), I was both surprised and amused to learn that the primary focus of the conference was not Mary of Nazareth, as I had somewhat "naturally" presumed, but instead Mary of Magdala. Since the original, informal invitation identified the subject of the conference simply as "Mary," without any further clarification, I assumed almost instinctively that we would be discussing the mother of Jesus. I draw attention to this innocent mistake in order to highlight a considerable problem in the study of the "Gnostic Mary." As this anecdote rather clearly illustrates, the name Mary used alone in reference to a figure from early Christianity, without any further qualification, can potentially refer to a number of different individuals. Several figures are simultaneously suggested, of whom Mary of Nazareth and Mary of Magdala are perhaps merely the most obvious choices.

For better or worse, this is basically the circumstance we meet in the ancient "Gnostic Mary" traditions. These are a set of early Christian apocrypha that include a character named "Mary," to whom the Savior has revealed knowledge of the "Gnostic" mysteries and who is an associate, or sometimes a rival, of the apostles. In most cases, the identity of this figure is not specified any further: she is known only as Mary without any further clarification. Yet in spite of this ambiguity, modern scholars have not hesitated to identify this Mary repeatedly and quite confidently with Mary of Magdala, explicitly rejecting any connections with Mary of Nazareth. Nevertheless, as I have demonstrated elsewhere, this apocryphal woman's identity with the Magdalene is nowhere near as certain as it has frequently been made out to be, and Mary of Nazareth's contribution to her representation is equally significant, and in some instances possibly more so.[1] Only the Gospel of Philip and the Pistis Sophia explicitly identify this Mary with the Magdalene, but both of these texts also make strong, unambiguous connections between this same woman and Mary of Nazareth. Despite the frequent appeal to these two texts as if they somehow resolve the matter, they in fact do not; instead, they underline the complexity and uncertainty of this woman's identity, as a few scholars have occasionally recognized.[2] In general, students of early Christianity have all too often looked past this problem, to the effect that this Mary's identification with Mary of Magdala has become such an orthodoxy of early Christian studies that one might hardly think to question it. As a result, it has proved somewhat difficult to reassess this interpretation, since it is so frequently assumed or asserted rather than explained,[3] making it sometimes unclear exactly what one is arguing against.[4]

Can We Use the Classification "Gnostic?"

Before proceeding any further with this issue, however, we must pause briefly to clarify, insofar as is possible, what has lately become a vexing problem of early Christian studies, namely the so-called Gnostic traditions of late antiquity. No doubt by this point many readers are already troubled by my rather free and easy use of the adjective "Gnostic." Recent studies by several scholars have raised serious questions about the value and meaning of the term "Gnostic," with some suggesting that we should abandon it altogether and others urging that its use may be continued but only in reference to a very specific early Christian group (or perhaps groups). Michael Williams, for instance, argues that "Gnosticism" has become "such a protean label that it has all but lost any reliably identifiable meaning for the larger reading public," suggesting that we replace the adjective "Gnostic" with the description "biblical demiurgical."[5] While Williams has undeniably served us all with his convincing demonstration of the incredibly diverse traditions that have been collectively described as Gnostic, the alternative label proposed by Williams is, in my opinion, equally if not more problematic, for a number of reasons that I have detailed elsewhere.[6]

In a somewhat similar vein is Karen King's recent work *What Is Gnosticism?* where she likewise dismantles the traditional interpretive category of "Gnosticism" and its related adjective "Gnostic." Unlike Williams, however, King does not propose alternative vocabulary: her study very perceptively traces the manifold problems with "Gnosticism" and "Gnostic," but it fails to provide a clear path out of the morass that it uncovers. In many ways the question of the book's title is left unanswered, and instead, King concludes with some very provocative and challenging thoughts about adopting postmodern and postcolonial strategies for interpreting the highly variegated landscape of early Christianity.[7] Indeed, after reading *What Is Gnosticism?* one is left fumbling for words and wondering how to talk at all about the "Gnostic" traditions and even early Christianity in general; no doubt this is the point of the book.

Bentley Layton offers an alternative approach to the use and meaning of "Gnostic," which is not without some problems of its own, but which at least for the present moment offers a useful and well-reasoned basis for using the term "Gnostic" in reference to a specific group within early Christianity. Layton basically adopts a social-historical approach (King calls it "nominalist") to the problem of determining who the Gnostics were.[8] Layton begins with the observation that the terms γνωστικός/γνωστικοί (Gnostic/Gnostics) were used in late antiquity to refer not to a particular set of beliefs, but to a particular group of people, who appear to have used this moniker as their self-designation. Opponents of this group identify a particular cosmological myth belonging to the Gnostics. Layton argues persuasively on several grounds that this myth is distinctive and can be relied upon to identify textual material deriving from Gnostic Christianity, a tradition that other scholars have also named "Sethian" or "Sethian Gnostic." Altogether, Layton identifies fourteen works that belong to the Gnostic Christian literary corpus, and through study of these we may know this ancient Christian community more clearly. Layton additionally notes a variety of similarities between the beliefs of Valentinian Christianity, as well as a report that Valentinian Christianity developed as an offshoot of the Gnostic (Sethian) community. Consequently, he suggests that the Valentinians may also properly be designated Gnostics.

Overall, Layton's approach to the problem of the Gnostics is attractive, and it brings the issue to a rather pragmatic and orderly solution that is well grounded in the sources and a social-historical approach to early Christianity.

It is not without its problems, however, as others have noted. King, for instance, sees Layton's approach as ultimately essentializing the Gnostics in much the same way that previous approaches based on the search for Gnostic origins or the construction of various typologies have worked to represent the Gnostics as a discrete, well-defined community that was clearly separated from other early Christian groups. This runs counter to the more fluid model built around the concept of "hybridity" that King urges her readers to adopt.[9]

Perhaps even more problematic, however, is Layton's assumption that the ancient polemicists who wrote against the Gnostics carefully and accurately referred to the same specific group by this name. Although the final results of Layton's method display a certain consistency that can to some degree allay such concerns, we must not completely rule out the possibility that these reconstructed Gnostics are to some degree either a polemicist's illusion[10] or only a part of a larger picture, as seems more likely. For instance, Layton's argument depends a great deal on Irenaeus's connection between the Gnostics and the summary that he gives of the cosmological myth found in the Apocryphon of John. Nonetheless, as Christoph Markschies notes in his recent publication *Gnosis: An Introduction*, it appears that Irenaeus and other early Christian writers had more than a single, discrete group in mind when using the term "Gnostics."[11] Layton himself even observes that "Irenaeus notes (1,30–31) that several versions of Gnostic myth were circulating about 180 c.e."[12] It seems that Irenaeus and other writers identified as "Gnostic" other groups who were not necessarily Sethian or even Valentinian. Indeed, Irenaeus famously compared the many different groups that arose from the Valentinians (whom Layton recognizes as being Gnostic in some significant sense) with the many-headed hydra of Greek mythology.[13] In light of this, King's concerns regarding the potential essentialism of Layton's hypothesis and her call for thinking more in terms of "hybridity" are both important.

Markschies, however, has in his recent book articulated what I find to be the most useful answer to the question posed by the title of King's book. In many ways Markschies's approach is reminiscent of Layton's, particularly in its effort to define the terms "Gnostic" and "gnosis" through careful analysis of the ancient sources.[14] But Markschies is careful to recognize that early Christian sources used the terms "Gnostic" and "gnosis" in reference to a wide variety of groups. These terms did not refer to either a single discrete group or a clearly defined set of ideas but were applied to a number of diverse groups and intellectual currents. In order to define the complex ancient phenomena referred to by these terms, Markschies proposes a "typological model," which reflects well both the ancient sources and the modern tradition of scholarship.[15] Although King and Williams have strongly critiqued such typologies as highly problematic,[16] as Markschies explains, "in historical study, it can make sense to work with such typological constructs if they also help to see phenomena with related content."[17] Moreover, Markschies is keenly aware that "gnosis" (which he uses instead of the problematic term "Gnosticism") is a highly diverse phenomenon, and his typology seems to allow for the sort of fluidity and "hybridity" both inside and alongside of "gnosis" that King advocates. While his typology is heuristic, it does not essentialize, in my opinion, nor does it imagine Gnostics as a discrete or particularly well-defined community that was clearly separated from other early Christian groups. It allows for overlap and shades of gray, which make it an especially useful model for talking about this complex and highly variegated phenomenon.

Inasmuch as the primary goal of this study is "to see phenomena with related content," Markschies's typological definition forms the primary basis for my use of the term "Gnostic." Nonetheless, in most instances Layton's definition can also apply to those sources and ideas that I have identified as "Gnostic." Therefore, for the sake of avoiding what has become for the time being an intellectual minefield, my use of the term "Gnostic" rests on the definitions advanced by both of these scholars, although I suspect that "Gnostic" may actually have been a more inclusive term than Layton's reconstruction envisions and perhaps somewhat less inclusive than Markschies proposes.

The Composite "Apocryphal" Mary

With regard to the Gnostic Mary, as we have so called her, the use of the adjective "Gnostic" is even more problematic, and for a variety of reasons I find it helpful to adopt different terminology. For some time now it has been rather widely recognized that not all of the apocryphal texts relating traditions of this Mary are "properly" Gnostic, even in the more traditional sense. For instance, there has long been doubt concerning the Gospel of Mary's status as a Gnostic text, and likewise the Gospel of Thomas is now understood as belonging to an intellectual milieu rather distinct from Gnostic Christianity.[18] In view of this, it seems preferable to develop some other means of referring to this woman. Other students of these traditions have avoided the problem by identifying this Mary with Mary Magdalene, but given the particular issues to be addressed in this article, this is clearly not an option here. Instead, I propose that we refer to this Mary as the "apocryphal Mary." This designation has the added advantage of breaking down the hermeneutic barriers between the so-called Gnostic traditions concerning Mary ("Magdalene") and other early Christian apocrypha relating traditions about Mary, an interpretive move for which I argue both in this article and elsewhere. With this removal of the illusion of a coherent "Gnosticism" that binds together certain apocryphal traditions about Mary, the effort to interpret these Marian traditions as a special corpus in isolation from other Marian apocrypha is seen to be highly problematic. In light of the fluidity and diversity that King invites us to find in earliest Christianity, we must also recognize that the interpretation of this Mary, long thought to be the Magdalene, is in many ways much less hermeneutically closed than once was thought; consequently, these traditions must be brought into dialogue with the other Marian traditions of early Christianity.

In most previous scholarship, the primary argument given for identifying the apocryphal Mary with the Magdalene is almost always the particular form of the name Mary that a particular text uses. In fact it would be quite conservative to say that more than 90 percent of the time this is the only reason that is given for identifying the apocryphal Mary with the Magdalene.[19] Beginning it seems with Carl Schmidt's early work on the Pistis Sophia at the end of the nineteenth century, scholars have repeatedly maintained that any references in early Christian apocrypha to a woman named either Mariamme or Mariam are failsafe indicators of Mary Magdalene's presence in the story.[20] This hermeneutic principle has been repeated as recently as Antti Marjanen's study of the apocryphal Mary traditions, where he follows this tradition in maintaining that "in all those Coptic texts where Mary is explicitly defined as the (virgin) mother of Jesus, the name is without exception spelled ⲘⲀⲢⲓⲀ while the form of the name used of Mary Magdalene is almost always ⲘⲀⲢⲓⲀⲘⲘⲎ."[21] Marjanen further explains that Christian Greek prefers the use of Μαρία to Μαριάμ in reference to the Virgin,[22] and throughout his study, he repeatedly returns to these nominal variants as an important means of identifying the apocryphal Mary with the Magdalene.[23] As I have clearly demonstrated elsewhere, however, the form of Mary's name is in no way a reliable indicator of her identity, and if anything, the evidence is actually stronger for identifying a character named Mariam or Mariamme with Mary of Nazareth, both in Coptic and in Greek literature.[24]

To this other arguments are only occasionally added, and the works of Marjanen and Karen King in particular are commendable in this respect for pursuing the question of Mary's identity beyond the mere form of the name, the latter focusing especially on the Magdalene's importance in the canonical gospels.[25] Nevertheless, the Magdalene's importance in the writings of the New Testament unfortunately cannot tip the balance in her favor. It is of course undeniable that Mary Magdalene figures prominently in the four gospels and may even have been a prominent leader in the early Christian community. But the same can be said for Mary of Nazareth as well. Like the Magdalene, the Virgin Mary is said to have stood at the foot of the cross, and John's gospel relates her involvement in her son's ministry. Much more remarkable is Luke's report in the book of Acts that Mary was present with the apostles in the upper room for the foundation of the Christian church. Of course, one could rightly object that the Gospel of Mark's description of conflict between Jesus and his mother and brothers makes Mary of Nazareth's actual participation in Jesus' ministry highly unlikely. It must be admitted that from an historical-critical vantage, the involvement of Christ's mother in his public ministry is quite improbable.[26]

This does not, however, somehow resolve the issue of the apocryphal Mary's identity in the Magdalene's favor, at least not for our purposes. On the one hand, the eventual importance of Jesus' brother James in the earliest Christian community should caution us somewhat regarding Mary of Nazareth's possible participation in the earliest Christian community, as Luke reports in Acts. More importantly, however, it is not our intent to identify the "historical" figure behind apocryphal Mary, if indeed this woman actually existed.[27] If there was in fact a specific historical woman who is represented with more or less accuracy in the image of the apocryphal Mary, then we must admit that it is more likely that the Magdalene, as opposed to the Nazarene, stands behind this figure. But it is by no means a given that the actions and characterizations ascribed to this apocryphal woman reflect historical reality; it is far more likely in my opinion that the apocryphal Mary is a mythological figure who, while she may typify the roles played by women in certain early Christian communities, does not represent a single specific woman, be she Mary of Magdala, Mary of Nazareth, or anyone else.[28]

As such, this literary character draws into its composite many different women, including the Magdalene and the Nazarene especially. She is very much an "intertextual" figure, in the sense that certain postmodern literary theorists define this term, an aspect that is even clearer once we dissolve the ideological illusion of a certain group of "Gnostic" apocrypha that should be interpreted collectively and in relative isolation.[29] This figure's representation in a text is not closed off and limited by the bounds of a given text or even the aggregate of apocryphal Mary traditions. As with all texts, and ultimately all language in this view, the apocryphal Mary is a figure woven from a variety of preexisting texts and discourses that have been reworked into a new combination. As others have occasionally glimpsed, particularly in regard to the interpretation of the Gospel of Philip, this Mary's identity is not coherent or unified, but rather is a composite produced out of fragments from related cultural texts, images, and discourses.[30] Such a complex view of the apocryphal Mary's identity can best account for her multifaceted representation and should likewise caution us against weighting the perspectives of historical-critical New Testament scholarship too heavily in this case. Just because Mary of Magdala appears to modern biblical scholars as a more likely participant in Jesus' ministry than his mother, we cannot assume that the producers and consumers of early Christian apocrypha in the second, third, and fourth centuries somehow shared this modern view.

Returning more directly to the arguments that have been used to align the apocryphal Mary with the Magdalene, one finds that scholars have occasionally looked to a particular aspect of Mary of Magdala's representation in the New Testament as something of a trump card capable of cutting through all of the complications to connect the apocryphal Mary with the Magdalene, that being her role as *apostola apostolorum,* or "apostle to the apostles," at the conclusion of the fourth gospel.[31] In John's gospel, Mary Magdalene is the first to behold the risen Christ, who charges her to return to the apostles and announce his resurrection.[32] It must be recognized that this story, in which Christ appears to Mary Magdalene after his resurrection and entrusts her with delivering the good news to the apostles, compares somewhat favorably with the image of the apocryphal Mary, who in several texts learns the hidden mysteries from the risen Christ. When this is joined to the apostles' skepticism at the women's report of the empty tomb in both Luke and the longer ending of Mark, this looks even more like the apocryphal Mary.

Yet while these gospel traditions are suggestive and undoubtedly connected with the apocryphal Mary's representation, this is far from the end of the story. The effort to identify the apocryphal Mary with the Magdalene on the basis of the latter's role as *apostola apostolorum* is radically undermined by the subsequent history of this tradition in earliest Christianity. As is becoming increasingly clear, early Syrian Christianity replaced the Magdalene with the mother of Jesus in this important role rather early on. As early as the mid second century, the gospel traditions of this region had been altered to identify Mary of Nazareth, instead of the Magdalene, as the one to whom Christ first appeared, making Christ's mother the bearer of good news to the apostles.[33] On the one hand, this early dissonance within the gospel traditions casts considerable doubt in general on the hypothesis that we may somehow rely on this pericope alone to establish Mary's identity as the Magdalene in these early Christian apocrypha. Unless we can somehow

exclude the influence of this alternative tradition on the formation and interpretation of these particular Marian apocrypha, the fourth gospel's conclusion can in no way decide the matter. The problem runs much deeper
than this, however. With only one exception, it is likely that the Marian apocrypha in question had their origin in Syria, as Professor Marjanen has most
recently argued convincingly.[34] This creates a rather strong probability that
the early Syrian reinterpretation of John's gospel was an active influence on
the development of the apocryphal Mary traditions. In fact, we might well
view this textual variant as an important source of the apocryphal Mary's
markedly "intertextual" character. The formative influence of this tradition
goes a long way toward explaining the largely composite nature of Mary's
identity in the later apocrypha.

Early Christian Traditions about Mary of Nazareth

This reevaluation of the apocryphal Mary traditions rests on more than
just a critique of previous arguments in the Magdalene's favor, however.
There are in fact a number of significant but generally overlooked early Christian traditions about Mary of Nazareth that have important connections with
these more well known Marian apocrypha. In earlier articles I have already
considered much of this ancient evidence favoring the Virgin Mary's identity with the apocryphal Mary.[35] The bulk of these traditions appear in a variety of early Christian apocrypha that portray Mary of Nazareth as one who
is learned in cosmic mysteries and because of this is regarded by the apostles and others as an important teaching authority. Certain well-known Coptic apocrypha are important witnesses to this depiction of Mary of Nazareth,
including the Pistis Sophia especially, but several more neglected apocryphal
narratives offer compelling testimony that the ancient Christians did not
hesitate to envisage the Virgin Mary as a teacher of secret wisdom who enlightened the apostles.[36] The most important of these apocrypha, however,
are clearly the ancient traditions of the end of Mary's life, the so-called Dormition traditions, a group of frequently overlooked narratives to which we
now will turn.

The ancient traditions of the Virgin Mary's death, or Dormition, have
heretofore been rather poorly studied and understood.[37] This is undoubtedly a consequence of the often-confusing variety of the earliest narratives
as well as their preservation in nine ancient languages, ranging from Old Irish
to Old Georgian. The earliest of these traditions is a group of narratives
known collectively as the "Palm of the Tree of Life" traditions, so called on
account of the importance that these narratives ascribe to a palm branch from

this mythic tree.[38] Unfortunately, however, these traditions have proven, like many other early Christian apocrypha, rather difficult to date. The narrative of Mary's Dormition first appears in several Syriac fragments that were copied in the late fifth century, bearing the title the Book of Mary's Repose (or *Liber Requiei*). Since this Syriac version translates an even earlier Greek original, we may be rather certain that the Book of Mary's Repose was already in existence at least by the early fifth century. Other factors, however, suggest an even earlier date, the most important being the probability that the Apocalypse of Paul, written around 400, depends on this earliest narrative of Mary's Dormition. This locates the origin of this apocryphon sometime in the fourth century, again, at the latest.[39] Yet as one begins to examine the contents of the Book of Mary's Repose, one finds it rife with various "heterodox" doctrines, many of which resonate far more with early Gnostic Christianities than with the established dogmas of the later Christian empire, strongly suggesting an origin in the third century, possibly even the later second century. Clear references to a Gnostic myth of creation and redemption and the presence of an unambiguous angel Christology make such an early date rather likely.[40] Although this dating is admittedly speculative and based primarily on the theological content of the apocryphon, one should recall that the dating of much of the Nag Hammadi material relies equally on the doctrine of a given text. Our suggestion of a third-century date for the Book of Mary's Repose based on its rather peculiar theological content is thus no more speculative than the identification of similar dates for much of the Nag Hammadi material on the same basis.[41]

The earliest Dormition apocryphon, the Book of Mary's Repose, bears considerable evidence of some sort of contact with Gnostic Christianity, particularly as understood in the sense defined by Layton. The apocryphon refers to a cosmological myth with striking similarities to those found in Sethian and Valentinian Gnostic texts, and it shares a number of other theological features with these traditions, including a focus on esoteric knowledge. The possible origins of the earliest Dormition traditions within a Gnostic milieu was first suggested in 1953 by W. H. C. Frend, in a somewhat impressionistic article,[42] but more recently a handful of scholars have drawn attention to the presence of many important Gnostic themes in the earliest Palm narratives. Mario Erbetta, for instance, in commenting on his Italian translation of the Book of Mary's Repose, notes the presence of several key Gnostic terms and ideas in the narrative, yet without going so far as to draw specific conclusions regarding the narrative's origin on the basis of these connections.[43] The editors of certain Coptic fragments of this apocryphon, however, Leslie MacCoull and Philip Sellew, have each noted various elements in the narrative that suggest its production within some sort of a Gnostic milieu.[44] Frédéric Manns has also in his recent study of the early Dormition traditions identified a variety of very strong connections between this apocryphon and the Gnostic Christianities of late antiquity. In spite of this, Manns rejects the significance of these Gnostic elements on the rather peculiar grounds that the early Dormition traditions place "such great importance on the Scriptures" and therefore cannot possibly come from a Gnostic source.[45] Following in the tradition of the Jerusalem Franciscan school, of which he is the director, Manns attributes the narrative's origin to a Johannine "rabbinic school" with Jewish-Christian tendencies.[46] Yet given the by now well-known Gnostic fondness for the Scriptures, both Hebrew and Christian, this is hardly a serious reason for excluding the possibility that the early history of the Book of Mary's Repose is connected with some sort of Gnostic Christianity.[47] While we cannot attribute the origin of this apocryphal narrative with any certainty to a particular ancient Gnostic group, the Book of Mary's Repose betrays unmistakable evidence of considerable contact with such a milieu at an early stage in its history, and the numerous parallels with Valentinian traditions are particularly suggestive.

The formative influence of some sort of Gnostic Christianity is most clearly visible in the lengthy revelation dialogue that opens the narrative. As the story of Mary's departure from this life begins, Christ, who is identified as a manifestation of the Great Cherub of Light, appears to his mother Mary to inform her of her impending death. This second Annunciation develops into an extended revelation discourse between the Christ-Angel and Mary, which accounts for about one-third of this roughly sixty-page apocryphon. Immediately as the narrative begins, we find the Christ-Angel entrusting his mother with a book containing the cosmic mysteries, which she is instructed to deliver to the apostles. When later in the story the apostles are brought by miraculous means to be present for the Virgin's death and burial, she hands the book over to the apostle John, telling him to "take this book in which is the mystery. For when he was five years old the teacher revealed all the things of creation, and he also put you, the twelve, in it."[48]

At first, however, Mary does not recognize just who it is that has appeared to her and entrusted her with the book of mysteries. When she asks the Christ-Angel for his name, he responds as follows:

> Why do you ask me my name? For it is a great wonder to be heard. When I have come, I will tell you what my name is. Then tell the apostles in secret, so that they will tell no one. And they will know my authority and the power of my strength: not because of the book alone, but also be-

cause of my name, since it will be a source of great power. And it will be
a revelation to all those in Jerusalem, and to those who believe, it will
be revealed. Go then to the Mount of Olives, and you will hear my name,
because I will not speak it to you in the midst of Jerusalem, lest the whole
city be destroyed.[49]

After ascending the Mount of Olives, Mary immediately recognizes this Great
Angel as the power that was manifest in her son, Jesus. Once the Christ-
Angel's identity has been established, Mary asks him: "What will we do when
we rest our body, because we do not want to abandon it on earth, because
it is before us? And as it suits us to dwell in this form of ours, we want our
body to be with us in that place."[50] Before he answers, the Christ-Angel explains to Mary that although the apostles had previously asked for this same
knowledge, they were denied. Now, however, he agrees to provide her with
the answer, instructing her to share the secret, soteriological knowledge that
he is going to reveal with the apostles when they arrive for her funeral. The
primary content of this revelation is a secret prayer, which the Christ-Angel
instructs Mary to recite as she goes forth from her body,[51] since one "cannot ascend without this prayer";[52] the prayer must be observed "with every
world," for without it, "it is not possible to pass by the beast with the head
of a lion and the tail of a serpent, so as to pass through every world."[53] The
prayer, he orders Mary, must be kept secret from those who love the world
and have not desired and kept word of the Lord.[54]

This secret prayer, which serves as a password enabling the soul to pass
through various "worlds" during its ascent after death, brings to mind similar notions from ancient Gnostic literature. A frequent theme of Gnostic
Christianities is the belief that a "spark of light" from the transcendent realm
lies imprisoned in the body of each Gnostic believer, and that possession of
the salvific "gnosis" enables this "spark" to ascend through the cosmic spheres
and return to the realm of light and spirit.[55] The various regions lying between the spiritual and material worlds, however, are guarded by the demiurge and his rulers, who attempt to prevent this escape, forcing the "spark
of light" to return to the earth, where it will live and die again. In light of
this understanding of the universe and salvation, the secret "knowledge" that
many early Christian traditions offered their followers had a very practical
content, consisting of passwords that would allow the soul to pass by the
guardians of the various cosmic spheres during its ascent. By speaking these
words at the appropriate time and in the proper order, one could force the
cosmic rulers to allow passage through the spheres and into the spiritual
realm.[56] The secret prayer in the Book of Mary's Repose appears to have a

similar function, a connection that is underscored by the description of the one who impedes ascent as a "beast with the head of a lion and the tail of a serpent." This description matches the frequent depiction of the demiurge or chief ruler in the Coptic Gnostic texts as "lion-like" or "lion-faced," or, in the case of the Apocryphon of John, as a "lion-faced serpent."[57]

Following the secret prayer's disclosure, the Christ-Angel continues to reveal mysteries to his mother, but unfortunately the text becomes somewhat garbled at this point in both of its manuscripts (no doubt because of its heterodox content); yet despite these obstacles, we can still tease the general outline and content out of the text. This section of the narrative is especially important because it refers directly to the distinctive Gnostic cosmological myth, including specific indication of the world's creation by a "demiurge," known as the "Ruler." In the key passage, the Christ-Angel explains for Mary certain aspects of Adam's creation:

> But on that day the body of Adam was in the glory that dwelled upon him, the body that sat lying on the earth, which he made with the Father, who was with him in counsel and participation. And this is that which was from the beginning and was even before the angels and the archangels, before the creation of the powers by me, until he sat and he was moved by the Ruler, when it was apparent that he could not arise. And God knew what was in the soul; and he rested and placed rest in his heart so that it would pray to him. And when the Father said this to Adam, he arose and was in the custody of the Father and the Son and the Holy Spirit until this day.[58]

As it stands now the passage is admittedly somewhat confusing; nevertheless, its content can clearly be seen to refer (however obliquely) to the events of creation as often described in the ancient Gnostic traditions. According to a fairly common Gnostic creation myth, some sort of "power" from the transcendent realm has fallen into the material realm, presenting the problem of how to restore this "spiritual power" to the "Pleroma," by which name the transcendent or spiritual realm is often known in ancient Gnostic texts, as well as in the Book of Mary's Repose. A plan is devised to effect the restoration of this "spiritual power" through the creation of humanity: this "power" is placed in humanity, through whom it will ultimately be returned to the Pleroma. In the first act of Adam's creation, the demiurge forms his physical body, and sometimes his soul as well, but at this point Adam still lies motionless. Only when a "spiritual" component is added, consisting of the "spiritual power" from the transcendent realm, does Adam finally come to life.[59]

These are the mythic events referred to by this extract from the Book of Mary's Repose, knowledge of which can help us to better understand what is otherwise a very opaque passage. This allusion to a Gnostic creation myth follows immediately after the Christ-Angel's revelation of the secret prayer, which he concludes with a promise that the secret prayer "will raise the dead and give life to all, and they will behold the steadfastness of God."[60] Given this context it would seem that the reference in this passage to Adam's body being "in the glory that dwelled upon him" is an allusion to the final restoration to the Pleroma. In this event humanity, here represented collectively in Adam, will be returned to the glory of the transcendent realm, thus restoring to the Pleroma the lost "spark of light" that presently lies trapped within humanity.

At first glance, the involvement of Adam's "body" in this restoration may seem rather peculiar, given a frequent tendency in the Gnostic traditions to describe instead the ascent of the "naked mind," "spirit," or "soul." Although belief in the "resurrection of the body" is somewhat uncommon among the ancient Gnostic traditions, it is by no means unprecedented, as certain writings found among the Nag Hammadi collection alert us.[61] The Treatise on Resurrection, for instance, a work with close connections to Valentinian Christianity, expresses belief in the resurrection in no uncertain terms:

> So, never doubt concerning the resurrection, my son Rheginos! For if you were not existing in flesh, you received flesh when you entered this world. Why will you not receive flesh when you ascend to the Aeon? That which is better than the flesh is that which is for it (the) cause of life. That which came into being on your account, is it not yours? Does not that which is yours exist with you?[62]

As the tractate elsewhere makes clear, the "flesh" of the resurrected body is not the same material flesh that presently clothes the human soul and spirit. Rather, the author seems to have adopted Paul's notion that "not all flesh is alike," and that at the resurrection the physical body will rise transformed into a spiritual body.[63] In this regard, one is reminded of Origen's view of embodiment and resurrection, according to which an originally incorporeal "spirit" or "mind" has come into the body, but at the resurrection and final restoration, it will continue to be embodied, albeit in a more glorious, spiritual body.[64]

Similar affirmation of a bodily resurrection occurs in the Gospel of Philip, a writing also identified with Valentinian Christianity. In a rather complicated passage, this apocryphon also describes the resurrection of a spiritual body in terms reminiscent of 1 Corinthians 15: "It is necessary to rise in this flesh, since everything exists in it. In this world those who put on garments are better than the garments. In the kingdom of heaven the garments are better than those who have put them on."[65] As in the Treatise on Resurrection, the notion of "flesh" in this passage clearly is not limited to just the material body but also encompasses the spiritual body that will clothe the elect after their restoration to the heavenly realm. Thus, while some Christian Gnostic groups may have opposed belief in the resurrection of the body, we now know that others definitely embraced it, albeit in a slightly unusual, but nevertheless very biblical, form. Consequently, it is neither surprising nor problematic to find a belief in bodily resurrection associated with the Gnostic traditions of the Book of Mary's Repose.

Following this brief mention of the future resurrection and restoration, the Christ-Angel next refers to Adam's creation by the chief Ruler (Archon), whom the following sentence identifies explicitly by this name. After the Ruler formed Adam's body, the Book of Mary's Repose reports that the body lay lifeless on the earth, unable to move as in many Gnostic accounts, until Adam was somehow "moved by the Ruler," enabling him to rise. Adam's mobility was presumably effected by the addition of some element from the transcendent realm, as in other Gnostic creation myths, a spiritual substance that was probably once described by the Book of Mary's Repose's now otherwise obscure reference here to "that which was from the beginning and was even before the angels and the archangels, before the creation of the powers by me [i.e., the Christ-Angel]."

Rather peculiar in this passage are the indications that the Ruler created with the "counsel and participation" of the Father, and that the Christ-Angel was himself responsible for the establishment of the archontic powers. Nevertheless, as with the resurrection of the body, both of these concepts, while not exactly commonplace among the Gnostic traditions, are attested in the ancient sources. The Valentinian tradition, for instance, is well known for having a much less negative view of the demiurge, his rulers, and the cosmos, and a number of ancient texts describe Gnostic systems that portray the cosmic powers as acting in harmony (sometimes unwittingly) with the higher powers of the transcendent realm.[66]

A good example of this tendency is the Tripartite Tractate, a Valentinian Gnostic treatise that offers several nice parallels to this passage from the Book of Mary's Repose.[67] In the Tripartite Tractate, it is the Logos, rather than Sophia, whose well-intended error leads to an imperfect begetting and his expulsion from the Pleroma. In contrast to many other Gnostic traditions, the Tripartite Tractate does not condemn the Logos's activity, affirming instead "it is not fitting to criticize the movement of the Logos." On the contrary, the actions of the Logos brought into existence a "system which has been destined to come about."[68] Thus the existence of the material world is not a mistake in the Tripartite Tractate but is explicitly identified as the fulfillment of the "Father's" will, as it is also in the Book of Mary's Repose. Moreover, according to the Tripartite Tractate, the Logos, after his imperfect begetting and expulsion, creates the worldly "powers," appointing several "rulers" to maintain order in the material realm, including the "chief Ruler" or demiurge, and all of these cosmic powers receive a positive assessment.[69] Then, the Logos and the chief Ruler both cooperate in the creation of humanity,[70] all of which amounts to a cosmogonic myth very similar to the one expressed in the passage from the Book of Mary's Repose. If we may equate the Christ-Angel of the Book of Mary's Repose with the Tripartite Tractate's Logos, we find that both traditions agree in attributing the material world's existence and the creation of humanity to the will of the transcendent Father, as well as in identifying the Christ-Angel/Logos as the creator of the Ruler and his minions. Similar notions attributed to Valentinian Christianity in other writings compare favorably with this feature of the Book of Mary's Repose, including Heracleon's equation of the demiurge with the Logos in the Gospel according to John and Irenaeus's report that the Valentinians identified the demiurge with a "great angel."[71] Thus, the Book of Mary's Repose's rather positive assessment of the material creation and the demiurge in this passage finds parallels in the Christian Gnostic traditions, and particularly with the Valentinian traditions.

As the Book of Mary's Repose continues with its revelation dialogue, the Christ-Angel explains to his mother that the mystery that he has just revealed was previously hidden from "the wise, and it is not even written in the Scriptures, so that the scribes would not see it and the ignorant would not hear it among their children."[72] Mary is in fact the first person to whom he has entrusted these secrets, and she in turn is commanded to share them with the apostles. Following this cosmological excursus, the Christ-Angel suddenly resumes discussion of the secret prayer, posing the question "who are they who will say this with their heart and soul completely?" In answer to his own question, he explains: "For before creation are those who boast before humanity, saying, 'We belong to God.' His memory arouses them as they seek recovery from their illness."[73] Several Gnostic themes are echoed in this statement. For instance, as we have already noted, the ancient Gnostic traditions generally identify the human "spirit" as something from the transcendent realm that has become imprisoned in the material realm, and more specifically, within humanity. According to many traditions, however, this "spirit" is not present in all human beings, but only in certain people, the spiritual race, to whom the Gnostic message of salvation is primarily addressed. This would seem to be implied in the Book of Mary's Repose, since it appears to assume that only some of humanity is from before creation and may boast accordingly, "We belong to God." Moreover, because this "spirit" was originally from the spiritual world, which preexisted the physical universe, those who possess it truly are from before the creation of the material world, as the Christ-Angel here describes them.[74] The language of remembrance and the notion of material existence as an "illness" in the passage are also reminiscent of the ancient Gnostic traditions. The present condition of humanity is frequently identified in ancient Gnostic texts as a "sick" or "drunken" state into which the spiritual essence of humanity has fallen, losing all memory of its divine origin.[75] Only by regaining the knowledge of one's divine origin can one be freed from the confines of the material world and return to the transcendent realm. This remembrance is the knowledge that the Gnostic redeemer brings into the world, enabling the human spirit to be restored to the Pleroma, as seemingly described here in the Book of Mary's Repose.

As the revelation dialogue between Mary and the Christ-Angel continues, the latter explains to Mary that in addition to those who are "before creation" and can boast, "We belong to God," there are also those who make requests of God, but "God does not hear them, because the will of God is not among them."[76] The cryptic story that then follows is presumably an effort to explain the difference between these two peoples.[77] The Christ-Angel asks Mary to recall the time when a "thief . . . was taken captive among the apostles," and he begged them to intercede with their master on behalf of himself and some others. When the apostles approached Jesus on the "thief's" behalf, he replied, "These are the shepherds of the house of Israel, who are beseeching on behalf of the sheep, so that they will be pardoned and glorified before humanity. And they cannot sanctify themselves, because they exalt themselves like the strong. Did I not give them many signs?" The apostles still do not understand, and so Jesus inflicts the following "parable" on them in an effort to enlighten them.

Taking his apostles onto a mountain, Jesus causes them to become hungry. When they complain of hunger, Jesus commands that a grove of trees, full of fruit, come forth on the mountaintop. Jesus sends the apostles to go and pick fruit from the trees, but they return empty-handed, explaining that when they came to the trees, they found no fruit on them. Jesus then persuades the apostles that they failed to see the fruit because the trees were too tall, telling them that if they go over again, he will cause the trees to bend so that the apostles can take their fruit. The apostles' return from the trees a second time, again with no fruit, and, having become frustrated, they demand of Jesus, "What is this, a mockery?" Jesus then bids them to go to the trees a third time and sit underneath them. When the apostles do so, "immediately the trees released stinking worms." When the apostles return to Jesus a third time, he offers an explanation, telling them to turn and look again at the trees. Then the apostles see that the trees have suddenly become human beings, who "stand and pray and are prostrate on their knees, while repenting," yet "there is no fruit to God in the repentance."

Although this "parable" is admittedly quite peculiar, it seems to elaborate on the Christ-Angel's identification of those whom God refuses to hear, who are distinguished from those belonging to God in the passage immediately preceding the parable. As the parable's conclusion continues to explain, when those people symbolized by the trees attempt to ascend, "they are returned to the world," and God turns away from them. These would appear to be the "non-Gnostics," who lack the spirit from the transcendent realm possessed by the Gnostics and thus are unable to ascend. The division of humanity into two distinct classes, one belonging to God and another condemned to this world, is a frequent Gnostic theme. Although the division between these two groups is sometimes permeable in the ancient Gnostic traditions, it is nevertheless yet another important point of contact between the Book of Mary's Repose and these ancient religious traditions.[78]

The Book of Mary's Repose echoes this theme in another parable, told much later in the narrative, during Peter's all-night sermon. On the eve of Mary's death, Peter suggests that someone should give a sermon, and when the apostles nominate him, he obliges them with an all-night discourse on death and the afterlife.[79] Before very long, however, Peter begins to speak too openly, and he is interrupted by a great light and a voice admonishing him not to disclose any secrets but to speak instead in terms that his audience can receive.[80] After acknowledging the authority of this divine intervention, Peter resumes with a lengthy tale of two servants, the gist of which is that it is better to remain a virgin than to marry. In expounding its meaning at the conclusion, however, Peter tells the crowd that has gathered for Mary's death,

> You then, the human race, are those with whom God became angry in the beginning, and he placed them in the world as in a prison and as spoils in the world for those to whom he abandoned us because of this. But the last days have come, and they will be transferred to the place where our ancient fathers Abraham, Isaac, and Jacob are. And there each one will be in the Pleroma.[81]

The identification of the present world as a prison is frequently met in the ancient Gnostic traditions, as is the belief in the final restoration of humanity's spirit to the Pleroma.[82] The presence of both these themes in the Book of Mary's Repose is further confirmation of a connection with some sort of Gnostic Christianity.

Likewise, the clear and persistent angel Christology of the Book of Mary's Repose can be explained by its development within a Gnostic milieu, since a number of ancient Gnostic groups identified the Gnostic redeemer or revealer as an angel.[83] The notion that Christ was an angel appears in a number of the Gnostic writings found at Nag Hammadi,[84] as well as in the famous Flavia Sophe inscription, a Gnostic epitaph found on a third-century Roman tomb. This inscription exhorts Flavia Sophe, the deceased, to "hasten to gaze at the divine features of the aeons, the Great Angel of the great council (i.e., the Redeemer), the true Son."[85] The inscription's explicit mention of Christ elsewhere ensures us that Flavia Sophe was a Christian Gnostic, and the inscription's specific reference to the bridal chamber might further suggest she was a Valentinian.[86] If this were the case, the inscription would comport with the witness of several early Christian writers who report that the Valentinians believed Christ to have been an "angel from the Pleroma."[87]

Finally, the presence of various Gnostic "technical terms" scattered throughout the Book of Mary's Repose would seem to indicate contact with the ancient Gnostic traditions. These include, for instance, in the earliest Greek version of this narrative such terms as γνῶσις, πλήρωμα, ἀνάπαυσις, ταμεῖον, and ἐπιγνῶσις, among others.[88] Consider, for example, the following prayer, spoken by Mary when she returns home after learning of her coming death:

> I bless you, sign that appeared from heaven on the earth, until you chose me and dwelt in me. I bless you and all of my relatives, those who will receive me [τοὺς παραλήμπτωράς μου], who came forth invisibly before you, in order to bring you along. I bless you because you gave me a measure of virility for the parts of your body, and [because] I have been found worthy of the kiss of your bridal chamber [νυμφών], as you promised me before. I bless you so that I will be found worthy to partake of the perfect Eucharist and your sweet-smelling offering, which is an abundance for all the nations. I bless you so that you will give me the garment that you promised me, saying: "By this you will be distinguished from my relatives," and [so that] you will cause me to be taken to the seventh heaven, so that I will be found worthy of your perfect fragrance

with all of those who believe in you, so that you will gather them together with me in your kingdom. For you are hidden among the hidden, observing those who are not seen. You are the hidden race [Τὸ γένος
τὸ κρυπτὸν], and you are also the Pleroma; you are the Pleroma, and I
have painfully given birth first to you and then to all of those who hope
in you.[89]

Here we encounter several Gnostic "technical terms," including references
to the Pleroma and the "bridal chamber," as well as the "racial" identity often
espoused in the Gnostic sources.[90] Particularly revealing, however, is the use
of the word παραλή[μ]πτωρ, a very uncommon word in Christian Greek,
but one that is frequently met in the Coptic Gnostic texts. Here it appears
to be used, as in the Coptic Gnostic texts, as a technical term for heavenly
powers that meet the soul at its separation from the body and guide it safely
past the demiurge and his minions to the Pleroma.[91] Although the presence
of such terms alone might not be seen as especially significant, in conjunction with the references to various Gnostic themes discussed above, it seems
altogether likely that this language derives from early contact with some sort
of Gnostic milieu.

Thus the Book of Mary's Repose bears strong evidence of development
in some sort of Gnostic Christian milieu, perhaps Valentinian Christianity
or something close to it, almost certainly before the fifth century, and most
likely during the third century or possibly even later second century. As a
result, this earliest narrative of the Virgin Mary's Dormition presents the
mother of Jesus in a light that is strongly reminiscent of the Mary figure
known primarily from certain apocrypha preserved in Coptic. In the Book
of Mary's Repose, Mary of Nazareth receives instruction from the Great Angel who was born as her son, sometime several years after the events of the
crucifixion. The Christ-Angel reveals to Mary the creation of the material
world by the Archon or Ruler, who with his minions seeks to keep the hidden race of Gnostics imprisoned in matter. He further informs her that the
spirit imprisoned within the human body needs to escape from the material world, to return to its home in the Pleroma, as the luminous, transcendent realm is often named in this text as well as elsewhere. The liberation of
this spirit, however, depends on soteriological knowledge, which the Christ-
Angel brings to Mary of Nazareth in the form of a secret prayer that will allow passage by the demiurge and his powers and a heavenly book that contains all the mysteries of heaven and earth. The Christ-Angel then charges
his mother specifically with the task of revealing this saving knowledge to

the apostles, who then will themselves share it with those who are worthy and capable of receiving it. This portrait of Jesus' mother compares rather favorably with images of the unnamed "Mary" of early Christian apocrypha. While this certainly does not prove beyond any shadow of a doubt that the apocryphal Mary is in fact a representation of the Nazarene, instead of the Magdalene, it does clearly indicate that there were some in the early church who imagined Mary of Nazareth is such a role. In this way the earliest Dormition traditions offer strong confirmation of the apocryphal Mary's ambiguous identity. Not only do the apocryphal Mary traditions themselves fail to establish this woman's identity firmly, but the ancient Dormition traditions assure us that there were in fact early Christians who would easily have recognized Mary of Nazareth in this fictional character.

NOTES

1. See Stephen J. Shoemaker, "A Case of Mistaken Identity? Naming the Gnostic Mary," in *Which Mary? The Marys of Early Christian Tradition*, ed. F. Stanley Jones, SBL Symposium Series 19 (Atlanta: Society of Biblical Literature, 2002), 5–30, and idem, "Rethinking the 'Gnostic Mary': Mary of Nazareth and Mary of Magdala in Early Christian Tradition," *JECS* 9 (2001): 555–95. Some of this material has also been covered in Stephen J. Shoemaker, *Ancient Traditions of the Virgin Mary's Dormition and Assumption*, Oxford Early Christian Studies (Oxford: Oxford University Press, 2002), ch. 4.

2. See esp. Shoemaker, "Rethinking the 'Gnostic Mary,'" 569–75; Enzo Lucchesi, "Évangile selon Marie ou Évangile selon Marie-Madeleine?" *Analecta Bollandiana* 103 (1985): 366; J. Kevin Coyle, "Mary Magdalene in Manichaeism?" *Le Muséon* 104 (1991): 39–55; Deirdre Good, "Pistis Sophia," in *Searching the Scriptures*, ed. Elisabeth Schüssler Fiorenza, vol. 2: *A Feminist Commentary* (New York: Crossroad, 1994), 696, 703–704; Jorunn Jacobson Buckley, "'The Holy Spirit' Is a Double Name," in *Female Fault and Fulfilment in Gnosticism* (Chapel Hill: University of North Carolina Press, 1986), 105; Robert Murray, *Symbols of Church and Kingdom: A Study in Early Syriac Tradition* (London: Cambridge University Press, 1975), 333. See also Ernest Renan, *Histoire des origines du Christianisme*, 6th ed., vol. 7: *Marc-Aurèle et la fin du monde antique* (Paris: Calmann Lévy, 1891), 145, n. 1, where the "Gnostic" Mary's identity with Mary of Nazareth was perhaps first proposed.

3. See Coyle, "Mary Magdalene in Manichaeism?" 41–42, where he notes that despite this figure's significant ambiguities, "undaunted, virtually all commentators on the Gnostic writings identify their 'Mary' (or one of them) as the Magdalene, although this identification is explicit only in *The Gospel according to Philip* and *Pistis Sophia*"; as we will see, however, the identity of "Mary" even in these texts is more complex than Coyle here suggests.

4. The closest thing that I have found to a systematic investigation of the matter would be Antti Marjanen's recent study *The Woman Jesus Loved: Mary Magdalene in the Nag Hammadi Library and Related Documents,* Nag Hammadi and Manichaean Studies 40 (Leiden: Brill, 1996), 3.

5. See Michael A. Williams, *Rethinking Gnosticism: An Argument for Dismantling a Dubious Category* (Princeton, N.J.: Princeton University Press, 1996), 3, 51–52.

6. Shoemaker, *Ancient Traditions,* 232–38. Despite the many strengths of Williams's work, I find his proposed solution problematic because it is jargonistic and it ultimately "re-reifies" the "Gnostic" traditions according to a typology that I find no less problematic than the one Williams dismantles. See also Karen L. King, *What Is Gnosticism?* (Cambridge: Harvard University Press, 2003), 168–69.

7. See esp. King, *What Is Gnosticism?* 228–47.

8. Bentley Layton, "Prolegomena to the Study of Ancient Gnosticism," in *The Social World of the First Christians: Essays in Honor of Wayne A. Meeks,* ed. L. Michael White and O. Larry Yarbrough (Minneapolis: Fortress Press, 1995), 334–50. See also King, *What Is Gnosticism?* 14–15.

9. King, *What Is Gnosticism?* 15. King also remarks (168) that a shortcoming of this approach is that "it limits the category of Gnosticism to a relatively small portion of those materials that had previously been so designated." Nonetheless, it seems that this will be the outcome of nearly any effort to radically reevaluate this material and the categories that are used to describe it.

10. As Frederik Wisse argues, taking a much more skeptical approach to the information given by Irenaeus and other polemicists; see "Stalking Those Elusive Sethians," in *The Rediscovery of Gnosticism: Proceedings of the International Conference on Gnosticism at Yale, New Haven, Connecticut, March 28–31, 1978,* vol. 2: *Sethian Gnosticism,* ed. Bentley Layton, Studies in the History of Religions (Supplements to *Numen*) 41 (Leiden: Brill, 1981), 563–76; idem, "The Nag Hammadi Library and the Heresiologists," *VC* 25 (1971): 205–23. I do not find at all persuasive, however, Wisse's proposal that the various Gnostic texts are to be understood as the products of individuals rather than communities.

11. Christoph Markschies, *Gnosis: An Introduction,* trans. John Bowden (London: T and T Clark, 2003), 7–11.

12. Layton, "Prolegomena," 341.

13. Irenaeus, *Haer.* 1,30,15 (in Adelin Rousseau and Louis Doutreleau, eds., *Irénée de Lyon: Contre les hérésies,* 9 vols., SC 100, 152–53, 210–11, 263–64, 293–94 [Paris: Les Éditions du Cerf, 1969–82]), Book 1, vol. 2 (294), 385–86.

14. Markschies, 1–13.

15. Ibid., 16–17.

16. King, *What Is Gnosticism?* 11–14, 73–79, 119–29; Williams, 29–31, 43–51.

17. Markschies, 15.

18. Regarding the Gospel of Mary, see King, *What Is Gnosticism?* 151, 163; Marjanen summarizes the main issues on this point rather nicely, although he argues that one can still regard the text as a Gnostic writing: *Woman Jesus Loved,* 94, n. 1.

On the Gospel of Thomas, see Bentley Layton, *The Gnostic Scriptures* (Garden City, N.Y.: Doubleday, 1987), 359–64; King, *What Is Gnosticism?* 151, 162–63.

19. See, e.g., Silke Petersen, *'Zerstört die Werke der Weiblichkeit!': Maria Magdalena, Salome und andere Jüngerinnen Jesu in christlich-gnostischen Schriften,* Nag Hammadi and Manichaean Studies 48 (Leiden: Brill, 1999), 94; Anne Pasquier, *L'Évangile selon Marie,* Bibliothèque copte de Nag Hammadi, Section textes, 10 (Québec: Les Presses de l'Université Laval, 1983), 23, n. 75; Coyle; Susan Haskins, *Mary Magdalene: Myth and Metaphor* (New York: Harcourt Brace, 1993), 37; Richard Atwood, *Mary Magdalene in the New Testament Gospels and Early Tradition* (Bern: P. Lang, 1993), 186–96 (Atwood largely assumes the identity of this figure with the Magdalene, but the repeated emphasis on the form of the name seems to suggest that Atwood has this principle in mind); Esther de Boer, *Mary Magdalene: Beyond the Myth* (Harrisburg, Pa.: Trinity International Press, 1997), 81; Renate Schmid, *Maria Magdalena in gnostischen Schriften* (Munich: Arbeitsgemeinschaft für Religions-und Weltanschauungsfragen, 1990), 93, n. 9, and 101, n. 29. François Bovon, "Le privilège pascal de Marie-Madeleine," *New Testament Studies* 30 (1984), 50–62, repeatedly emphasizes the significance of the form of the name, assuming its importance without ever really explaining why. In her recent book, Jane Schaberg raises the issue of the form of the name. Although she indicates awareness of the problems with using the form of the name Mary to identify which Mary is speaking, she does not engage the matter and determines to follow the position of most scholars that this criterion makes the identity of Mary "reasonably clear"; *The Resurrection of Mary Magdalene: Legends, Apocrypha, and the Christian Testament* (New York: Continuum, 2002), 127.

20. Although it is somewhat difficult to trace the development of this hermeneutic principle, it appears to have its origin in Schmidt's early decisions concerning the different Marys of the Pistis Sophia. Firstly, Schmidt suggests that the character known simply as Mary in the Pistis Sophia is always to be identified as Mary of Magdala, whether or not her identity as the Magdalene is specified, while the mother of Jesus is present in the dialogue only when Mary of Nazareth is explicitly indicated. Schmidt's second contribution was to identify this Mary with a woman (or perhaps women?) named Mariamme, whom Origen (actually, Celsus) and Hippolytus associate with early Christian heterodoxy. Presumably, it was this equation that birthed the notion that the names Mariamme and, by association (?), Mariam were infallible indicators of the Magdalene's presence in a text. See especially Carl Schmidt, *Koptisch-gnostische Schriften,* vol. 1, 4th ed., GCS 45 (Berlin: Akademie Verlag, 1981), 452–54; 563–64.

21. Marjanen, *The Woman Jesus Loved,* 63–64.

22. Ibid., n. 33, where he gives a few references to the anti-heretical works of Irenaeus, Hippolytus, and Epiphanius, noting only one major exception to his claim, the use of Μαριάμμη in the Protevangelium of James.

23. This argument is most prominently featured in Marjanen's discussion of Sophia of Jesus Christ, where he explains the importance of the different variants

(ibid., 62–63), a passage that is often cross-referenced in discussion of subsequent texts. Other texts for which this is the primary or only argument given for Mary's identity with the Magdalene include: Gospel of Thomas (ibid., 39); Gospel of Mary (94–95); 1 Apocalypse of James (131); Pistis Sophia (173–74 and 184, n. 43); the Manichean Psalm Book (206–207; see especially n. 11 here, where the importance of name spelling is emphasized). Although Marjanen sometimes gives the appearance of relying on other criteria, such as conflict with the apostles (Gospel of Thomas), the "Philip group" (Sophia of Jesus Christ), etc., many of these will be seen to rest ultimately on decisions about Mary's identity in other texts, where the decision is based primarily on this criterion.

24. See Shoemaker, "Case of Mistaken Identity?" 9–17.

25. This is true especially of Karen L. King, "The Gospel of Mary," in *Searching the Scriptures* vol. 2, 618–20, and seemingly also of Michel Tardieu, *Écrits gnostiques: Codex de Berlin,* Sources gnostiques et Manichéenes 1 (Paris: Editions du Cerf, 1984), who for the most part simply assumes this, but at one point he does suggest that her identity is related to her status as the first witness to the resurrection (225). Jane Schaberg proposes to identify a profile that "indicates when Mary Magdalene is in mind." Nevertheless, this "profile" begs the question: It is constructed only after assuming the Magdalene's presence in a corpus of texts that are used to construct the profile, relying (it would seem) on the form of Mary's name to identify the character in question. As such, this profile cannot then subsequently be used to confirm the Magdalene's identity; *Resurrection of Mary Magdalene,* 127–85, esp. 127–30.

26. See the more detailed discussion of this material in Shoemaker, "Case of Mistaken Identity?" 17–24.

27. This is, it would seem, the goal of several other scholars working on this subject, including King, Bovon, Marjanen, and Schaberg: see *Resurrection of Mary Magdalene,* 225–53.

28. See in particular Elizabeth A. Clark, "The Lady Vanishes: Dilemmas of a Feminist Historian after the 'Linguistic Turn,'" *CH* 67 (1998), 1–31, where she describes the considerable problems with attempting to perceive "real women" through the textual remains of early Christianity: what we find instead is a representation of individual women crafted primarily by the men who control the culture.

29. For an excellent brief discussion of "intertextuality" and a fine example of its application, see Stephen J. Davis, "Crossed Texts, Crossed Sex: Intertextuality and Gender in Early Christian Legends of Holy Women Disguised as Men," *JECS* 10 (2002), 1–36, esp. 11–14.

30. Buckley, 105; Murray, 333; Marjanen, *The Woman Jesus Loved,* 160–61; Elaine H. Pagels, "Pursuing the Spiritual Eve: Imagery and Hermeneutics in the Hypostasis of the Archons and the Gospel of Philip," in *Images of the Feminine in Gnosticism,* ed. Karen L. King (Philadephia: Fortress Press, 1988), 202.

31. See, e.g., King, "Gospel of Mary Magdalene," 618; Marjanen, *The Woman Jesus Loved,* 94–95, n. 2; Tardieu, 225.

32. John 19:25–27.

33. See Shoemaker, "Case of Mistaken Identity?" 24–30, and idem, "Rethinking the 'Gnostic Mary,'" 560–69.

34. Excepting only the Pistis Sophia, whose Egyptian origin seems likely, Marjanen identifies a probable origin for each of the "Gnostic" Mary texts in Syria: Gospel of Thomas: Marjanen, *The Woman Jesus Loved,* 37; Sophia of Jesus Christ: ibid., 74; Dialogue of the Savior: ibid., 77–78; Gospel of Mary: ibid., 99; First Apocalypse of James: ibid., 127–28; Gospel of Philip: ibid., 147–48.

35. See Shoemaker, "Case of Mistaken Identity?" and "Rethinking the 'Gnostic Mary.'"

36. These are discussed in some detail in Shoemaker, "Rethinking the 'Gnostic Mary'" esp. 569–89.

37. See now, however, Shoemaker, *Ancient Traditions.*

38. Ibid., 32–46.

39. For a more thorough discussion, see ibid., 38–46, 254–56, 284–85.

40. In addition to what follows, see the discussion in ibid., 238–56.

41. A perusal of the introductions to the various Nag Hammadi and related texts in the Nag Hammadi and Manichean Studies series will confirm this fact.

42. W. H. C. Frend, "The Gnostic Origins of the Assumption Legend," *Modern Churchman* 43 (1953): 23–28.

43. Mario Erbetta, *Gli Apocrifi del Nuovo Testamento,* vol. 1/2, *Vangeli: Infanzia e passione di Cristo, Assunzione di Maria* (Torino: Marietti, 1966), 410–11, 473, nn. 11, 17, 23.

44. Leslie S. B. MacCoull, "More Coptic Papyri from the Beinecke Collection," *APF* 35 (1989): 31–32; Philip Sellew, "An Early Coptic Witness to the *Dormitio Mariae* at Yale: P.CtYBR inv. 1778 Revisited," *Bulletin of the American Society of Papyrologists* 37 (2000): 37–70, see 49–50.

45. Frédéric Manns, *Le récit de la dormition de Marie (Vatican grec 1982), Contribution à l'étude de origines de l'exégèse chrétienne,* Studium Biblicum Franciscanum, Collectio Maior 33 (Jerusalem: Franciscan Printing Press, 1989), 115–16.

46. Ibid., 118–19.

47. Indeed, Williams has proposed a biblical orientation as one of the primary criteria for "rethinking gnosticism." See, e.g., Williams, *Rethinking Gnosticism,* 54–79; Elaine H. Pagels, *The Gnostic Paul: Gnostic Exegesis of the Pauline Letters* (Philadelphia: Fortress Press, 1975); idem, *The Johannine Gospel in Gnostic Exegesis: Heracleon's Commentary on John,* Society of Biblical Literature Monograph Series 17 (Nashville: Abingdon Press, 1973).

48. Liber Requiei 44, in Victor Arras, ed., *De Transitu Mariae Apocrypha Aethiopice,* vol. 1, CSCO, 342–43, 351–52 (Louvain: Secrétariat du CorpusSCO, 1973), 27 (Eth) and 17–18 (Lat); Antoine Wenger, *L'Assomption de la T. S. Vierge dans la tradition byzantine du VIe au Xe siècle; études et documents,* Archives de l'Orient Chrétien, 5 (Paris: Institut Français d'Études Byzantines, 1955), 220–21; trans. Shoemaker, *Ancient Traditions,* 316, 360. The translation reflects the Greek version.

49. Liber Requiei 2, in Arras, *De Transitu,* 1–2 (Eth) and 1 (Lat); Wenger, 210–11; trans. Shoemaker, *Ancient Traditions,* 290–91, 353.

50. Liber Requiei 12, in Arras, *De Transitu* 1, 7 (Eth) and 4 (Lat); trans. Shoemaker, *Ancient Traditions,* 297–98. In the Georgian version, the Christ-Angel tells Mary of the time when this question was posed by the apostles and then answers it for her: Michel van Esbroeck, "Apocryphes géorgiens de la Dormition," *Analecta Bollandiana* 92 (1973): 55–75; 73 (Geor) and 75 (Lat).

51. Wenger, 214–15. The Ethiopic parallel is rather nonsensical, but seems to center around the same idea; Liber Requiei 13, in Arras, *De Transitu* 1, 7 (Eth) and 5 (Lat). See also the commentary on this passage in "Appendix II de Libro Requiei," in Arras, *De Transitu,* 79–81 (Lat).

52. Liber Requiei 14, in Arras, *De Transitu* 1, 7–8 (Eth) and 5 (Lat); trans. Shoemaker, *Ancient Traditions,* 299.

53. Liber Requiei 15, in Arras, *De Transitu* 1, 8 (Eth) and 5 (Lat); trans. Shoemaker, *Ancient Traditions,* 299.

54. Wenger, 214–15; Liber Requiei 14–15, in Arras, *De Transitu* 1, 7–8 (Eth) and 5 (Lat).

55. See the extensive survey of different traditions in Kurt Rudolph, *Gnosis: The Nature and History of Gnosticism,* trans. Robin McLachlan Wilson (San Francisco: Harper and Row, 1987), 171–204, esp. 171–72.

56. See Arras, *De Transitu,* 81 (Lat). Examples include the (First) Apocalypse of James 32,28–35,9 in Douglas M. Parrott, ed., *Nag Hammadi Codices V,2–5 and VI with Papyrus Berolinensis 8502, 1 and 4,* NHS 11 (Leiden: Brill, 1979), 84–89; the Books of Jeu 33–38, 49–52, in Carl Schmidt, ed., and Violet MacDermot, trans., *The Books of Jeû and the Untitled Text in the Bruce Codex,* NHS 13 (Leiden: Brill, 1978), 83–88, 116–38. For a general discussion, see Rudolph, *Gnosis,* 172–80, 244. Cf. Irenaeus, *Haer.,* 1,21,5 (Rousseau and Doutreleau, *Irénée de Lyon,* Book I, vol. 2 [294]: 304–308).

57. E.g., Apocryphon of John, synopsis 25, in Michael Waldstein and Frederic Wisse, eds., *The Apocryphon of John: A Synopsis of Nag Hammadi Codices II,1, III,1, and IV,1 with BG 8502,2,* NHS 33 (New York: Brill, 1995), 60–61; Pistis Sophia 30–39, 47–57, in Schmidt and MacDermot, *Pistis Sophia,* 45–63, 86–111, passim; Hypostasis of the Archons 94,17, in Layton, *Nag Hammadi Codex II,* vol. 1, 252–53; On the Origin of the World 100,7, 26, in Layton, *Nag Hammadi Codex II,* vol. 2, 34–35.

58. Liber Requiei 17, in Arras, *De Transitu* 1, 9 (Eth) and 6 (Lat); trans. Shoemaker, *Ancient Traditions,* 300.

59. See the survey of different traditions in Rudolph, *Gnosis,* 67–113, esp. 76 and 94.

60. Liber Requiei 16, in Arras, *De Transitu* 1, 9 (Eth) and 6 (Lat); trans. Shoemaker, *Ancient Traditions,* 300.

61. See, e.g., Rudolph, *Gnosis,* 189–94; Elaine H. Pagels, "'The Mystery of the Resurrection': A Gnostic Reading of 1 Cor 15," *JBL* 93 (1974): 276–88.

62. Treatise on Resurrection 47,1–13, in Harold W. Attridge, ed., *Nag Hammadi Codex I [The Jung Codex],* vol. 1, NHS 22–23 (Leiden: Brill, 1985), 153. Regarding various points of contacts between this text and Valentinian Christianity, see Attridge,

Nag Hammadi Codex I, vol. 1, 133; and Malcolm L. Peel, *The Epistle to Rheginos* (Philadelphia: Westminster, 1969), 175–80.

63. 1 Cor. 15:39–44. Some have tried to interpret this tractate as expressing the more "traditional" Gnostic belief in the ascent of the naked soul, but without success in my opinion: see, e.g., Bentley Layton, *The Gnostic Treatise on Resurrection from Nag Hammadi* (Missoula, Mont.: Scholars Press, 1979). In order to read the text in this way, Layton asks us to assume that certain statements are essentially "rhetorical questions" that suppose a negative answer. In his translation, he in several places adds parenthetical statements to the text such as "Now (you might wrongly suppose) . . ."; "(furthermore, you might suppose) . . ."; "Surely then (so might run the argument) . . .": Layton, *Gnostic Treatise,* 23, 25. These are not necessary, and without their addition, the text presents a coherent understanding of a resurrection body whose substance consists of *pneuma* (spirit) rather than *sarx* (flesh). See the convincing interpretation by Peel, 139–55. See also, e.g., Elaine Pagels, "'The Mystery of the Resurrection'"; J. É. Ménard, "La notion de 'résurrection' dans l'*Épître à Rhèginos,*" in *Essays on the Nag Hammadi Texts,* ed. Martin Krause (Leiden: Brill, 1975), 110–24; Kurt Rudolph, "Die Gnosis: Texte und Übersetzungen," *Theologische Rundschau* 55 (1990): 113–52, at 141–42.

64. Origen's views regarding the resurrection are admittedly somewhat debated. Daniélou, for instance, reads Origen as believing in the mind's restoration to its original, incorporeal state; *Origen,* trans. Walter Mitchell (New York: Sheed and Ward, 1955), 219. Other scholars, however, with whom I tend to agree, have identified the above pattern in Origen's thought: see, e.g., Henri Crouzel, *Origen,* trans. A. S. Worrall (San Francisco: Harper and Row, 1989), 249–57; Henry Chadwick, "Origen, Celsus, and the Resurrection of the Body," *HTR* 41 (1948): 83–102; Thomas Corbett, "Origen's Doctrine of the Resurrection," *ITQ* 46 (1979): 276–90.

65. Gospel of Philip 57,18–22, in Layton, *Nag Hammadi Codex II,* 154–55. Regarding the resurrection in the Gospel according to Philip, see A. H. C. van Eijk, "The Gospel of Philip and Clement of Alexandria: Gnostic and Ecclesiastical Theology on the Resurrection and the Eucharist," *VC* 25 (1971): 94–120.

66. Rudolph, *Gnosis,* 321–23; King, *What Is Gnosticism?* 159–60. Regarding both Valentinian Christianity in general and the Gospel According to Philip in particular, see Einar Thomassen, "How Valentinian Is the Gospel of Philip?" in *The Nag Hammadi Library after Fifty Years: Proceedings of the 1995 Society of Biblical Literature Commemoration,* ed. John D. Turner and Anne McGuire, NHS 44 (Leiden: Brill, 1997), 273. Examples of this tendency in Valentinian Christianity are found in the following sources: Ptolemy, *Ep.* (in Epiphanius, *Haer.* 33,3,1–7,10, esp. 33,3,1–8, *Epiphanius: Ancoratus und Panarion,* vol. 1, ed. Karl Holl, ed., GCS 25 [Leipzig: J. C. Hinrichs, 1915], 450–57); Clement of Alexandria, *Excerp. Theod.* 47,2, 49,1, 53,4 (François Sagnard and Louis Marie Matthieu, eds., *Clément d'Alexandrie: Extraits de Théodote,* SC 23 [Paris: Éditions du Cerf, 1948], 158–63, 168–69); Irenaeus, *Haer.* 1,5,1–6 (Rousseau and Doutreleau, *Irénée de Lyon,* Book I, vol. 2 [294], 77–91); Hippolytus, *Haer.* 6,28–29 (Miroslav Marcovich, *Hippolytus: Refutatio omnium haere-*

sium, Patristische Texte und Studien 25 [Berlin: Walter de Gruyter, 1986], 236–69). See also A Valentinian Exposition 34,34–35,37, in Charles W. Hedrick, ed., *Nag Hammadi codices XI, XII, XIII,* NHS 28 (Leiden: Brill, 1990), 130–33, where Jesus and Sophia together initiate the creation of the material world.

67. In fact, Einar Thomassen regards this as perhaps the most classically Valentinian text: Einar Thomassen, "Notes pour la delimitation d'une corpus Valentinien à Nag Hammadi," in *Les Textes de Nag Hammadi et le Problème de leur Classification. Actes du colloque tenu à Québec du 15 au 19 septembre 1993,* ed. Louis Painchaud and Anne Pasquier (Quebec: Les Presses de l'Université Laval, 1995), 243–59, esp. 258.

68. Tripartite Tractate 75,10–80,11, in Harold W. Attridge, ed., *Nag Hammadi Codex I [The Jung Codex],* vol. 1, NHS 22 (Leiden: Brill, 1985), 230–39.

69. Ibid., 82,10–24, 99,9–12, 100,19–101,5 (ibid., 242–43, 272–75).

70. Ibid., 104,31–105,10 (ibid., 282–83).

71. Heracleon, *Frag.* 1, in Origen, *Jo.* 2,14 (E. Preuschen, ed., *Origenes Werke,* vol. 4: *Der Johanneskommentar,* GCS 10 [Leipzig: J. C. Hinrichs, 1903], 70–71); Irenaeus, *Haer.* 1,5,2 (Rousseau and Doutreleau, *Irénée de Lyon,* Book I, vol. 2 [294], 80–81).

72. Liber Requiei 17, in Arras, *De Transitu* 1, 9 (Eth) and 6 (Lat); trans. Shoemaker, *Ancient Traditions,* 300.

73. Liber Requiei 18, in Arras, *De Transitu* 1, 10 (Eth) and 6 (Lat); trans. Shoemaker, *Ancient Traditions,* 300.

74. Rudolph, *Gnosis,* 88–95.

75. Ibid., 109–11, 119–21.

76. Liber Requiei 18, in Arras, *De Transitu* 1, 10 (Eth) and 6 (Lat); trans. Shoemaker, *Ancient Traditions,* 300.

77. This parable is found in Liber Requiei 18–23, in Arras, *De Transitu* 1, 10–12 (Eth) and 7–8 (Lat); and William Wright, *Contributions to the Apocryphal Literature of the New Testament* (London: Williams and Norgate, 1865), 63–65 (Syr) and 50–51 (Eng); trans. Shoemaker, *Ancient Traditions,* 300–303.

78. Rudolph, *Gnosis,* 91–92; King, *What Is Gnosticism?* 161; see also Williams, *Rethinking Gnosticism,* 189–212, on the often permeable nature of these two classes.

79. Liber Requiei 54–65, in Arras, *De Transitu* 1, 32–39 (Eth) and 21–26 (Lat).

80. Liber Requiei 57, in Arras, *De Transitu* 1, 33–34 (Eth) and 22 (Lat). See also Wenger's ancient Latin version (L4): "et facta est uox dicens: «Petre uide ne reuelaris hoc, quia uobis solis datum est hec cognoscere et loqui scientiam»" (251). John of Thessalonica preserves the same scene, but there the voice only rebukes Peter for speaking in terms that his audience cannot understand, without any mention of secrets; *Dorm. BMV A* 9, in Martin Jugie, *Homélies mariales byzantines: textes grecs,* vol. 2, PO 19.3 (Paris: Firmin-Didot, 1926), 390.

81. Liber Requiei 65, in Arras, *De Transitu* 1, 38 (Eth) and 25 (Lat); trans. Shoemaker, *Ancient Traditions,* 324. Somewhat unsurprisingly, John of Thessalonica has altered this particular passage to read as follows: "[B]eing angry with our race at the beginning, God cast Adam into this world. Under his displeasure, then, and in a kind of exile, we live in it, but we will not be allowed to remain in it. For the day of each

of us is coming, and it will bring us to where our fathers and ancestors are, Abraham and Isaac and Jacob" (John of Thessalonica, *Dorm. BMV A* in Jugie, vol. 1, 394–95, trans. Brian E. Daley, *On the Dormition of Mary: Early Patristic Homilies* [Crestwood, N.Y.: St. Vladimir's Seminary Press, 1998], 61). Thus, the fall of preexistent "souls" has been transformed into Adam's fall, and references to the world as a prison and the restoration to the Pleroma stricken.

82. Rudolph, *Gnosis* 109, 196–99.

83. Ibid., 131; Layton, *Gnostic Scriptures* 24, 52–53, 122, 142; Joseph W. Trigg, "The Angel of Great Counsel: Christ and the Angelic Hierarchy in Origen's Theology," *JTS* n.s. 42 (1991): 35–51, 41. Examples include, in addition to those in the following notes, Hypostasis of the Archons 93,7–97,21, in Bentley Layton, ed., *Nag Hammadi Codex II, 2–7*, vol. 1, NHS 20–21 (Leiden: Brill, 1989), 250–51; On the Origin of the World 124,12–14, in Bentley Layton, ed., *Nag Hammadi Codex II, 2–7*, vol. 2, NHS 20–21 (Leiden: Brill, 1989), 84–85; Melchizedek 14,26–15,7, in Birger A. Pearson, ed., *Nag Hammadi codices IX and X*, NHS 15 (Leiden: Brill, 1981), 66–69; Justin the Gnostic, *Book Baruch* (preserved in Hippolytus, *Haer.* 5,26,1–27,5 [Marcovich, *Hippolytus*, 200–209]).

84. In addition to those mentioned in n. 83 above, the Sophia of Jesus Christ 91,12–13/78,15–17, in Douglas M. Parrott, ed., *Nag Hammadi Codices III, 3–4 and V, 1*, NHS 27 (Leiden: Brill, 1991), 39; Pistis Sophia 7–8, in Carl Schmidt, ed., and Violet MacDermot, trans., *Pistis Sophia*, NHS 9 (Leiden: Brill, 1978), 12–13. See also Gospel of Philip 56,13–15, 57,35–58,1, in Bentley Layton, ed., *Nag Hammadi Codex II, 2–7*, vol. 1, NHS 20–21 (Leiden: Brill, 1989), 54–55; Testimony of Truth 68,10–20, in Birger A. Pearson, ed., *Nag Hammadi Codices IX and X*, NHS 15 (Leiden: Brill, 1981), 186–87. See in addition Carl Schmidt's discussion of the Gnostic texts from the Codex Brucianus: *Gnostische Schriften in koptischer Sprache aus dem Codex Brucianus*, TU 8.1 (Leipzig: J. C. Hinrichs'sche Buchhandlung, 1892), 433. See also Martin Werner, *The Formation of Christian Dogma: An Historical Study of Its Problem*, trans. S. G. F. Brandon (New York: Harper and Brothers, 1957), 134, where he notes the identification of Christ with an angel in several Christian Gnostic sources.

85. Translation is from Rudolph, *Gnosis*, 212, where he also provides a clear photograph of the inscription. The inscription has been published with commentary in Carlo Cecchelli, *Monumenti cristiano-eretici di Roma* (Rome: Fratelli Palombi, 1944), 149–53; and in A. Ferrua, "Questioni di epigrafia eretica romana," *Revista di Archeologica Christiana* 21 (1944/45): 185–89.

86. Rudolph (among others) identifies the bridal chamber specifically with the Valentinians in *Gnosis*, 245–47.

87. Clement of Alexandria, *Excerp. Theod.* 35,1, in Sagnard and Matthieu, 136; Irenaeus, *Haer.* 1,2,6 (Rousseau and Doutreleau, *Irénée de Lyon*, Book I, vol. 2 [294], 48); Hippolytus, *Haer.* 6,51,1, in Marcovich, *Hippolytus* 271. Irenaeus also attributes this belief to the followers of Marcus: Irenaeus, *Haer.* 1,15,3 (Rousseau and Doutreleau, *Irénée de Lyon*, Book I, vol. 2 [294], 242–45). See also Antonio Orbe, *Estudios Valentinianos*, vol. 1: *Hacia la primera teologica de la procesion del Verbo*, Analecta Gregoriana 99 (Rome: Gregorian University, 1958), 408–10.

88. See Manns, 115–16.

89. Wenger, 214–17. See also Liber Requiei 36–37, in Arras, *De Transitu* 1, 20–21 (Eth) and 13–14 (Lat); trans. Shoemaker, *Ancient Traditions,* 311, 356–57.

90. Rudolph, *Gnosis,* 58. Regarding the "bridal chamber" theme in the ancient Gnostic traditions, see ibid., 245–47. On the use of "racial" identity by ancient Gnostics, see ibid., 91–92 and Williams, 193–202. The members of this "race" are hidden to the extent that they themselves do not even recognize their true identity until the "Redeemer" (Christ in Gnostic Christianity) brings them to knowledge of this fact (Rudolph, *Gnosis,* 119–21).

91. See, e.g., Gospel of the Egyptians III, 64,22, 66,5; IV, 76,12, 78,7, Alexander Böhlig and Frederik Wisse, eds., *Nag Hammadi Codices III, 2 and IV, 2: The Gospel of the Egyptians,* NHS 4 (Grand Rapids, Mich.: Eerdmans, 1975), 148–49, 154–55; Second Book of Jeu 42–43, in Schmidt and MacDermot, *The Books of Jeû,* 99,15–16; 101,24; Untitled Text in the Bruce Codex 9, in ibid., 241,18; Pistis Sophia 55,11 and passim, in Schmidt and MacDermot, *Pistis Sophia,* 105; see also the entry for παραλήμπτωρ in the index of Greek words, 790; Zostrianos 47,24, in John H. Sieber, ed., *Nag Hammadi Codex VIII,* NHS 31 (Leiden: Brill, 1991), 116; and Apocryphon of John, synopsis 69,10, in Waldstein and Wisse, 148–49. On the meaning of this term, see esp. the discussion in Böhlig and Wisse, 194–98.

9

"Idhan Maryam Nabiyya" ("Hence Maryam is a Prophetess"): Muslim Classical Exegetes and Women's Receptiveness to God's Verbal Inspiration

HOSN ABBOUD

*I*n this essay, I show how Muslim classical exegetes of medieval Andalusia argued for the prophethood of Maryam, mother of Jesus, and for women's receptiveness to God's verbal inspiration through the angels or directly from God. These exegetes, contrary to the exegetes of Eastern medieval Islam (who emphasized gender bias), based their arguments on Qur'ānic scriptural evidence and prophetic tradition. My feminist analysis of the doctrine of Maryam's prophethood not only exposes the androcentric readings imposed by Eastern exegetes but also demonstrates that signs of Maryam's prophethood (*'alāmāt nubuwwat Maryam*) are well established in the Qur'ānic vision.

Andalusian and Eastern Medieval Muslim Exegetes on Maryam's Prophethood

"About women's prophethood, ibn Ḥazm said: This treatise (*faṣl*) had only caused a great controversy in Cordoba and in our days, since a group (*ṭā'ifa*) negated Prophethood to women altogether and accused those who claimed it of heresy (*bid‘a*); so, there are those (*ṭā’ifa*) who admitted women to prophethood and others who preferred to take a neutral position."[1]

These are the words of ibn Ḥazm the Andalusian (d. 1064), the Zāhirite[2] ("literalist") jurist who is well known for his *Treatise of Differentiation between the Prophet's Companions* (*Risāla fī al-Mufāḍala bayna al-Ṣaḥāba*).[3] In this treatise, he argues that the wives of prophet Muḥammad are superior to all male companions of the prophet and that women are equally entitled to perfection (*al-kamāl*), that is, messengerhood and prophethood (*ar-rissāla wa-l-nubuwwa*), as referred to in the prophetic tradition, *Ḥadīth*.[4] His opinion rests on scriptural evidence and authority, since, in his own words, "Prophethood is verbal inspiration (*waḥī*)[5] designed for those whom God intends to inspire with what God wills to inform them about. This verbal inspiration takes the form of the appearance of an angel or a recited speech which the inspired addresses to himself; in this case the speech is derived from God's knowledge without an intermediate teacher."[6] In the first form of delivery, ibn Ḥazm said that the Qur’ān mentions God's sending of angels to women to give them glad tidings from His true revelation (*laqad jā’a l-Qur’ān bi-anna llāha ‘azza wa-jal ‘arsala malā’ka ila n-nisā’ l-‘akhbārihinna bi-waḥyin ḥaqqin min-llāh*). Thus, Maryam mother of Jesus, Sara mother of Isaac, and the mother of Moses are to be reckoned among God's prophets because angels spoke to them, and God, therefore, inspired them. The angel said to Maryam: "I am only a messenger from your Lord (to announce) to you the gift of a holy boy" (*qāla innamā anā rasūlu rabbiki li’ahaba laki ghulāman zakiyyan*) (Q: *Sūrat Maryam* 19/19).

Al-Qurṭubi the Andalusian, who died two hundred years (d. 1273) after ibn Ḥazm, authored a Qur’ānic exegesis with a focus on the legal aspects of the Qur’ān.[7] Al-Qurṭubi shares ibn Ḥazm's opinion on women's prophethood. Citing "the choosing verse" of "The Family of ‘Imrān" (*sūrat Al‘Imrān*):

> Behold! The angels said:
> "O Maryam! God had chosen you
> And purified you— chosen you
> Above the women of all nations." (Q: 3/42)

Al-Qurṭubī interprets "God's choosing of Maryam" (*‘iṣtifā’u llāhi li-Maryam*) as an admission of Maryam to prophethood. He insists: "truly Maryam is a prophetess because God (may He be praised) inspired her through the angel in the same way He inspired the rest of the male prophets."[8] He quotes the following *Ḥadīth* (prophetic tradition) to corroborate the Qur’ānic evidence: "many were perfect among men but only Maryam the daughter of 'Imrān and Āssia the wife of Pharaoh were perfect among women and the favor of 'Ā'isha over other women is like the flavor of bread [soaked with stock] (*tharīd*) over the rest of food." He explains that absolute perfection is for God, and certainly the most perfect among humankind are prophets, followed by saints (*siddīqīn*), martyrs (*al-shuhadā'*), and the righteous (*al-ṣāliḥīn*). If this is comprehensible, al-Qurṭubī adds, then the perfection mentioned in the *Ḥadīth* implies prophethood, and accordingly, Maryam (peace be upon her) and Āssia are two prophets. He quotes another *Ḥadīth* to confirm his interpretation and is careful to attest its reliable chain of transmitters from the prophet Muḥammad himself: "the best women of the world are four: Maryam, the daughter of 'Imrān; Āssia b. Muzāḥim, the wife of Pharaoh; Khadīja, the daughter of Khuwaylid and Fāṭima, the daughter of Muḥammad." He concludes that according to the apparent meaning in the Qur'ān and the *Ḥadīth*s, "Maryam is preferable to all women of the world, from Eve to the last woman till the Hour of Resurrection; for the angels had inspired her verbally by way of entrustment (*taklīf*), glad tidings and annunciation, in the same way they gave news to the rest of the male prophets. Thus, Maryam is a prophetess (*idhan Maryam nabiyya*) and a prophet is preferable to a saint and she is preferable to all women entirely: those who passed and those who shall come."[9] He further adds:

> In consequence of this preference, the Holy Spirit spoke to her, appeared to her, and blew in her coat and came close to her, while this had never happened to any woman before. Also, Maryam believed God's words and did not ask for a sign when she was given the annunciation, the way Zachariah asked for a sign, and accordingly, God named her in His revelation "she who believed in God's Words," *al-ṣiddīqa*. She also believed in His Books and was from among the God-fearing people.[10]

One is impressed by al-Qurṭubī's high esteem of Maryam and his keen effort to give from the sacred Scriptures proofs of her prophethood. Does al-Qurṭubī's interpretation of the doctrinal issue of Maryam's prophethood reflect his training in the Mālik school of law, or does it rather suggest that the "liberal" status of thirteenth-century Andalusian women allowed them wider space within the sacred?[11] Since this question is not germane to the subject at hand, it will not be addressed here, but it should not be neglected for future inquiry.

Al-Qurṭubī (and ibn Ḥazm) expounded on the Qur'ānic vision of a woman's receptiveness to God's verbal inspiration. My contribution, however, is to emphasize that Maryam is an important link in a genealogically determined chain of prophets, from the posterity of Adam to the posterity of Abraham (Q: 19/58). My contention that Maryam is a prophetess in Islam relies on the matrilineal naming of Jesus: Jesus, the son of Maryam. Though certainly given to the fatherless Jesus to emphasize his human nature and avoid attributing any paternity to God, Jesus' matrilineal name does, if Qurʾānic tradition is to be adhered to, suggest the prophethood of both mother and son. For, if the prophets Zachariah and his son John, Maryam and her son Jesus, Abraham and his sons Isaac and Jacob *are from the offspring* (the same genealogical line as Q: 19/58 indicates) of Adam, Noah, Abraham, and Israel, *then* for Jesus to be a prophet, being the son only of a mother, that mother must be a prophetess.[12] In other words, if Jesus is to remain firmly embedded in the line of prophets, Maryam must also be considered a prophetess.

Muslim classical exegetes of the Islāmic East do not share ibn Ḥazm's or al-Qurṭubī's opinions of Maryam's prophethood. Abū Jaʿfar ibn Jarīr al-Tabarī (d. 923), in his comprehensive compilation of the first two and a half centuries of Muslim exegesis, was particularly interested in incorporating a tremendous number of exegetical *Ḥadīths*.[13] In his interpretation of the annunciation to Maryam, he was more interested in identifying the angel than in addressing the issue of verbal inspiration to Maryam. As to the exegetical *Ḥadīths* that support "God's choosing of Maryam," he quotes three different *Ḥadīths* that revolve around the same idea of *Ḥadīth al-kamāl*, which is but an elaboration of the status of the most prestigious women in Islam, that is, Maryam, Āssia, Khadīja, and Fāṭima. In the three variations of the *Ḥadīth*, Maryam, as the most perfect woman among all women, was never superseded by any of the other women. Al-Tabarī, on the other hand, does not relate this privilege of Maryam to the doctrinal issue of prophethood (*nubūwwa*).

Al-Zamakhsharī (d. 1144), closely associated to "rationalist" Muʿtazilī[14] ideas, is famous for his study of Qurʾānic philology and syntax in his exegesis, *al-Kashshāf*.[15] In his interpretation of the annunciation event, Zamakhsharī, like his predecessor al-Tabarī, is interested only in identifying the angel, since, as a rule, the Qurʾān does not name the angels.[16] Zamakhsharī, however, has something to say on behalf of Zachariah, whose story in the Qurʾān is entwined with that of Maryam. He writes: "the angels spoke orally to Maryam as *muʿjiza* (miracle) to Zachariah, whose story is a prelude to Maryam's story, and as a sign of Jesus' prophethood." As for "God's choosing of Maryam" (*Iṣṭifāʾu llāhi li-Maryam*) he adds: "God chose Maryam in the first place because He accepted her to serve in the temple, raised her up and made her distinguished by the exalted charisma (*al-karāma al-sannīyya*); and in the second place, God had chosen her when He gave her Jesus without a father and this had never happened before." Even though Zamakhsharī does not discuss the issue of women's prophethood, we know that *karāma* (marvel of a saint) is associated with sainthood while *muʿjiza* (miracle) is unique to prophethood.[17] Zamakhsharī, therefore, interprets Maryam's conceiving "the Word of God"[18] neither as a miracle nor as a sign given to her for her own person, that is, as a woman equipped to receive Godly verbal inspiration.[19]

Fakhr al-Dīn al-Rāzī's (d. 1210) massive work of thirty-two volumes of Qur'ānic exegesis (*tafsīr*) combines philosophical and theological erudition.[20] Al-Rāzī discussed, in his usual way of dividing the topics into issues or questions, Zechariah's questioning Maryam about the source of her miraculous sustenance. Al-Rāzī then interpreted this miraculous sustenance as a *karāma* to her and related "God's choosing of Maryam" to the *karāma,* which was permissible to saints "because no prophethood was granted to Maryam as is well known (*wa-stadal bil-'āya ʿala jawāz l-karāma lil-awliyā' li-'anna Maryam la nubuwwata laha ʿalā l-mashhūr*). This is the opinion of mainstream Sunna and the Shī'ites, and the Muʿtazilites held a different opinion."

After identifying Gabriel as the angel, al-Rāzī tells us: "Maryam was not a prophet because God states: 'Nor did We send before you (as apostles) any but men, whom We did inspire (men) living in human habitations *etc.* (*wamā 'arsalna min qablika 'illa rijālan nūḥī ilayhim min ahl l-qura etc.*)'" (Q: 12/109). To justify the sending of Gabriel to Maryam, al-Rāzī spoke of the event as a *karāma* and informed us that those who admitted *karāma* to saints took this position. He also informs us that there were those who saw the annunciation to Maryam as a sign to Jesus and that he and al-Ka'bī the Muʿtazilite accepted this opinion but that there were those who saw it as a miracle to Zachariah, which was the opinion of most of the Muʿtazilites. Thus, al-Rāzī did not interpret the annunciation to Maryam as a sign given to her, but merely to Jesus—that is, not as a sign of woman's receptiveness to God's verbal inspiration—when, in fact, the Qur'ān (23/50) expressly identifies it as such: "And We made the son of Maryam and his mother as a Sign: We gave them both shelter on high ground, affording rest and security and furnished with springs." Moreover, al-Rāzī did not, as he should have, see Maryam's sign in God choosing her like that of Adam, Noah, the family of Abraham, and the family of 'Imrān above all people as "offspring, one of the other" (*dhuriyyatan baʿḍoha min baʿḍ*).[21]

Maryam's Prophethood in the Qur'ān

Contemporary Muslim exegetes do not address Maryam's prophethood, as if the doctrine of inability of women to receive prophethood is already determined.[22] Rather than engaging in a discussion of the relative merits of the two opposing arguments carried by the Andalusian and the Eastern classical exegetes, I will endeavor in the rest of this paper to offer a modern, admittedly feminist, interpretation of Maryam's prophethood as apparently envisioned in the Qur'ān. Moreover, it is important, at this point, to be aware of the Qur'ānic ordinances of Jesus' apostleship and Maryam's religious title since these ordinances are equally critical to the argumentations used by Tabarī, Zamakhsharī, and Rāzī in negating Maryam's prophethood:

> "Nor did We send before thee (as apostles) any but men,
> Whom we did inspire (Men) living in human habitations *etc.*"
> (*wa-mā arsalna min qablika illā rijālan nūḥī ilayhim min ahl li-qura
> etc.*) (Q: 12/109)

> "And before thee also the apostles We sent were but men, to whom
> We granted inspiration: if ye realize this not, ask of those who possess
> the Message."
> (*wa-mā ʿarsalnā min qablika ʿill rijālan nūḥī ilayhim fasʾalu ʿahala-
> dhikrī ʿin kuntum lā taʿlamūn.*) (Q: 15/43)

In fact, a plausible interpretation of these Qur'ānic polemic ordinances is that they argue against those who said to Muḥammad: "if God wanted to send a messenger, He would have sent an angel, and not a messenger in human form." They thus seek to confirm Muḥammad's claim of apostleship within his capacity as a human being and not within his capacity as a male messenger. Tabarī, however, reads them as follows: "we did not send before you Muḥammad to inspire except men, i.e., neither women nor angels,"[23] and al-Rāzī says: "when all messengers were human beings, how come they had wondered about your truth O Muḥammad, and the verse shows that God had never sent a messenger from among women and, also God had never sent a messenger from the people of the desert."[24] Al-Qurṭubī, the Andalusian exegete who spoke vigorously of Maryam's prophethood, interprets these verses as a rebuttal to those who asked Muḥammad "for an angel to be sent from God." He points out that those who maintain that "men were sent but that there were no women, jinn and angels from among them" are in fact contradicting the *Ḥadīth* that admits four women to prophethood: Eve, Āssia, the mother of Moses, and Maryam.[25] He does not fail to mention, however, the opinion of al-Hassan al-Ashʿarī, who argued that God never sent a prophet from the desert or from among women or jinn, and that (religious) scientists believe that it is necessary that the messenger be human, a man, and urban.

Furthermore, the following Qur'ānic polemic verse reveals Jesus' status as an apostle and Maryam's religious status as a woman of truth (*ṣiddīqa*):

Christ, the son of Maryam was no more than
An Apostle; many were the apostles that passed away before him.
His mother was a woman of truth (*ṣiddīqa*).
They had both to eat their (daily) food.
See how God doth make His Signs clear to them;
Yet see in what ways they are deluded away from the truth. (Q: 5/75)

Clearly, the focus is on the human nature of Jesus and Maryam: Jesus being strictly an apostle and Maryam "the woman who always confirms the truth," *al-ṣiddīqa*.[26] If we recall the two previous verses, which identified only men as messengers (Q: 12/109 and 16/43) and put them together with the verse that calls Maryam a *ṣiddīqa*, then we think that the androcentric readings by Ṭabarī, Zamakhsharī, and al-Rāzī are justified. Their readings, however, collapse when we learn that there is a distinction between *nabī* ("giver of news from God") and *rasūl* ("God's messenger"), on the whole established in the Qur'ānic text, and recognized and elaborated upon by mainstream orthodox theologians. *Nabī* to them generally means a divine envoy without a revealed book, while *rasūl* is an emissary with a law and a revealed book.[27] Vigilant analysis indicates that *nabī* tends to be applied to biblical figures (including Zachariah, John the Baptist, and Jesus) that "are exclusively among the descendents of Ibrāhīm."[28] The term *rasūl*, on the other hand, which appears more than four times as often as *nabī*, usually denotes "above all those who had been sent to a certain folk or community, in particular to warn them of impending disaster."[29] Although these theologians have always restricted both categories of envoys to males, ibn Ḥazm insists that no one claims that God sent a woman-apostle, but he distinguishes *nubuwwa* (prophethood) from *risāla* (messengerhood), the latter restricted to men.[30] Moreover, he employs two interesting scriptural evidences, which make him by today's feminist standards a precedent to the Moroccan feminist Fāṭima Mernīssi by nine centuries.[31] First, he brings to our attention the location of Maryam's account among the accounts given of male prophets in *Sūrat Maryam*. Second, he argues precisely that Joseph (Yūsuf) is a *ṣiddīq* but nonetheless is a prophet-messenger. Following the same logic of Qur'ānic nomenclature, ibn Ḥazm argues that, as with Joseph, Maryam's address as a *ṣiddīqa* does not negate her prophethood.

Also, ibn Ḥazm's commonsense reading is confirmed by Maryam's prophetic signs (*ʿalāmat nubuwwat Maryam*), which are clearly manifested in the Qurʾānic account of her life story: her being accepted by God to serve in the temple, her purity and sinlessness (*ʿiṣma*), her righteous upbringing and miraculous sustenance, the angelic annunciation from God (*al-bishāra*), and her being impregnated by the Holy Spirit (*min rūḥina*).[32]

Placing Maryam's Qurʾānic story within the context of Muḥammad's Meccan struggle (*Sūrat Maryam* is a Meccan *sūra*) would, I believe, add further weight to the thesis that Maryam is put in the Qurʾānic tradition on the same level with other male prophets.

The Immediate Relevance to Muḥammad's Situation in Mecca of Maryam's Story

Muḥammad recited Qurʾānic stories about the messengers sent before Muḥammad, in a spirit of concern for religious history, and also with reference to the events around him.[33] These stories or accounts in essence alternate on one basic model or prototype.[34] They portray a messenger or a prophet sent by God who preaches to his people, is rejected by them, but is finally vindicated when God intervenes to punish the unbelievers. "These stories or accounts are so often repeated in the Meccan period that it is natural to assume that they are particularly relevant to Muḥammad at Mecca: they reflect his situation as an embattled preacher of monotheism and his hopes of vindication through God's intervention."[35] The messengers or prophets in these stories therefore serve as exemplars to Muḥammad and believers in Mecca; their stories are an encouragement to him and his followers in their difficult situation. Kenneth Cragg in *The Event of the Qurʾān* alludes to the same implied reading:

> The wide canvas from Adam to Jesus depicts for Muḥammad's people the meaning and destiny of their own cause. Biblical material, in independent shape, is rehearsed in lively corroboration of Qurʾānic authority. All prophecy accumulates towards it, so that revelation may culminate. Other Scriptures are mentors, not masters. It is the ruling theme of prophecy as crisis, which they consistently serve.[36]

Looking closely at the extended narrative from the whole of the Meccan period (Q: 19/16–33) where Jesus equally features with other male prophets: Zachariah, John the Baptist, Abraham, Moses, Ishmāʿīl, and Idrīss, we notice that the narrative, in reality, focuses rather more attention on Maryam than on Jesus.[37] An angel is sent by God (literally "our spirit" 19/17) to announce to Maryam the gift of a holy son (Q: 19/19). Maryam is surprised by the news and wonders how she can have a son when no man has touched her and she has not been unchaste (Q: 19/20). She is assured that it is easy for God and that the child will be appointed "as a sign for people and mercy from God" (Q: 19/21). Maryam conceives him and retires to a remote place, where she will deliver her child under the palm tree. She becomes fearful and sad, but soon "the one inside her" comforts her and tells her that she will have water, food, and comfort and that if she does see any human being, she must declare that she has vowed not to talk with anyone (Q: 19/23–26). On her return to her people, she is accused of a shameful thing, but her son speaks from the cradle to vindicate her against these slanders (Q: 30–33). At the end of the narrative, Jesus makes a compassionate statement on his own and his mother's behalf, expressing deep respect for his mother or motherhood in general: "He hath made me kind to my mother, and not overbearing or miserable" (wa-barran bi-wālidatī wa-lam yajʿalnī jabbāran shaqiyya).

Now, what is the relevance to Muḥammad in Mecca of Maryam's drama? Like Muḥammad, Maryam received a divine message delivered to her personally by means of the appearance of an angelic being. Like Muḥammad, Maryam was abandoned and slandered by her own people because of this divine choosing of her out for a special task. Like Muḥammad and his followers, she experienced fear, hunger, thirst, and insecurity. Then, miraculously God vindicated her before those who ridiculed her, exemplifying the end that the rejected Muḥammad waited for and anticipated.

This means Muḥammad is identifying with Maryam. This identification with Maryam is not farfetched, but, on the contrary, is of a piece with his identification with Arab women of his own household. Arab women in early Islam had strong characters and were, like Maryam, models to Muḥammad: Khadīja, Muḥammad's first wife, was such a model. She arranged religious consultations with her uncle, the Christian priest (qiṣṣ) Waraqa b. Nawfal when Muḥammad passed through a crisis of faith. Her prestige as a rich woman-merchant from the elite family of Asad b. Abd al-ʿUzza gave support to the politically rising Muḥammad against his Meccan opposition. No wonder Muḥammad described the year Khadīja died as "the year of sadness" (ʿām al-ḥuzn).[38] During the Caliphate of ʿUthmān (644–656 CE), the first written sheets of Muḥammad's recitations (ṣuḥuf), later "gathered" to form the Qurʾān, were entrusted to Hafṣa, the caliph Omar ibn al-Khaṭṭāb's daughter and Muḥammad's second wife.[39] Al-Khansāʾ, a contemporary of Muḥammad, celebrated as the greatest poetess of the Arabs, used to run for contests against other male poets in the ʿUqāz market. She, like Maryam, carried the "word" (with a small *w*), which in old Arabic is also an ode.[40] After the death of Muḥammad and during the wars of apostasy (*ḥurūb ar-ridda*), at least two women claimed prophethood: Sajāḥ b. al-Hārith (d. 675), described as a famous spokesperson for God (*mutanabbi'a*), a poet, a woman of letters, knowledgeable in news and renowned among her people.[41] Sajāḥ, as the sources inform us, was from the Arabic Christian tribe of Taghlib, and the revelation she recited to her people is still readable in today's Arabic. Many other women claimed prophethood at this period, and many Arabic tribes gathered around them "until they became dangerous to the new religion."[42] The phenomenon of leading Arab women well equipped to receive verbal inspiration, hence, could not have been an alien phenomenon to the rising prophet Muḥammad at Mecca.

But what is unusual, in addition to Maryam's being, with other male prophets, a model to prophet Muḥammad, is Muḥammad's identifying more with Maryam than with Jesus (Jesus does not feature in a story in all the Meccan period). That is, Muḥammad identifies more with a Christian woman/ mother figure than with Jesus Christ, who was God's messenger and his Word (Q: 3/45). And since Maryam carried the Word[43] and Muḥammad carried the Qur'ān (the Revealed message) and since Jesus is the Word[44] revealed to Maryam and the Qur'ān is the Recitation revealed to Muḥammad, does not it make Jesus analogous to the Qur'ān, and Maryam analogous to Muḥammad?[45]

In this essay, I contrast the authority of Andalusian exegetes, who argue for Maryam's prophethood, with the authority of Eastern exegetes, who are androcentric in their Qur'ānic interpretations. Calling attention to Maryam's signs of prophethood, well established in the text, will eventually inaugurate Maryam on equal level with other male prophets within the Qur'ānic representation of salvation history. My logical argument concerning Jesus' matrilineal name, in that the Qur'ān identifies Jesus solely in relation to his mother, highlights the Qur'ānic vision of Maryam's prophethood. In retelling Maryam's story, I show how Muḥammad identified more with Maryam than with Jesus, which jibes with the status of elite Arab women of early Islam.

Finally, what do we gain from critiquing classical exegetes of medieval Islam and claiming Maryam's status as a prophetess?

We confirm that Qur'ānic traditional exegesis is disputable and open to feminist interpretation. By excluding Maryam's prophethood, the traditional interpretation has excluded women from religious authority in general and has deprived them from claiming their equal spiritual rights. Alternatively, emphasizing the essentially egalitarian Islamic vision (ethical and spiritual) between the sexes serves as a counterweight to the ubiquitous forces seeking to perpetuate a hierarchically structured marriage model, a model that more reflects the norms of classical Islam than the ability of modern Islam to adapt to ever-changing situations in different times and places. Moreover, Muḥammad's identification with Maryam in carrying God's verbal inspiration should motivate both Christian and Muslim women to come together in a spirit of mutual understanding.

NOTES

I would like to express my thanks to Professor Jane McAuliffe for encouraging me to participate in the conference, to Professor Deirdre Good for inviting me to contribute to the conference and to this volume, to Professor Ridwān al-Sayyed for his valuable comments on the Islamic doctrine of prophethood, and to Khalīl al-Hindī for editing the last draft of this paper.

1. Ibn Ḥazm al-Andalusī, *Al-Faṣl fīl-Milal wa l-Ahwā' wa l-Niḥal* (Cairo: Dār al-Muttahida lil-Nashr, 1347 AH), 3(12).

2. Al-Ẓāhiriyya, a school of law, which would derive the law only from the literal text (ẓāhir) of the Qur'ān and the Sunna. "Ibn Ḥazm in keeping with the Zahirite tradition rejected all kinds of inference (*qiyās*) or deduction and adhered to the literal, narrow signification of the sacred text considering that the different theological schools, the conservative or the liberal, Mu'tazilite or Ash'arite, had gone astray." See Mājid Fakhrī, *Tārīkh al-Falsafa al-Islāmiyya* (*History of Islamic Philosophy*) (New York: Columbia University Press, 1970), 431.

3. Ibn Ḥazm, *ibn Ḥazm war-Risāla fīl-Mufāḍala bayna al-ṣaḥāba*, ed. Saʿīd al-Afghānī (Beirut: Dār al-Fikr, 1969), 223.

4. *Ḥadīth* is the term used for Tradition, being an account of what the Prophet said or did, or of his tacit approval of something said or done in his presence. *Ḥadīth*, along with the Qur'ān (the book revealed by God) and *ijmā'* (general consensus), formed the source of law and the standard for distinguishing the true from the false, the permitted from the forbidden—they both shaped Muslim ethics and values. See Ṣubḥī al-Ṣāliḥ, *'Ulūm al-ḥadīth* (Beirut: Dār al-'Ilm lil-Malāyīn, 1966), 3.

5. For the theory of revelation in the Islam, see Ibrāhīm Madkūr, *Fī al-Falsafa al-Islāmiyya: Manhaj wa-Taṭbīqah* (Cairo: Dār al-Maʿarif, 1947), 93. See Joseph van Ess, "Verbal Inspiration? Language and Revelation in Classical Islamic Theology," in *The Qur'an as Text,* ed. Stefan Wild (Brill: Leiden, 1996), 177–94.

6. *Al-Faṣl fī al-Milal wa l-Ahwā' wa l-Niḥal,* 13.

7. Abu Abd Allah Muḥammad al-Anṣārī al-Qurṭubī, *Al-Jāmiʿ li-Aḥkām l-Qur'ān* (Beirut: Dār Iḥyā' al-Turāth al-Arabī, 1965), 4 (82–83).

8. Ibid.

9. Ibid.

10. Ibid.

11. For a very good article on the progressive situation of Andalusian women, see Maria J. Viguera, "Aṣluhu lil-Maʿālī: On the Social Status of Andalusī Women," in Salma Khadra Jayyusi, ed., *The Legacy of Muslim Spain* (Brill: Leiden, 1994), 710–24.

12. The significance of lineage and the relative importance of matrilineal and patrilineal ascription to the Arabs did not stop with the coming of Islam. See the genealogy of Khadīja, the first wife of Muḥammad in ibn Saʿd's (d. 845) biographical dictionary, *Kitāb al-Tabaqāt al-Kubra,* ed. Iḥsān ʿAbbās (Beirut: Dār Ṣadīr, 1958), 8 (14).

13. Abū Jaʿfar Muḥammad b. Jarīr al-Ṭabarī, *Jāmiʿ al-bayān ʿan taʾwīl Āy l-Qurʾān* (*The Comprehensive Clarification of the Interpretation of the Verses of the Qurʾān*), ed. Maḥmūd M. Shākir (Cairo: Dār al-Maʿārif, 1969), 6 (395–98).

14. *Al-Muʿtazila,* the name of a religious movement founded at Baṣra, in the first half of the second century/eighth century by Wāṣil b. ʿAṭāʾ, became one of the most important theological schools of Islam, considering that certain awareness is accessible to man by means of his intelligence alone in the absence of, or prior to, revelation.

15. Abū al-Qāsim Maḥmūd b. ʿUmar al-Zamakhsharī, *Al-Kashshāf ʿan ḥaqāʾiq ghawāmid al-tanzīl wa-ʿuyūn al-aqāwīl fī wujūh al-taʾwīl* (*Unveiler of the Real Meanings of the Hidden Matters of What Was Sent Down and the Choicest Statements about the Various Aspects of Its Interpretation*) (Beirut: Dār al-Kitāb al-ʿArabī, 1966), 1 (189).

16. Only three times does the Qurʾān mention the names of the angels: see Q: 2/97–98 and Q: 66/4.

17. "While the miracle is a public act, preceded by a 'proclamation' (*daʿwa*) and a 'challenge' (*taḥaddī*), by means of which the prophet demonstrates incontrovertibly the 'impotence' (*ājiz*) of his hearers to reproduce likewise the miracle thus brought about, the *karāma* is a simple, personal favour. It should be kept secret, and is in no way the sign of a prophetic mission." See L. Gardet, "*Karāma,*" in *Encyclopedia of Islam* (Leiden: Brill, 1960), 4 (615).

18. The annunciation verse in the chapter "the family of ʿImran" speaks of Jesus as a Word from God and being the son of Maryam at the same time: "Behold! The angels said: O Maryam! God gives thee Glad tidings of a Word from Him: his name will be Jesus, the son of Maryam, held in honor in this world and the Hereafter and of (the company of) those nearest to God" (Q: 3/45).

19. *Al-Kashshāf.*

20. Fakhr al-Dīn al-Rāzī, *Mafātīḥ al-ghayb* (*The Keys of the Unseen*) or *al-Tafsīr al-Kabīr* (The Great Commentary) (Beirut: Dār al-Fikr, 1981), 8 (47). *Al-Tafsīr al-Kabīr* is al-Rāzī's magnum opus. Jane McAuliffe says of al-Rāzī's *tafsīr:* "in terms of method and arrangement, the closest, near contemporary Western parallel to *al-Tafsīr al-kabīr* would be the *Summa Theologiae* of Thomas Aquinas." In a manner analogous to the structure of that work, Fakhr al-Dīn frequently divides his analysis of a particular verse into a series of "questions (*masāʾil*)." Each *masʾala* may then

be further subdivided to present a full range of possible interpretations. See Jane Dammen McAuliffe, *Qur'ānic Christians: An Analysis of Classical and Modern Exegesis* (Cambridge: Cambridge University Press, 1991), 69.

21. See how "God's choosing of Maryam" as the offspring of the family of Abraham and the family of 'Imrān is a prelude to the narrative of the nativity of Maryam in the chapter of "the Family of 'Imrān," Q: 3/33.

22. See Muḥammad 'Abdu (d. 1905) and Rashīd Riqa (d. 1935), *Tafsīr al-Qur'ān al-Ḥakīm, al-shahīr bi-Tafsīr al-Manār (1917–1934);* cf. Rida, al-Sayyed Muḥammad Rashid (Beirut: Dār al-Ma'rifa lil-Ṭibā'a wa-l-Nashr, n.d.); Sayyed Quṭb (d. 1966), *Fī Ẓilāl al-Qur'ān* (Beirut: Dār al-Shurūq, 1979).

23. Ṭabarī, 16 (293).

24. Al-Rāzī, 9 (230).

25. Al-Qurṭubī, 9–10 (274).

26. *Ṣiddīq* or *ṣiddīqa,* meaning "the eminently veracious" and "she or he who always confirms the truth," is a sobriquet, also applied to the first caliph Abū Bakr al-ṣiddīq. Its etymology is derived from Aramaic-Hebrew *ṣaddi*—"pious" in rabbinic literature. See *EncIs,* 9 (535).

27. Fazlur Raḥmān, *Major Themes of the Qur'ān* (Chicago: Bibliotheca Islamica, 1980), 81–82.

28. Cf. Michael Zwettler, "A Mantic Manifesto: The Sūra of 'The Poets' and the Qur'ānic Foundations of Prophetic Authority," in *Poetry and Prophecy: The Beginnings of a Literary Tradition,* ed. James L. Kugel (Ithaca, N.Y.: Cornell University Press, 1990), 86.

29. Ibid.

30. Ibn Ḥazm, *Al-Milal wa l-Niḥal,* 12. See the similar argument discussed by Barbara Freyer Stowasser in *Women in the Qur'ān: Traditions, and Interpretation* (New York: Oxford University Press, 1994), 67.

31. Fāṭima Mernīssī, a Moroccan sociologist, was the first feminist to use the technique of "*'ilm r-rijāl,*" which Muslim scholars employed to check the trustworthiness of religious men who transmitted *Hadith* from prophet Muḥammad. See Fāṭima Mernīssī, *The Veil and the Male Elite: A Feminist Interpretation of Women's Rights in Islam,* trans. Mary Jo Lakeland (New York: Addison-Wesley, 1991).

32. The focus on Maryam's signs of prophethood is mine. See the sign of prophethood (*'alāmāt al-nubuwwa*) in *Ibn Khaldūn's Muqaddima* (Beirut: Lajnat al-Bayān al-'Arabi, 1957), 1 (345). In classical Islam, a literary genre grew to defend the prophethood of Muḥammad and to clarify the signs of prophethood (*'alāmāt al-nubuwwa*). See Fakhr al-Dīn al-Rāzī, *al-Nubuwwāt wa-mā yata 'allaq bihā* (Cairo: Dār al-Ittiḥād al-'Arabī lil-Ṭibā'a, n.d.); Al-Qāqī Abd al-Jabbār al-Hamadhānī, *Tathbīt Dalā'il al-Nubuwwa* (Beirut: Dār al-'Arabiyya, n.d.), vol. 2; 'Alī b. Muḥammad al-Māwūrdī al-Shābi'ī, *A'lām al-Nubuwwa* (Beirut: Dār al-Kitāb al-'Arabi, 1987).

33. See the important study "Christianity in the Qur'ān," by David Marshall in *Islamic Interpretations of Christianity,* ed. Lloyd Ridgeon (Richmond, Surrey, U.K.: Curzon, 2001), 4. Here, I follow Marshall's thinking about the relevance to Muḥam-

mad's situation in Mecca of the different Qur'ānic stories; however, I introduce some understanding of the form and the meaning of the story (as an account also), and I add the term "prophet" with the term "messenger" since the Qur'ān seems either to put them together or to differentiate between them.

34. The Qur'ānic stories, with the exception of the story of Joseph Q: 12 (*qiṣṣat Yūsuf*), can be considered short stories (*uqṣuṣāt*) since they are short accounts that do not meet the usual components of the story. The artistic and psychological effects of the narration on the hearers, however, necessitated calling them stories.

35. David Marshall, 4.

36. Kenneth Cragg, *The Event of the Qur'ān: Islam in Its Scripture* (London: Allen and Unwin, 1971), 17.

37. As far as I know, David Marshall is the first scholar on Qur'ānic Christianity to have established this important observation.

38. See the important role Khadīja played in the initiation of Muḥammad's mission in Khalīl Abd al-Karīm, *Fatrat al-Takwīn fī Hayāt al-Sāqiq al-Amīn* (Cairo: Mirit lil-Nashr wa-l Ma'lumat, 2001), 327.

39. Jalāl al-Dīn al-Suyūṭi, *Al-Itqān fī 'Ulūm al-Qur'ān*, ed. Abū al-Faql Ibrāhīm (Saida: Al-Maktaba al-'Asriyya, 1997), 1 (169).

40. Ibn Manẓūr, *Lisān al-'Arab* (Beirut: Dār Ṣadir, 1997), 5 (431).

41. Mamdūḥ al-Zūby, *Al-Mutanabbi'ūn: Sirat ashhar mudda'ī al-nubuwwa wamu'taqadātihim* (Beirut: Mu'assat al-Imān, 1995), 32.

42. Ibid. See how Umm Ziml claimed prophecy and the Arab tribes of Ghaṭafān, Tay', Salīm, and Hawāzin gathered around her until she became dangerous to the new religion (94).

43. Jesus' name as a "Word" is also Christian, but his name as Jesus, son of Maryam, is strictly Qur'ānic.

44. See Donald F. Winslow, "Logos," in *The Encyclopedia of Early Christianity*, ed. Everett Ferguson, vol. 1 (New York and London: Garland, 1997), 688. Winslow says: "No wonder that the early Christians would think of scripture itself as the 'word of God'; and no wonder they would think of Christ, 'the Word,' as the divinely planned fulfillment of God's creative and redemptive plan, to which the whole of Hebrew scriptures they believed, bore ample testimony."

45. See "*Theorie de la reception*" and the analogy between Jesus and the Qur'ān in Muḥammad Arkoun, *Al-Qur'ān min al-Tafsīr al-mawrūth ila taḥlīl al-khiṭāb al-dīnī*, translated from French by Hāshim Sāliḥ (Beirut: Dar al-Tali'a, 2001), 23. M. Arkoun's book, translated from Arabic by Hāshim Sāliḥ, contains four essays or lectures originally written in French.

10

~

Twelve Years Later: Revisiting the "Marys" of Manichaeism

J. KEVIN COYLE

*T*o my knowledge, the article I published in 1991 under the title "Mary Magdalene in Manichaeism?" was the first sustained attempt at addressing personages named "Mary" in Manichaean texts.[1] In that article I asked: "Does a figure corresponding to the prominent 'Mary' of Gnosticism appear as well in the literature of Gnosticism's spiritual heir, Manichaeism? And, if so, is she the Magdalene?"[2] My attempt to answer these questions attracted a number of responses,[3] in light of which I wish to update my thoughts on the "Mary" figures in the Manichaean religion.[4]

Manichaeism and the New Testament

For nearly three centuries, scholars have discussed Manichaeism's exact relationship with other religious movements, including what became orthodox Christianity and various forms of Gnosticism. Scholarship now leans toward the view that Manichaeism's founder, Mani (216–277 CE), was more strongly influenced by some form of Christian ideas than by any other religious factor. Still, the Christian elements were emphasized to a greater or lesser degree by the religion's proponents according to significant religious traditions in whatever geographical region they sought to proselytize; but their emphasis did not overlook acknowledged and profound differences with the Judeo-Christian traditions.

Its docetism was one of the main points of contention between Manichaeism and "mainstream" Christianity: Manichaeism's "true Jesus" could not have been born of Mary, not having been born at all. Further, Manichaeism repudiated the presentation of creation found in Genesis, along with its creator God (identified with the principle of evil). It went on to reject the Old Testament itself, as well as everything it considered "Jewish interpolations" in the New Testament. Nevertheless, Manichaeans attributed a revelatory (albeit imperfect) character to what remained of the New Testament after appropriate "decontamination." Manichaeism also made use of some of the pseudepigrapha, in particular those they found in use among Gnostics of Egypt, such as the Acts of Thomas and the Acts of Peter.[5] These they sometimes revised for their own purposes.[6]

The "Marys" of Manichaeism

Until early in the twentieth century, what was known about Manichaeism was sparse and wholly dependent on information supplied by its detractors. Discoveries in northwest China in the early 1900s, and in Egypt in the 1930s and since the mid '80s, have given us a more balanced view, for the first time providing access to documents from Manichaeism itself.

In the Egyptian Manichaica, two figures appear whose names may be translated as "Mary." These appearances are confined to a collection of psalms, part of a fourth-century library of Manichaean writings, all of them in Coptic (dating in that language from about 340 CE)[7] and discovered at an abandoned oasis in 1930.[8] Two hundred eighty-nine of the psalms are numbered, with still others unnumbered but grouped under general titles (e.g., Psalms of the Wanderers). All are contained in a single codex, only the second half of which has been edited.[9] In these psalms, the name forms approximating "Mary" are ΜΑΡΙΑ (Maria), ΜΑΡΙ2ΑΜΜΗ (Marihammē), and ΜΑΡΙ2ΑΜΑ (Marihama)[10]—though the last two likely refer, as we shall see, to the same figure.

Throughout both halves of the psalter, the name ΜΑΡΙΑ (corresponding to the form in the Coptic of John 20:1–8)[11] appears in virtually every legible doxology at the end of a psalm, whereas ΜΑΡΙ2ΑΜΜΗ is confined to the psalm group attributed to the authorship of Heracleides (one of twelve disciples of Mani himself).[12] Of the seven unnumbered psalms composing what Siegfried Richter has identified as the fourth Heracleides cluster,[13] three—the first, fifth, and sixth—refer to ΜΑΡΙ2ΑΜΜΗ (or ΜΑΡΙ2ΑΜΑ).[14] The fifth Psalm of Heracleides contains the following lines:

A net-caster is ΜΑΡΙϨΑΜΑ, hunting for the eleven others that
were wandering. . . .
A joyous servant is Martha her sister also.
Obedient sheep are Salome and Arsenoe.[15]

Here ΜΑΡΙϨΑΜΑ[16] is the first of eleven women named in a list, which
immediately follows the names of eleven of the apostles, from Peter through
Paul. The first two names following ΜΑΡΙϨΑΜΜΗ's are biblical, while
those of Arsenoe and the seven other women are drawn from various apocryphal (but not necessarily Gnostic) Acts of apostles.[17]
    The reference to "Martha (ΜΑΡΘΑ) her sister" strongly, if not ir-
refutably, indicates that in ΜΑΡΙϨΑΜΑ the psalmist has Mary of Bethany
in mind (see Luke 10:38–41); this would not preclude the association with
Mary of Magdala[18] that both early Christian and Gnostic traditions make.[19]
The Manichaean ΜΑΡΙϨΑΜΑ plays a role more active than the canonical
Marys: she hunts, she casts the net, and later, like her Gnostic counterpart,
she becomes talkative.[20] The Manichaean Martha, on the other hand, is a servant (though a joyful one), and the other two women are "obedient sheep."
A Martha and a Mary are associated in two other Western Manichaean
sources,[21] the Cologne Mani Codex (92,15–22),[22] and the Latin fragment from
Tebessa.[23] The other two names, Salome and Arsenoe, we will take up shortly.
    The "net-caster" theme, when coupled to ΜΑΡΙϨΑΜΑ as hunting,
recalls another Coptic Manichaean document, the *Kephalaia*, in which the
"four Light-hunters" cast their nets to bring souls to redemption. Of these,

> The third hunter is Je[sus the Splendor who came from the] great[ness],
> who hunts after the light and lif[e; and he leads?] it to the heights. His
> net is his wisdom (σοφία), [the] lig[ht wisdom] with which he hunts
> the souls, catching them in the n[et . . .]. The sea is the error of the uni-
> verse, the law o[f sin . . .] the souls that are drowning in it [. . .] He
> catch[es] them in his net.[24]

There is, then, a link between ΜΑΡΙϨΑΜΜΗ's hunting and her net-casting, and another between Jesus the hunter, his net (which is "wisdom"), and
ΜΑΡΙϨΑΜΑ the net-caster,[25] rendered explicit in the next text:

> He chose ΜΑΡΙϨΑΜΜΗ, the spirit of wisdom.
> He gave life to Martha, the breath of discretion.
> He summoned Salome, the grace of peace.
> He called Arsenoe, he set her in the garland of Truth.[26]

These lines appear in the long sixth Psalm of Heracleides where, again, they immediately follow a list of eleven apostles (not in all respects the same as the preceding,[27] though Peter is once more named first[28]). This time only three, rather than ten, female names accompany MⲀⲢⲒⲀMMH's: These are Martha, Salome (CⲀⲖⲰMH), and Arsenoe (ⲀⲢCⲈⲚOH), in the same order as in the fifth Psalm of Heracleides, with MⲀⲢⲒⲀMMH (rather than MⲀⲢⲒⲀMⲀ) retaining the first place. Their presence together in two Psalms of Heracleides suggests that the four names held special significance for Manichaeans.[29] In addition, a Turfan fragment (M18, Middle Persian) mentions two of the four together:

> On Sunday, at the birdsong's beginning, there came Maryam Salome Maryam among the many other women, bringing aromatic nard-plants . . .[30]

This is an apparent allusion to Mark 16:1: ("Mary Magdalene, Mary the mother of James, and Salome brought spices . . ."); but the allusion is problematic, in that further on in the same fragment "Maryam," "Šalöm," and "'Arsanî'âh" are the women who visit Jesus' tomb on Easter morning (see Luke 24:5).[31] Unmentioned in both groups is Martha (who is not placed at the tomb by John or the Synoptics, either, although in the Letter of the Apostles [9] she is an ointment-bearer).

The association of Salome with Mary of Magdala in Mark 15:40 and the possible allusion to Mark 16:1 recall that the Manichaean psalmist is thinking specifically of the Magdalene. Mark 15 and 16 are the only New Testament appearances of a Salome other than Herodias's daughter, though the name is common enough in apocryphal writings. The original inspiration for the Manichaean Salome (the name reappears in the sixteenth Psalm of Thom)[32] is probably the New Testament, since "Salome seems to have been a peculiarly Palestinian name."[33] However, she also appears in the Gospel of the Egyptians (if we may believe Clement of Alexandria),[34] the Pistis Sophia (132, along with MⲀⲢⲒⲀ) and the Gospel of Thomas (61),[35] where we also find MⲀⲢⲒⲀM (though not in the same logion).[36]

The name of Arsenoe (who seems to attract more attention from Manichaeism than from any other religious tradition of antiquity)[37] has no biblical witness, but appears in 3 Maccabees 1:1, 4 and once in the First Apocalypse of James (40:26). In fact, all four women appear here (40:22–29)—insofar as the text is legible—although one cannot simply argue, as Petersen does, that the list is "probable, because the names of these four women are mentioned in the Manichaean psalms" (*wahrscheinlich, weil in zwei mani-chäischen Psalmen diese vier Frauennamen zusammen genannt werden*).[38]

ⲘⲀⲢⲒϨⲀⲘ (or ⲘⲀⲢⲒⲀ), Martha, and Salome are all named in the Pistis Sophia (Martha in 38–39, 57, 73, and 80)[39] as well as in Origen's *Contra Celsum* (5:62), where, speaking of Gnostic groups, he mentions "Harpocratians from Salome, others from Mariamme, others from Martha." As Mary, even though accompanied by Martha, is specifically identified as the Magdalene in the Pistis Sophia and the First Apocalypse of James (40:25), we have a strong basis for seeing here a mix of the Magdalene with Mary of Bethany.[40]

If the Manichaean ⲘⲀⲢⲒϨⲀⲘⲘⲎ is meant to personify or recall something about Wisdom, it is not, as in the Gnostic Gospel of Philip, of Wisdom as fallen.[41] But Richter and Silke Petersen were right to challenge my observation that ⲘⲀⲢⲒϨⲀⲘⲘⲎ is identified with Wisdom *tout court* rather than with the *spirit* of wisdom.[42] I now believe that here we have a demonstration of Geo Widengren's insight that "wisdom" is a frequent term for Mani's teaching.[43] It remains that the connection between ⲘⲀⲢⲒ-ϨⲀⲘⲘⲎ and the spirit of wisdom (ⲡⲡ̅ⲛ̅ⲁ̅ ⲛ̅ⲧⲥⲟⲫⲓⲁ) constitutes the passage's prime interest.

The final appearance of ⲘⲀⲢⲒϨⲀⲘⲘⲎ under consideration here comes in the first Psalm of Heracleides, all of which (save for her response, in two strophes) is addressed to her by Jesus:[44]

> "ⲘⲀⲢⲒϨⲀⲘⲘⲎ, ⲘⲀⲢⲒϨⲀⲘⲘⲎ, know me: do not touch me.
> [. . . Stem] the tears of thy eyes and know me that I am thy master.
> Only touch me not, for I have not yet seen the face of my Father.
> Thy God was not stolen away, according to the thoughts of thy littleness: thy God did not die, rather he mastered death.
> I am not the gardener: I have given, I have received the . . ., I appeared (?) [not] to thee, until I saw thy tears and thy grief . . . for (?) me.
> Cast this sadness away from thee and do this service (λειτουργία): be a messenger for me to these wandering orphans.
> Make haste rejoicing, and go unto the Eleven. Thou shalt find them gathered together on the bank of the Jordan.
> The traitor persuaded them to be fishermen as they were at first and to lay down their nets with which they caught men unto life.
> Say to them, 'Arise, let us go, it is your brother that calls you.' If they scorn my brotherhood, say to them, 'It is your master.'
> If they disregard my mastership, say to them, 'It is your Lord.' Use all skill and advice until thou hast brought the sheep to the shepherd.

If thou seest that their wits are gone, draw Simon Peter unto thee; say
to him, 'Remember what I uttered between thee and me.
Remember what I said between thee and me in the Mount of Olives:
"I have something to say, I have none to whom to say it."'"
"Rabbi, my master, I will serve (διακονεῖν) thy commandment in the
joy of my whole heart.
I will not give rest to my heart, I will not give sleep to my eyes, I will
not give rest to my feet until I have brought the sheep to the fold."
"Glory to ΜΔΡΙϨΔΜΜΗ, because she hearkened to her master,
she] served (διακονεῖν) his commandment in the joy of her whole
heart. Glory and] victory to the soul of the blessed ΜΔΡΙϨ."[45]

The inspiration for the first five lines is the canonical John 20:11–18,[46] where
Mary of Magdala is explicitly named. Here the one who addresses her at the
tomb is also Jesus—but not the one of orthodox Christianity (who is "the
traitor": προδότης), and not risen, for there has been no death; but not yet
returned to the divine realm of Light, either. ΜΔΡΙϨΔΜΜΗ weeps, but is
not to touch the narrator, who has "not yet seen the face of my Father,"[47]
recalling John 20:16–17, but expressed in a very Manichaean manner: Jesus
has not yet seen the face of God. The fourth Psalm of Heracleides refers to
"the four-faced God," who is "the Father of Greatness," and to Jesus as "the
son of Amen."[48]

Of interest, too, is that ΜΔΡΙϨΔΜΜΗ is given a mission that essentially
spells out what "net-casting" and "hunting" mean: they are a *leitourgia*[49]—
work, task, or mission—as "a messenger [. . .] unto the Eleven," far more
explicit than even in John. And she is not just to carry a message, but also
to make herself the spokesperson of Jesus: she is to recall the eleven to the
real net-casting (for souls) from which the traitorous Jesus lured them. She
is to speak in the name of the real Jesus: "Say to them, 'Arise, let us go, it is
your brother that calls you' [. . .]. Say to them, 'It is your master' [. . .].
Say to them, 'It is your Lord'." And she is to bring "the sheep to the shepherd." The identification of Jesus with ΜΔΡΙϨΔΜΜΗ is especially striking in its reference to Peter (who, it will be remembered, is named first among
the eleven in the fifth and sixth psalms): she is to call him to remembrance.
"Say to him: 'Remember what I uttered [. . .]. Remember what I said. . . .'"

ΜΔΡΙϨΔΜΜΗ's two-strophed response is to the effect that she will be
true to the mission entrusted to her: She is, then, a model of obedient fidelity,[50]
although the verb διακονεῖν implies ministry or service rather than passive
obedience. She promises not to rest "until I have brought the sheep to the
fold"—curiously, not now to the shepherd, as per Jesus' instruction, although

the psalmist's intention may be to draw on the proximity of the Coptic (Sub-achmimic) word ⲰⲈⲓⲣⲈ (sheepfold) to ⲰⲎⲣⲈ (child).[51] The psalm does not inform whether ⲘⲀⲣⲓϨⲀⲘⲘⲎ actually keeps her promise; but just before the usual doxology (with its customary mention of ⲘⲀⲣⲓⲀ)[52] is one just for her: "Glory to ⲘⲀⲣⲓϨⲀⲘⲘⲎ, because she hearkened to her mas-ter [i.e., took him seriously, apparently unlike the eleven], she served (δια-κονεῖν = ministered?) his commandment in the joy of her whole heart." Again, we note the emphasis on faithful (though active) obedience.

Clarifications

The dozen years since my first article on this subject have seen the pub-lication of many new studies on Mary Magdalene.[53] Among them is Antti Marjanen's, in which he judges that my "claim that the figure of Mary Mag-dalene is somehow mirrored in the Mary of the doxologies remains un-founded."[54] Petersen is more blunt: I have, she says, "tried *without basis* to establish a connection [of ⲘⲀⲣⲓⲀ] to Mary Magdalene."[55] A claim and a connection I would cheerfully retract—had I made them. But I fear they are due to misreading the orientation of my question: "Besides these conclu-sions on the doxological ⲘⲀⲣⲓⲀ, can any other be made at this point re-garding the presence of Mary *Magdalene* in Manichaeism?"[56] It is all a mat-ter of inflection, in a query immediately following the statement that: "This ⲘⲀⲣⲓⲀ does not seem to be the same personage as ⲘⲀⲣⲓϨⲀⲘⲘⲎ, not only because each has her own name-form, but also because each has a dis-tinct mention within the same doxology."[57]

In an intensive article published in 2001, Stephen Shoemaker argues for a rethinking of the general consensus that "Mary" in Gnostic writings signifies Mary of Magdala rather than Mary of Nazareth. He quotes my re-mark that Mary Magdalene is explicitly identified as such only in the Gospel of Philip and the Pistis Sophia, then cautions that "the identity of 'Mary' even in these texts is more complex than Coyle here suggests."[58] This is an evaluation with which I have no quarrel, since I was merely noting the in-frequency with which she is specifically called the Magdalene. Shoemaker goes on to observe that the identity of the Gnostic Mary "must be supplied from one or a combination of at least two possibilities, Mary of Nazareth and Mary of Magdala."[59] That is as may be where Gnostic, canonical, and Christian nonbiblical literatures are concerned; but when it comes to Manichaeism, there is no danger of confusing Mary of Magdala with Mary of Nazareth, for Manichaeism never pays attention to a woman who would have, at best, mothered the wrong Jesus and, at worst, desecrated him with her womb.[60] As noted, the favored Jesus is a docetic one: He has no earthly mother. This does not mean, however, that the Manichaean ⲘⲀⲢⲓ-ϨⲀⲘⲘⲎ could not bear traits of more than one New Testament "Mary";[61] but Mary of Nazareth would not be one of them.[62] The Marys of Magdala and of Bethany are much more likely candidates for the sort of conflation Shoemaker suggests. To that conclusion five others can be added:

(1) In 1991 I quoted Victor Gold as affirming that it is the Magdalene who is the popular Mary in Manichaeism.[63] If that is truly the case, the affirmation might still be valid only for Western Manichaeans, and then not (at least in some cases) to the exclusion of Mary of Bethany. But unlike the composite formed of her in Christian tradition, Manichaeism's Mary Magdalene does not include the sinner.[64]

(2) In the Egyptian Manichaean psalms, ⲘⲀⲢⲓϨⲀⲘⲘⲎ plays a role that may not be as important as in some Gnostic writings, but that is certainly more pronounced than in the canonical gospels: She is a guide, a teacher, even a stand-in for Jesus.[65]

(3) In contrast with Gnostic tendencies, she engages in conflict with neither Peter nor any other apostle.[66] Her teaching is entirely positive and nonconfrontational. But if in Gnostic writings (notably, the Gospel of Mary and Gospel of Thomas) Mary provides a teaching of her own, the Manichaean ⲘⲀⲢⲓϨⲀⲘⲘⲎ does not. Yet she resembles her Gnostic homologue in her leadership role over the eleven and (as in canonical writings as well) in bringing the first message from the risen Jesus. Nevertheless, the influence of Gnostic (or at least pseudepigraphical) writings on the form Manichaeism gives to her name is certain.[67] But, while there is explicit mention of ⲘⲀⲢⲓⲀ ⲦⲘⲀⲅⲆⲀⲗⲎⲚⲎ in some Gnostic works,[68] we never find this form in Manichaean documents, which is one reason why a composite figure cannot be ruled out.

(4) The Manichaean ⲘⲀⲢⲓϨⲀⲘⲘⲎ is associated with Jesus who is the Wisdom of God (see 1 Cor. 1:24, a favorite Manichaean passage). The intention, therefore, may be to express Jesus' feminine side through ⲘⲀⲢⲓϨⲀⲘⲘⲎ. I emphasize, though, that I advanced this in 1991 only as a *possibility,* in terms of the Magdalene both as (the spirit of) Wisdom and as "an essential complement to the Christ-Saviour figure."[69]

(5) As in both Gnostic and non-Gnostic Christian groups, the Manichaean Miriamic (or should we say, Marihammic?) figure plays the role of the ideal believer; that is, she embodies the virtues—in the

event, obedience and fidelity—of the appropriate group: in the event, of Manichaeism.

NOTES

1. J. K. Coyle, "Mary Magdalene in Manichaeism?" *Le Muséon* 104 (1991): 39–55.

2. Coyle, "Mary Magdalene," 44–45.

3. Especially by S. Richter, *Exegetisch-literarkritische Untersuchungen von Her-akleidespsalmen des koptisch-manichäischen Psalmenbuches*, Arbeiten zum spätantiken und koptischen Ägypten, 5 (Altenberge: Oros Verlag, 1994), passim. See also P. Nagel, "Mariammê—Netzwerferin und Geist der Weisheit," in *Divitiae Aegypti: Koptologische und verwandte Studien zu Ehren von Martin Krause*, ed. C. Fluck et al. (Wiesbaden: L. Reichert Verlag, 1995), 223–28; A. Marjanen, *The Woman Jesus Loved: Mary Magdalene in the Nag Hammadi Library and Related Documents*, Nag Hammadi and Manichaean Studies, 40 (Leiden: Brill, 1996), 206–15; S. J. Shoemaker, "Rethinking the 'Gnostic Mary': Mary of Nazareth and Mary of Magdala in Early Christian Tradition," *JECS* 9 (2001): 555–95; and J. Schaberg, *The Resurrection of Mary Magdalene: Legends, Apocrypha, and the Christian Testament* (New York: Continuum, 2002), ch. 4, passim.

4. For a brief survey of Mani and Manichaeism, see the pertinent article in A. Fitzgerald, ed., *Augustine Through the Ages: An Encyclopedia* (Grand Rapids, Mich., and Cambridge: William B. Eerdmans, 1999), 520–25. A more thorough treatment is supplied by S. N. C. Lieu, *Manichaeism in the Later Roman Empire and Medieval China*, 2nd ed., Wissenschäftliche Untersuchungen zum Neuen Testament 63 (Tübingen: Mohr, 1992).

5. See below, n. 17.

6. On Manichaean use of New Testament apocrypha, especially from Gnostic sources, see G. Bornkamm, *Mythos und Legende in den apokryphen Thomas-Akten: Beiträge zur Geschichte der Gnosis und zur Vorgeschichte des Manichäismus*, Forschungen zur Religion und Literatur des Alten und Neuen Testaments 49 (Göttingen: Vandenhoeck and Ruprecht, 1933), 103–11; P. Nagel, "Die apokryphen Apostelakten des 2. und 3. Jahrhunderts in der manichäischen Literatur: Ein Beitrag zur Frage nach den christlichen Elementen im Manichäismus," in *Gnosis und Neues Testament: Studien aus Religionswissenschaft und Theologie*, ed. K. W. Tröger (Gütersloh: Gerd Mohn, 1973), 149–82; J.-D. Kaestli, "L'utilisation des Actes apocryphes des apôtres dans le manichéisme," in *Gnosis and Gnosticism: Papers Read at the Seventh International Conference on Patristic Studies (Oxford, September 8th–13th 1975)*, NHS 8, ed. M. Krause (Leiden: Brill, 1977), 107–16; Coyle, "Mary Magdalene," 48; and H.-J. Klimkeit, "Die Kenntnis apokrypher Evangelien in Zentral- und Ostasien," in *Manichaica Selecta: Studies Presented to Julien Ries on the Occasion of His Seventieth Birthday*, ed. A. van Tongerloo and S. Giversen, Manichaean Studies 1 (Leuven: n.p., 1991), 149–75. Kaestli thinks (114) that in such usage "it is not a matter of a second-

ary development, nor of an adaptation to the requirements of the mission to the Christians, but of a primitive trait of the new religion with roots in the spiritual evolution of Mani himself" (translation mine).

7. For the date, see C. R. C. Allberry, *A Manichaean Psalm-Book, Part II*, Manichaean Manuscripts in the Chester Beatty Collection, vol. 2 (Stuttgart: Kohlhammer, 1938), xix–xx. If Kaestli (114–15) is right in considering the Coptic collection as derived from a Greek model, "itself dependent on a Syriac original" (*lui-même dependant d'un original syriaque*), then the original psalter must date, according to him, from the last quarter of the third century.

8. On this discovery, see C. Schmidt, H. J. Polotsky, and H. Ibscher, "Ein Mani-Fund in Aegypten: Originalschriften des Mani und seiner Schüler," *Sitzungsberichte der Preussischen Akademie der Wissenschaften zu Berlin, Philosophisch-historische Klasse, Jhg. 1933*, 4–90. Polotsky's contribution (63–82) is reproduced in his *Collected Papers* (Jerusalem: Magnes Press, 1971), 673–98.

9. With an English translation by Allberry, *A Manichaean Psalm-Book*. The "Corpus Fontium Manichaeorum," collection (Turnhout: Brepols) offers a new edition and German translation of the Manichaean psalms in its Series Coptica, vol. 1 (Liber Psalmorum). To date, two fascicles have appeared in this volume: G. Wurst, *Die Bema-Psalmen* (1996), and S. G. Richter, *Die Herakleides-Psalmen* (1998).

10. On these forms, see Silke Petersen, *"Zerstört die Werke der Weiblichkeit!": Maria Magdalena, Salome und andere Jüngerinnen Jesu in christlich-gnostischen Schriften,* Nag Hammadi and Manichaean Studies, 48 (Leiden: Brill, 1999), 95 and 189; and Marjanen, *The Woman Jesus Loved,* 78.

11. Jesus calls Mary of Magdala ΜΑΡΙΑΜ in the Coptic John 19:25 and 20:11,18. On the forms "Maria" and "Mariam," see J. D. M. Derrett, "Miriam and the Resurrection (John 10, 16)," *Downside Review* 111 (1993): 176–78 and 183.

12. Richter, who has studied them intensively, identifies five clusters of Psalms of Heracleides, in addition to a freestanding psalm: *Exegetisch-literarkritische,* 3–4; *Die Herakleides-Psalmen,* 3–5.

13. Richter, *Die Herakleides-Psalmen,* 51–103.

14. I agree with Richter (*Exegetisch-literarkritische,* 16, n. 63) that "all three instances of the Psalms of Heracleides have the same Mary in mind" (*alle drei Belege der Herakleidenpsalmen die gleiche Maria meinen*).

15. Allberry, 192.21–24.

16. Marjanen, *The Woman Jesus Loved,* 208, n. 18, considers this "a spelling error or variant" for ΜΑΡΙϨΑΜΜΗ.

17. Thecla in the Acts of Paul and Thecla; Maximilla and Iphidam(i)a in the Acts of Andrew; Aristobula and Drusiana in the Acts of John; Eubula in the Acts of Peter and Acts of Paul; and Mygdonia in the Acts of Thomas.

18. See Nagel, "Mariammê," 224, n. 13: "The link Manichaeans made (and not only they) of Mary Magdalene with Mary of Bethany does not alter the fact that Mary Magdalene is meant" (*Daß Maria Magdalena bei den Manichäern [und nicht nur bei*

diesen] sekundär mit Maria von Bethanien verbunden werden ist, ändert nichts daran, daß Maria Magdalena intendiert ist).

19. See Coyle, "Mary Magdalene," 40–42; Marjanen, *The Woman Jesus Loved,* 208; A. Feuillet, "Le récit johannique de l'onction de Béthanie," *Esprit et Vie* 95.14 (April 1985): 198–201; P.-E. Dauzat, *L'invention de Marie-Madeleine* (Paris: Bayard, 2001), 39–45, 63–65, and 73–85; and especially V. Saxer, "Marie-Madeleine dans les évangiles: La femme coupée en morceaux?" *RevTh* 92 (1992): 674–701 and 818–33.

20. See Dauzat, 148–57; and Schaberg, 141–44.

21. See Coyle, "Mary Magdalene," 45, n. 37. On Martha and Mary in the New Testament, see Silke Petersen, 254–55.

22. Greek text and English translation by R. Cameron and A. J. Dewey, *The Cologne Mani Codex (P. Colon. inv. nr. 4780) "Concerning the Origin of His Body"* Texts and Translations, 15: Early Christian Literature Series, 3 (Missoula, Mont.: Scholars Press, 1979), 74–75.

23. On this text, see F. Decret, "Aspects de l'Église manichéenne: Remarques sur le manuscrit de Tebessa" in *Signum Pietatis: Festgabe für Cornelius Petrus Mayer OSA,* ed. A. Zumkeller, Casiciacum 40 (Würzburg: Augustinus-Verlag, 1989), 138–43; and J. BeDuhn and G. Harrison, "The Tebessa Codex: A Manichaean Treatise on Biblical Exegesis and Church Order," in *Emerging from Darkness: Studies in the Recovery of Manichaean Sources,* ed. P. Mirecki and J. BeDuhn, Nag Hammadi and Manichaean Studies 43 (Leiden: Brill, 1997), 33–87, esp. 43, 69–70, 79–80, and 85–86.

24. *Kephalaion 5*: Coptic in H. Ibscher et al., *Kephalaia, 1. Hälfte, Lieferung 1–10,* Manichäische Handschriften der Staatlichen Museen Berlin 1 (Stuttgart: Kohlhammer, 1940), 28.26–33; trans. I. Gardner, *The Kephalaia of the Teacher: The Edited Coptic Manichaean Texts in Translation with Commentary,* Nag Hammadi and Manichaean Studies 37 (Leiden: Brill, 1995), 32.

25. Already noted by Nagel, "Mariammê," 226–27, although he thinks that the Magdalene's "personality is transferred to the πνεῦμα σοφίας—but not to ⲥⲟⲫⲓⲁ herself" (*Persönlichkeit wird überholt zum πνεῦμα σοφίας—aber nicht zur ⲥⲟⲫⲓⲁ selbst*). His association (225–28) of her as Spirit of Wisdom with the "net-caster" theme via the notion of the four "hunters of light" and the Virgin of Light is interesting, but more problematic: See Silke Petersen, 193.

26. Allberry, 194.19–22.

27. On the two lists, see Richter, *Exegetisch-literarkritische,* 193–210.

28. But F. S. Pericoli Ridolfini, "Il salterio manicheo e la gnosi giudaico-cristiana," in *The Origins of Gnosticism: Colloquium of Messina, 13–18 April 1966,* ed. U. Bianchi, Studies in the History of Religions 12 (Leiden: Brill, 1967), 598, reads too much into this when he claims that "Mary appears there as coordinator of the apostles, and Simon Peter as the principal recipient of the Gnostic revelation of Jesus" (*Maria vi appare como coordinatrice degli apostoli e Simone Pietro como il principale depositario della rivelazione gnostica di Gesù*).

29. See R. Bauckham, "Salome the Sister of Jesus, Salome the Disciple of Jesus,

and the Secret Gospel of Mark," *NovT* 33 (1991): 264–65, who says that, for the author of *The Testament of Our Lord* (Syriac, fourth century), "Martha, Mary and Salome are the most prominent female disciples of Jesus, just as Peter, John, Thomas, Matthew, Andrew and Matthias are the most prominent of the twelve."

30. In F. W. K. Müller, "Handschriften-Reste in Estrangelo-Schrift aus Turfan, Chinesisch-Turkistan" II, *Abhandlungen der Königlich Preussischen Akademie der Wissenschaften, Philologisch-historische Klasse, Jhg. 1904, Abh. 3,* 34–35 (my translation). For W. L. Petersen the quotation, "because of its length, complexity and uniqueness, establishes with absolute certainty the dependence of this Manichaean Fragment upon Tatian's Diatesseron": "An Important Unnoticed Diatesseronic Reading in Turfan Fragment M-18" in *Text and Testimony: Essays on New Testament and Apocryphal Literature in Honour of A. F. J. Klijn,* ed. T. Baarda et al. (Kempen: J.H. Kok, 1988), 189. There is a reference as well to a *myrm* in another Turfan fragment [M 380], though the reading is uncertain. See W. Sundermann, *Mitteliranische manichäische Texte kirchen-geschichtlichen Inhalts,* Schriften zur Geschichte und Kultur des Alten Orients, Berliner Turfantexte 11 (Berlin: Akademie Verlag, 1981), 140.2399.

31. See Coyle, "Mary Magdalene," 46.

32. Allberry, 222.19–20, 26–27: "Salome built a tower upon the rock of truth and mercy [. . .]. Salome gave a parapet to the tower. . . ." For a discussion of these lines, see Silke Petersen, 237–40. Oddly, not Salome, but Mary Magdalene is the one usually associated with the tower image: See M. Scopello, "Marie-Madeleine et la Tour: *pistis* et *Sophia,*" in *Figures du Nouveau Testament chez les Pères,* Cahiers de Biblia Patristica 3 (Strasbourg: Centre d'Anayse et de Documentation Patristiques, 1991), 179–96.

33. Bauckham, 254. See also T. Ilan, "Notes on the Distribution of Jewish Women's Names in Palestine in the Second Temple and Mishnaic Periods," *JJS* 40 (1989): 191–92; and Silke Petersen, 195–96.

34. Clement, *Stromata* III, 6:45.

35. In Bauckham's view (263) "Salome's prominence in Gnostic Gospel traditions should not be exaggerated. She appears only in the East Syrian tradition (from which the Manichaean tradition about her probably also derives) and the Egyptian tradition."

36. M. Fieger, "Die Frau im Thomasevangelium," in *Lingua restituta orientalis: Festgabe für Julius Assfalg,* ed. R. Schulz and M. Görg, Ägypten und Altes Testament 20, (Wiesbaden: O. Harrassowitz, 1990), 103: "By Mariham, a name encountered also in Logion 114, only Mary Magdalene can be meant" (*Mit Mariham, dieser Name begegnet auch in Spruch 114, kann nur Maria Magdalena gemeint sein*). On the various forms of the name "Mary" in Gnostic and other texts, see Schaberg, 126–27.

37. See Silke Petersen, 258–60.

38. Silke Petersen, 249.

39. See G. Casadio, "Donna e simboli femminili nella gnosi del II secolo," in *La donna nel pensiero cristiano antico,* ed. U. Mattioli, Saggi e richerche (Genoa: Marietti, 1992), 319: "In Pistis Sophia [. . .] Mary is the principal personality along with

Jesus: there she appears as the pneumatic figure par excellence, predestined to en-
ter the πλήρωμα, with the Kingdom of Light for her inheritance" (*Nella Pistis
Sophia [. . .] Maria e il personnagio principale insieme a Gesù: ivi essa appare come
la figura pneumatica per excellenza, predestinata a entrare nel* πλήρωμα, ereditando
il regno della luce).

40. Bauckham, 257: "throughout the whole of Gnostic literature no more than
six women disciples of Jesus are ever named (Mary [Magdalene], Martha, Salome,
Arsenoe, Mary the mother of Jesus, Mary the sister of Jesus) and no more than four
in any work." The Manichaean literature seems to follow the same pattern. According
to A. Veilleux, *La première Apocalypse de Jacques (NH V,3)*, Bibliothèque copte de
Nag Hammadi, Section "Textes" 17 (Quebec: Les Presses de l'Université Laval, 1986),
94, n. 54, "The reconstruction '[Ars]inoé' in 40,26 is fairly certain" (*La reconstruction "[Ars]inoé" en 40,26 est assez certaine*) but "the mention of Martha is more hy-
pothetical" (*la mention de Marthe est beaucoup plus hypothétique*). He admits that
his reconstruction, too, is based on the Manichaean psalmbook. On the "Mary" of
the First Apocalypse of James, see also Silke Petersen, 250–54.

41. On Sophia's fall, see G. C. Stead, "The Valentinian Myth of Sophia," *Journal of Theological Studies* n.s. 20 (1969): 75–104, esp. 78–89.

42. Richter, *Exegetisch-literarkritische* 212, referring to my article (p. 49); see also
Silke Petersen, 193, and above, p. 199. But that would not rule out the notion of a
spirit (which is) of wisdom: See G. W. MacRae, "The Jewish Background of the Gnostic Sophia Myth," *NovT* 12 (1970): 90.

43. G. Widengren, "La Sagesse dans le manichéisme," in *Mélanges d'Histoire
des Religions offerts à Henri-Charles Puech* (Paris: Presses universitaires de France,
1974), 501–15.

44. Richter, *Exegetisch-literarkritische*, 59, believes that the dialogue of this psalm,
which he dates between 275 and 300, is inspired by an earlier Manichaean work.

45. Allberry, 187.

46. For opposing views, see Coyle, "Mary Magdalene," 49, n. 66. On differences
with the canonical text, see Marjanen, *The Woman Jesus Loved*, 207, n. 16.

47. Allberry, 187, refers at this point to C. Schmidt, *Gespräche Jesu mit seinen
Jüngern nach der Auferstehung*, Texte und Untersuchungen 43 (Leipzig: Hinrichs,
1919), 38–39 (Ethiopic and Coptic).

48. Allberry, 191.12–14. On the four-faced God, see J. K. Coyle, *Augustine's "De
moribus ecclesiae catholicae": A Study of the Work, Its Composition, and Its Sources*,
Paradosis 25 (Fribourg: University Press, 1978), 32, n. 144.

49. On the meaning of this term here see Richter, *Exegetisch-literarkritische*, 46.

50. See Marjanen, *The Woman Jesus Loved*, 212 and 215.

51. See, e.g., the thirteenth Psalm of Thom (Allberry, 220.2–3): N̄ϢΗΡΕ
N̄ϹⲠⲀⲦⲞⲨϹ [. . .] N̄ϢΗΡΕ Ⲙ̄ⲠϨΗⲦ.

52. Every Coptic Manichaean psalm, edited or not, with a legible doxology mentions ⲘⲀⲢⲒⲀ, who cannot be our ⲘⲀⲢⲒϨⲀⲘⲘΗ, because each name form appears here in a juxtaposed but separate doxological passage. The phenomenon is so

unique as to have me agree with Marjanen (*The Woman Jesus Loved*, 206–207), that in this case the name difference is significant. See below, p. 203.

53. See—besides the references in preceding notes—B. Neipp, *Marie-Madeleine, femme et apôtre: La curieuse histoire d'un malentendu* (Aubonine, Switz.: Éd. du Moulin, 1991); V. Saxer, 674–701 and 818–33; R. Atwood, *Mary Magdalene in the New Testament Gospels and Early Tradition*, European University Studies: Series 23, Theology, vol. 457 (Bern: P. Lang, 1993); S. Haskins, *Mary Magdalen, Myth and Metaphor* (New York: Harcourt Brace, 1993); J. Moreno Garrido, "María Magdalena en los textos gnósticos de Nag Hammadi," *Seminarios de Filosofia*, volumen especial (1993): 135–54; C. Ricci, *Mary Magdalene and Many Others: Women Who Followed Jesus* (Minneapolis: Fortress, 1994), trans. of *Maria di Magdala e le molte altre*, La Dracone 2 (Naples: M. d'Auria Editore, 1995); H. van Reisen, "Verrezen tot leerlinge van de Haer.: Maria Magdalena in de verkundiging Augustinus," *Tijdschrift voor Liturgie* 79 (1995), 98–110; E. de Boer, *Mary Magdalene: Beyond the Myth* (London: SCM Press, 1997), trans. of *Maria Magdalena: De mythe vorbij: Op zoek naar wie zij werkelijk is* (Zoetermeer: Meinema, 1996); J.-Y. Leloup, *L'Évangile de Marie: Myriam de Magdala* (Paris: Éd. Albin Michel, 1997); K. L. King, "Canonization and Marginalization: Mary of Magdala," *Concilium* 3 (1998): 29–36; and M. R. D'Angelo, "Reconstructing 'Real' Women from Gospel Literature: The Case of Mary Magdalene," in *Women and Christian Origins*, ed. R. S. Kraemer and M. R. D'Angelo (New York: Oxford University Press, 1999), 105–28. Studies unavailable to me were those of H. Koivunen, *The Woman Who Understood Completely: A Semiotic Analysis of the Mary Magdalene Myth in the Gospel of Mary*, Acta Semiotica Fennica (Imatra, Finland: International Semiotics Institute, 1994); M. Arminger, *Die verratene Päpstin: Maria Magdalena, Freundin und Geliebte Jesu, Magierin der Zeitenwende* (Munich: List, 1997); E. Mohri, *Maria Magdalena: Frauenbilder in Evangelientexten des 1. bis 3. Jahrhunderts* (Marburg: N. G. Elwert Verlag, 2000); and *Which Mary? The Marys of Early Christian Tradition*, ed. F. S. Jones, SBL Symposium Series 19 (Atlanta: Society of Biblical Literature, 2002).

54. Marjanen, *The Woman Jesus Loved*, 207, n. 11.

55. Silke Petersen, 191, n. 436 (referring to 51–53 of my article): *"unbegrundeterweise versucht, einen Zusammenhang mit Maria Magdalena herzustellen."*

56. Coyle, "Mary Magdalene," 53. Richter, *Exegetisch-literarkritische*, 16, n. 63, cites this sentence, also with the conclusion that I implied that the ΜΑΡΙΑ of the doxologies is Mary Magdalene.

57. Coyle, "Mary Magdalene," 51. The first argument is also employed by Marjanen, *The Woman Jesus Loved*, 206. But see below, p. 204.

58. Shoemaker, "Rethinking," 557, n. 4.

59. Ibid., 589.

60. See Allberry, 121.29 and 175.16.

61. See Shoemaker, "Rethinking," 560: "there is much to suggest that the gnostic Mary is in fact a composite figure, and that she has absorbed elements of both

the Magdalene's and the Virgin's identities. Her simple identification with one or the other figure simply cannot accommodate all of the evidence."

62. *Pace,* Shoemaker, "Rethinking," 586–87.

63. Coyle, "Mary Magdalene," 39.

64. On this, see I. Maisch, *Mary Magdalene: The Image of a Woman through the Centuries* (Collegeville, Minn.: Liturgical Press, 1998), 43–46; trans. of *Maria Magdalena zwischen Verachtung und Verehrung: Das Bild einer Frau im Spiegel der Jahrhunderte* (Freiburg-Basel-Vienna: Herder, 1996), 51–54.

65. See Coyle, "Mary Magdalene," 48.

66. See Maisch, *Mary Magdalene,* 26–27 (*Maria Magdalena,* 34–35); and Schaberg, 156–66.

67. See, for example, the Gnostic Dialogue of the Savior, 126,17 and 131,39, and Sophia of Jesus Christ, NH III, 4, 98,9 and 114,9; also the forms ⲘⲀⲢⲓⲀⲘⲘⲎ (or ⲘⲀⲢⲓⲀⲘⲚⲎ) in one manuscript of the Pistis Sophia (Coyle, "Mary Magdalene," 41, n. 16) or ⲘⲀⲢⲓⳉⲀⲘ (Gospel of Thomas, 114; Gospel of Mary, 9–10, 17–19). On various forms of names for "Mary" in Gnostic writings, see Shoemaker, "Rethinking," 582–86.

68. As in Pistis Sophia, 113–21.

69. With respect to this issue, neither Nagel, "Mariammê," 225, n. 18 and 228, Marjanen, *The Woman Jesus Loved,* 214, nor Richter, *Exegetisch-literarkritische,* 212, has quoted me in toto. Casadio, 319, says that in the Gnostic writings "Magdalene (the "Mary" par excellence) is the ultimate incarnation of Sophia, the final feminine bearer of Gnostic revelation, and, like Eve and Norea, the σύζυγος of a Gnostic savior" (*Maddalena [la "Maria" per excellenza] è l'ultima incarnazione di Sophia, l'ultima detentrice al femminile della rivelazione gnostica, e, come Eva, come Norea, la σύζυγος di un salvatore gnostico*).

Works Cited

Abd al-Karīm, Khalīl. *Fatrat al-Takwīn fī Hayāt al-Sāqiq al-Amīn.* Cairo: Mirit lil-Nashr wa-l Maʿlumat, 2001.

Abrahams, Roger D. "Introductory Remarks to a Rhetorical Theory of Folklore." *JAF* 81 (1968): 143–48.

Abu Abd Allah, Muḥammad al-Anṣārī al-Qurṭubī. *Al-Jāmiʿ lá-Aḥkām l-Qurʾān.* Beirut, Dār Iḥyāʾ al-Turāth al-Arabī, 1965.

Abu al-Qāsim, Maḥmūd b. ʿUmar al-Zamakhsharī. *Al-Kashshāf ʿan ḥaqāʾiq gha-wāmid al-tanzīl wa-ʿuyūn al-aqāwīl fī wujūh al-taʾwīl (Unveiler of the Real Meanings of the Hidden Matters of What Was Sent Down and the Choicest Statements about the Various Aspects of Its Interpretation).* Beirut: Dār al-Kitāb al-ʿArabi, 1966.

Abu Jaʿfar, Muḥammad b. Jarīr al-Ṭabarī. *Jāmiʿ al-bayān ʿan taʾwīl Āy l-Qurʾān (The Comprehensive Clarification of the Interpretation of the Verses of the Qurʾān),* ed. Maḥmūd M. Shākir. Cairo: Dar al-Maʿārif, 1969.

Ackerman, Susan. "Why Is Miriam Also among the Prophets? (and Is Zipporah among the Priests?)." *JBL* 12 (2002): 47–80.

Aland, Kurt, and Barbara Aland. *The Text of the New Testament.* Grand Rapids, Mich.: Eerdmans, 1987.

Allberry, C. R. C. *A Manichaean Psalm-Book, Part II.* Manichaean Manuscripts in the Chester Beatty Collection, vol. 2. Stuttgart: Kohlhammer, 1938.

Apostolos-Cappadona, Diane. "The Art of *Seeing:* Classical Paintings and *Ben-Hur.*" In *Image and Likeness: Religious Visions in American Film Classics,* ed. John R. May, 104–15 and 190–91. New York: Paulist Press, 1992.

———. "A Daughter's Own Book: Cultural Reflections on Women's Literacy in Nineteenth-Century American Culture." *AAQ* 19.4 (Fall 2002): 8–13.

———. *Dictionary of Women in Religious Art.* 1996. Reprint, New York: Oxford University Press, 1998.

———. "Discerning the Hand of Fatima: An Iconological Investigation of the Role of Gender in Religious Art?" In *A History of Our Own: Muslim Women and the DeConstruction of Patriarchy,* ed. Amira El-Azhary Sonbol. Syracuse: Syracuse University Press, 2004.

———. *In Search of Mary Magdalene: Images and Traditions.* New York: American Bible Society, 2002.

————. "'The Lord has struck him down by the hand of a woman!': Images of Judith." In *Art as Religious Studies*, ed. Doug Adams and Diane Apostolos-Cappadona, 81–97. 1987. Reprint, Eugene: Wipf and Stock, 2001.

————. "Picturing Devotion: Rogier's *St. Luke Drawing the Virgin*." In *Rogier van der Weyden, "St. Luke Drawing the Virgin": Selected Essays in Context*, ed. Carol J. Purtle, 5–14. Turnhout: Brepols, 1997.

————. "Virgin/Virginity." In *Encyclopedia of Comparative Iconography: Themes Depicted in Works of Art*, ed. Helene E. Roberts, vol. 2. Chicago: Fitzroy Dearborn, 1998.

Arkoun, Muḥammad. *Al-Qurʾān min al-Tafsīr al-mawrūth ila taḥlīl al-khiṭāb al-dīnī*, translated from French by Hāshim Sāliḥ. Beirut: Dar al-Taliʾa, 2001.

Arnold, Bill T., and Bryan E. Beyer, eds. *Readings from the Ancient Near East*. Grand Rapids, Mich.: Baker Academic, 2002.

Arras, Victor. *De transitu Mariae apocrypha aethiopice*. 2 vols. CSCO 343, 352, Scriptores Aethiopici, 67, 69. Louvain: Secrétariat du CorpusSCO, 1973.

Attridge, Harold W. "Don't Be Touching Me: Recent Feminist Scholarship on Mary Magdalene." In *A Feminist Companion to John*, vol. 2, ed. Amy-Jill Levine, 140–66, Feminist Companion to the New Testament and Early Christian Writings Series 5. New York: Sheffield Academic Press, 2003.

————. *Nag Hammadi Codex I (The Jung Codex)*. 2 vols. NHS 22–23. Leiden: Brill, 1985.

Atwood, Richard. *Mary Magdalene in the New Testament Gospels and Early Tradition*. Bern: P. Lang, 1993.

Aune, David. *Early Christian Prophecy in Its Ancient Mediterranean Context*. Grand Rapids, Mich.: Eerdmans, 1983.

Avenary, Hanoch. "Jüdische Musik." In *Die Musik in Geschichte und Gegenwart: allgemeine Enzyklopädie der Musik*, ed. 1, vol. 7, 224–32. Kassel: Bärenreiter-Verlag, 1968.

Barnett, Richard D. "The Nimrud Ivories and the Art of the Phoenicians." *Iraq* 2 (1935): 179–210.

Bauckham, R. "Salome the Sister of Jesus, Salome the Disciple of Jesus, and the Secret Gospel of Mark." *NovT* 33 (1991): 245–75.

Bauer, Angela. *Gender in the Book of Jeremiah: A Feminist Literary Reading*. New York: Peter Lang, 1999.

Bauer, Walter. "The Picture of the Apostle in Early Christian Tradition: 1. Accounts." In *New Testament Apocrypha*, vol. 2: *Writings Relating to the Apostles, Apocalypses, and Related Subjects*, ed. E. Hennecke and W. Schneemelcher, trans. R. McL. Wilson. London: SCM Press, 1965.

Baumgarten, Albert. *The Flourishing of Sects in the Maccabean Era: An Interpretation*. Leiden: Brill, 1997.

————. "The Pharisaic Paradosis." *HTR* 80 (1987): 63–77.

Beard, Mary. "Re-reading (Vestal) Virginity." In *Women in Antiquity: A New Assessment*, ed. Richard Hawley and Barbara Levick. London: Routledge, 1995.

BeDuhn, Jason, and G. Harrison. "The Tebessa Codex: A Manichaean Treatise on Biblical Exegesis and Church Order." In *Emerging from Darkness: Studies in the Recovery of Manichaean Sources,* ed. Paul Mirecki and Jason BeDuhn. Nag Hammadi and Manichaean Studies 43. Leiden: Brill, 1997.

Behn, Friedrich. *Musikleben im Altertum und frühen Mittelalte.* Stuttgart: Hiersemann, 1954.

Bellis, Alice Ogden. "Feminist Biblical Scholarship." In *Women in Scripture: A Dictionary of Named and Unnamed Women in the Hebrew Bible, the Apocryphal/Deuterocanonical Books, and the New Testament,* ed. Carol Meyers, Toni Craven, and Ross S. Kraemer. Boston: Houghton Mifflin, 2000.

Bernard, Archbishop John Henry. *A Critical and Exegetical Commentary on the Gospel according to St. John.* Vol. 2. New York: Charles Scribner's Sons, 1929.

Best, Ernest. "'Concerning the Loaves': Comprehending Incomprehension in Mark 6:45–52." *JSNT* 83 (2001): 3–26.

———. *Disciples and Discipleship: Studies in the Gospel according to Mark.* Edinburgh: T and T Clark, 1986.

Bibliotheca Bodmeriana: La collection des Papyrus Bodmer. Muenchen: K. G. Saur, 2000.

Black, Clifton. *The Disciples according to Mark: Markan Redaction in Current Debate.* Sheffield: Sheffield Academic Press, 1989.

Black, Matthew. *An Aramaic Approach to the Gospels and Acts.* 3rd ed. Oxford: Clarendon Press, 1967.

Böhlig, Alexander, and Frederik Wisse, eds. *Nag Hammadi Codices III, 2 and IV, 2: The Gospel of the Egyptians.* NHS 4. Grand Rapids, Mich.: Eerdmans, 1975.

Bornkamm, Guenther. *Mythos und Legende in den apokryphen Thomas-Akten: Beiträge zur Geschichte der Gnosis und zur Vorgeschichte des Manichäismus.* Forschungen zur Religion und Literatur des Alten und Neuen Testaments 49. Göttingen: Vandenhoeck and Ruprecht, 1933.

Bovon, François. "Le privilège pascal de Marie-Madeleine." *New Testament Studies* 30 (1984): 50–62.

———. *Luke 1.* Hermeneia. Philadelphia: Fortress, 2002.

Braun, Joachim. *Music in Ancient Israel/Palestine.* Trans. Douglas W. Stott. Grand Rapids, Mich.: Eerdmans, 2002.

———. "Musical Instruments." In *Oxford Encyclopedia of Archaeology in the Near East,* vol. 4, 73–74. New York: Oxford University Press, 1997.

Brenner, Athalya. *The Israelite Woman: Social Role and Literary Type in Biblical Narrative.* Biblical Seminar 2. Sheffield: Sheffield Academic Press, 1985.

Brenner, Athalya, and Fokkelien van Dijk-Hemmes. *On Gendering Texts: Female and Male Voices in the Hebrew Bible.* Biblical Interpretation Series 1. Leiden: Brill, 1993.

Brenner, Martin L. *The Song of the Sea: Exod 15:1–21.* Berlin: Walter de Gruyter, 1991.

Brock, Sebastian P., and Susan Ashbrook Harvey. *Holy Women of the Syrian Orient.* Berkeley: University of California Press, 1987.

Brooke, George J. "The Long-Lost Song of Miriam." *BARev* (1994): 62–65.

Brooten, Bernadette. *Women Leaders in the Ancient Synagogue.* Brown Judaic Series 36. Chico, Calif.: Scholar's Press, 1982.

Brown, Peter. *The Body and Society: Men, Women and Sexual Renunciation in Early Christianity.* New York: Columbia University Press, 1988.

Brown, Raymond. *The Birth of the Messiah: A Commentary on the Infancy Narratives in the Gospels of Matthew and Luke,* 2nd ed., Anchor Bible Reference Library. New York: Doubleday, 1995.

———. *The Community of the Beloved Disciple.* New York: Paulist Press, 1979.

———. *The Gospel of John.* Vol. 2. Garden City, N.Y.: Doubleday, 1970.

———. "Roles of Women in the Gospel of John." *Theological Studies* 36 (1975): 688–99. Reprinted in *The Community of the Beloved Disciple: The Life, Loves and Hates of an Individual Church in New Testament Times,* 183–89. New York: Paulist Press, 1979.

Buckley, Jorunn Jacobson. "'The Holy Spirit' Is a Double Name." In *Female Fault and Fulfilment in Gnosticism.* Chapel Hill: University of North Carolina Press, 1986.

Bultmann, Rudolph. *History of the Synoptic Tradition.* Trans. John Marsh. New York: Harper and Row, 1963.

Burns, Rita. *Has the Lord Spoken Only through Moses? A Study of the Biblical Portrait of Miriam.* SBL Dissertation Series 84. Atlanta: Scholars Press, 1987.

Cahill, P. Joseph. "Narrative Art in John IV." *RSB* 2 (1982): 41–48.

Cameron, R., and A. J. Dewey. *The Cologne Mani Codex (P. Colon. inv. nr. 4780) "Concerning the Origin of His Body."* Texts and Translations 15: Early Christian Literature Series 3. Missoula, Mont.: Scholars Press, 1979.

Casadio, Giovanni. "Donna e simboli femminili nella gnosi del II secolo." In *La donna nel pensiero cristiano antico,* ed. U. Mattioli, 319. Saggi e richerché. Genoa: Marietti, 1992.

Cassuto, Umberto. *A Commentary on the Book of Exodus.* Trans. Israel Abrahams. 1951. Reprint, Jerusalem: Magnes Press, 1983.

Cecchelli, Carlo. *Monumenti cristiano-eretici di Roma.* Rome: Fratelli Palombi, 1944.

Chadwick, Henry. "Origen, Celsus, and the Resurrection of the Body." *HTR* 41 (1948): 83–102.

Clark, Elizabeth A. *Ascetic Piety and Women's Faith.* Lewiston, N.Y.: Edwin Mellen, 1986.

———. "The Lady Vanishes: Dilemmas of a Feminist Historian after the 'Linguistic Turn.'" *CH* 67 (1998): 1–31.

———. *Women in the Early Church.* Collegeville, Minn.: Liturgical Press, 1983.

Clark, Kenneth. *The Nude: A Study in Ideal Form.* New York: Pantheon, 1956.

Clayton, Mary. *The Apocryphal Gospels of Mary in Anglo-Saxon England.* Cambridge: Cambridge University Press, 1998.

Corbett, Thomas. "Origen's Doctrine of the Resurrection." *ITQ* 46 (1979): 276–90.

Corley, Kathleen E. "Feminist Myths of Christian Origins." In *Re-imagining Chris-*

tian Origins: Essays in Honor of Burton Mack, ed. Elizabeth Castelli and Hal Taussig, 60–61. Valley Forge, Pa.: Trinity, 1996.

———. "Women and the Crucifixion and Burial of Jesus." *Forum* n.s. 1.1 (1998): 181–226.

———. *Women and the Historical Jesus: Feminist Myths of Christian Origins.* Santa Rosa, Calif.: Polebridge Press, 2002.

Coyle, J. Kevin. *Augustine's "De moribus ecclesiae catholicae": A Study of the Work, Its Composition, and Its Sources.* Paradosis 25. Fribourg: University Press, 1978.

———. "Mary Magdalene in Manichaeism?" *Le Muséon* 104 (1991): 39–55.

Cragg, Kenneth. *The Event of the Qur'ān: Islam in Its Scripture.* London: Allen and Unwin, 1971.

Cross, Frank Moore. "Prose and Poetry in the Epic and Mythic Texts from Ugarit." *HTR* 67 (1974): 1–15.

———. "The Song of the Sea and Canaanite Myth." In *Canaanite Myth and Hebrew Epic.* Cambridge, Mass.: Harvard University Press, 1973.

Cross, Frank Moore, and David Noel Freedman. "The Song of Miriam." *JNES* 14 (1955): 237–50.

Cross, Frank Moore, and David Noel Freedman. *Studies in Ancient Yahwistic Poetry.* SBL Dissertation Series 21. Missoula, Mont.: Scholars Press, 1975.

Crossan, John Dominic. *The Cross That Spoke.* San Francisco: HarperCollins, 1988.

Crouzel, Henri. *Origen.* Trans. A. S. Worrall. San Francisco: Harper and Row, 1989.

Daley, Brian E. *On the Dormition of Mary: Early Patristic Homilies.* Crestwood, N.Y.: St. Vladimir's Seminary Press, 1998.

D'Angelo, Mary Rose. "Gender in the Origins of Christianity: Jewish Hopes and Imperial Exigencies." In *Equal at the Creation: Sexism, Society and the Christian Tradition,* ed. Joseph Martos and Pierre Hégy, 36–39. Toronto: University of Toronto, 1998.

———. "Intimating Deity in the Gospel of John: Theological Language and 'Father' in 'Prayers of Jesus.'" In *God the Father in the Gospel of John,* ed. Adele Reinhartz. *Semeia* 85 (1999): 59–82.

———. "Reconstructing 'Real' Women from Gospel Literature: The Case of Mary Magdalene." In *Women and Christian Origins,* ed. Ross Shephard Kraemer and Mary Rose D'Angelo. New York: Oxford University Press, 1999.

———. "Re-membering Jesus: Women, Prophecy and Resistance in the Memory of the Early Churches." *Horizons: Journal of the College Theology Society* 19 (1992): 199–218.

———. "(Re)presentations of Women in the Gospels: John and Mark." In *Women and Christian Origins,* ed. R. Kraemer and M. R. D'Angelo. New York: Oxford University Press, 1999.

———. "Re-Reading Resurrection." In *Crossroads in Christology: Essays in Honor of Ellen M. Leonard,* ed. Anne Anderson and Mary Rose D'Angelo. *TJT* (2000): 108–29.

———. "Women in Luke-Acts: A Redactional View." *JBL* 109 (1990): 441–61.

Daniélou, Jean. *Origen*. Trans. Walter Mitchell. New York: Sheed and Ward, 1955.

Dauzat, Pierre-Emmanuel. *L'invention de Marie-Madeleine*. Paris: Bayard, 2001.

Davies, W. D. *The Setting of the Sermon on the Mount*. Cambridge: Cambridge University Press, 1966.

Davis, Stephen J. "Crossed Texts, Crossed Sex: Intertextuality and Gender in Early Christian Legends of Holy Women Disguised as Men." *JECS* 10 (2002): 1–36.

de Boer, Esther. "The Gospel of Mary: Beyond a Gnostic and a Biblical Mary Magdalene." Dissertation, University of Kampen, 2002.

———. "The Lukan Mary Magdalen and the Other Women Following Jesus." In *A Feminist Companion to Luke*, ed. Amy-Jill Levine with Marianne Blickenstaff. Sheffield: Sheffield Academic Press, 2002.

———. *Mary Magdalene: Beyond the Myth*. London: SCM Press, 1997.

Decret, François. "Aspects de l'Église manichéenne: Remarques sur le manuscrit de Tebessa." In *Signum Pietatis: Festgabe für Cornelius Petrus Mayer OSA*, ed. A. Zumkeller, 138–43. Casiciacum 40. Würzburg: Augustinus-Verlag, 1989.

Derrett, J. D. M. "Miriam and the Resurrection (John 10,16)." *Downside Review* 111 (1993): 176.

Deutsch, Celia. *Hidden Wisdom and the Easy Yoke: Wisdom, Torah and Discipleship in Matthew 11:25–30*. JSNTSS 18. Sheffield: Sheffield Academic Press, 1987.

Dewey, Joanna. "The Gospel of Mark." In *Searching the Scriptures*, vol. 2: *A Feminist Commentary*, ed. Elisabeth Schüssler Fiorenza. New York: Crossroad, 1994.

Dijk-Hemmes, Fokkelein van. "Some Recent Views on the Presentation of the Song of Miriam." In *A Feminist Companion to Exodus to Deuteronomy*, ed. Athalya Brenner. Feminist Companion to the Bible, vol. 6. Sheffield: Sheffield Academic Press, 1994.

al-Dīn al-Rāzī, Fakhr. *Mafātīḥ al-ghayb (The Keys of the Unseen) or al-Tafsīr al-Kabīr (The Great Commentary)*. Beirut: Dār al-Fikr, 1981.

Dunderberg, Ismo. "The Beloved Disciple in John: Ideal Figure in an Early Christian Controversy." In *Fair Play: Diversity and Conflicts in Early Christianity: Essays in Honour of Heikki Räisänen*, ed. Ismo Dunderberg, Christopher Tuckett, and Kari Syreeni, 243–69. Supplements to *NT* 53. Leiden/Boston/Köln: Brill, 2002.

Ehrman, Bart. "Cephas and Peter." *JBL* 109.3 (1990): 463–74.

Elm, Susanna. *"Virgins of God": The Making of Asceticism in Late Antiquity*. Oxford: Clarendon Press, 1994.

Engle, James R. "Pillar Figurines of Iron Age Israel and Asherah/Asherim." Ph.D. dissertation, University of Pittsburgh, 1979.

Erbetta, Mario. *Gli Apocrifi del Nuovo Testamento*. 3 vols. Vol. 1/2: *Vangeli: Infanzia e passione di Cristo, Assunzione di Maria*. Torino: Marietti, 1966.

Fakhrī, Mājid. *Tārīkh al-Falsafa al-Islāmiyya (History of Islamic Philosophy)*. New York: Columbia University Press, 1970.

Farley, Margaret A. "Feminist Consciousness and the Interpretation of Scripture." In *Feminist Interpretation of the Bible,* ed. Letty Russell. Philadelphia: Westminster, 1985.

Ferguson, Everett, ed. *The Encyclopedia of Early Christianity.* New York: Garland, 1997.

Ferrua, Antonio. "Questioni di epigrafia eretica romana." *Revista di Archeologia Cristiana* 21 (1944/45): 185–89.

Feuillet, Andre. "Le récit johannique de l'onction de Béthanie." *Esprit et Vie* 95.14 (April 1985): 198–201.

Fieger, M. "Die Frau im Thomasevangelium." In *Lingua restituta orientalis: Festgabe für Julius Assfalg,* ed. Regina Schulz and Manfred Görg. Ägypten und Altes Testament 20. Wiesbaden: Otto Harrassowitz, 1990.

Finesinger, Sol Baruch. "Musical Instruments in the Old Testament." *HUCA* 3 (1926): 21–76.

Finnegan, Ruth H. *Oral Poetry: Its Nature, Significance, and Social Context.* Cambridge: Cambridge University Press, 1977.

Fitzgerald, A., ed. *Augustine through the Ages: An Encyclopedia.* Grand Rapids, Mich.: Eerdmans, 1999.

Foskett, Mary F. *A Virgin Conceived: Mary and Classical Representations of Virginity.* Bloomington: Indiana University Press, 2002.

Fox, Everett, trans. *Now These Are the Names: A New English Rendition of the Book of Exodus.* New York: Schocken Books, 1986.

Freedberg, David. *The Power of Images: Studies in the History and Theory of Response.* Chicago: University of Chicago Press, 1982.

Freedman, David Noel. "Pottery, Poetry, and Prophecy: An Essay in Biblical Poetry." *JBL* 96 (1977): 5–26.

Frend, W. H. C. "The Gnostic Origins of the Assumption Legend." *Modern Churchman* 43 (1953): 23–28.

Fretheim, Terence. *Exodus.* Interpretation: A Bible Commentary for Teaching and Preaching. Louisville: John Knox Press, 1991.

Galate, Linda Sue. "Evangelium: An Iconographic Investigation of an Ante Pacem Image." Ph.D. dissertation, Drew University, 1997.

Gardet, L. "*Karāma.*" In *EncIs,* 615. Leiden: Brill, 1960.

Gardner, I. *The Kephalaia of the Teacher: The Edited Coptic Manichaean Texts in Translation with Commentary.* Nag Hammadi and Manichaean Studies 37. Leiden: Brill, 1995.

Garrido, J. Moreno. "María Magdalena en los textos gnósticos de Nag Hammadi." *Seminarios de Filosofia,* volumen especial (1993): 135–54.

Genette, Gérard. *Narrative Discourse: An Essay in Method.* Ithaca, N.Y.: Cornell University Press, 1980.

Gerson-Kiwi, Edith. "Musique dans le Bible." In *Dictionnaire de la Bible,* suppl. vol. 5, 1411–68. Paris: Letouzey et Ane, 1957.

Ginsberg, H. Louis. "Women Singers and Wailers among Northern Canaanites." *BA-SOR* 72 (1938): 13–15.

Goitein, Shelomo Dov. "Women as Creators of Biblical Genres." *Prooftexts* 10 (1988): 1–33.

Good, Deirdre. "Pistis Sophia." In *Searching the Scriptures,* ed. Elisabeth Schüssler Fiorenza, vol. 2: *A Feminist Commentary,* 678–707. New York: Crossroad, 1994.

Gorali, Moshe. "Musical Instruments in Ancient Times." *Ariel* 29 (1971): 70.

Grabar, André. *Christian Iconography: A Study of Its Origins.* 1968. Reprint, Princeton, N.J.: Princeton University Press, 1980.

Graetz, Naomi. "Did Miriam Talk Too Much?" In *A Feminist Companion to Exodus to Deuteronomy,* ed. Athalya Brenner, 231–42. Feminist Companion to the Bible, vol. 6. Sheffield: Sheffield Academic Press, 1994.

Grant, Robert, and Glen Menzies. *Joseph's Bible Notes (Hypomnestikon).* Atlanta: Scholars Press, 1996.

Green, Alberto R. W. *The Role of Human Sacrifice in the Ancient Near East.* American Schools of Oriental Research Dissertation Series 1. Missoula, Mont.: Scholars Press for the American Schools of Oriental Research, 1975.

Green, Joel. "The Social Status of Mary in Luke 1.5–2.52: A Plea for Methodological Integration." *Bib* 4.73 (1992): 457–72.

Grønbæk, Jakob H. *Die Geschichte vom Aufstieg Davids (1. Sam. 15–2. Sam.5): Tradition und Komposition.* Acta Theologica Danica 10. Copenhagen: Munksgaard, 1971.

Haenchen, Ernst. *A Commentary on the Gospel of John.* Vol. 2: *Chapters 7–21.* Trans. Robert W. Funk. Hermeneia. Philadelphia: Fortress, 1980.

Hanna, Judith Lynne. *The Performer-Audience Connection: Emotion in Metaphor in Dance and Society.* Austin: University of Texas Press, 1983.

Haskins, Susan. *Mary Magdalen: Myth and Metaphor.* New York: Harcourt Brace, 1993.

Hedrick, Charles W., ed. *Nag Hammadi Codices XI, XII, XIII.* NHS 28. Leiden: Brill, 1990.

Herr, Larry G. "Ammonites." In *Oxford Encyclopedia of Archaeology in the Near East,* vol. 1, 103–105. Oxford: Oxford University Press, 1997.

Hock, Ronald F. *The Infancy Gospels of James and Thomas.* The Scholar's Bible (Santa Rosa, Calif.: Polebridge Press, 1995).

Holl, Karl, and Jürgen Dummer, eds. *Epiphanius.* 2nd ed. 3 vols. GCS 25, 31, 37. Leipzig: J. C. Hinrichs, and Berlin: Akademie-Verlag, 1915, 1980, 1985.

Hopkins, Denise Dombkowski. "Judith." In *Women's Bible Commentary,* ed. Carole A. Newsom and Sharon H. Ringe. Expanded ed. Louisville: Westminster John Knox Press, 1998.

Hornbostel, Erich M., and Curt Sachs. "Systematik der Musikinstrumente." *Zeitschrift der Ethnologie* 46 (1914): 553–90.

Houston, Walter. "Exodus." In *The Oxford Bible Commentary,* ed. John Barton and John Muddiman. Oxford: Oxford University Press, 2001.

Ibn Ḥazm al-Andalusī. *Al-Faṣl fīl-Milal wa l-Ahwā' wa l-Niḥal.* Cairo: Dār al-Muttahida lil-Nashr, 1347 AH.

———. *Ibn Ḥazm war-Risāla fīl-Mufāḍala bayna al-ṣaḥāba,* ed. Saʿīd al-Afghānī. Beirut: Dār al-Fikr, 1969.

Ibn Manẓūr. *Lisān al-ʿArab.* Beirut: Dar Sadir, 1997.

Ibrāhīm Madkūr. *Fī al-Falsafa al-Islāmiyya: Manhaj wa-Ta ṭbīqah.* Cairo: Dār al-Maʿarif, 1947.

Ibscher, I. *Kephalaia, 1. Hälfte, Lieferung 1–10.* Manichäische Handschriften der Staatlichen Museen Berlin 1. Stuttgart: Kohlhammer, 1940.

Iersel, B. "Failed Followers in Mark: Mark 13:12 as a Key for the Identification of the Intended Readers." *CBQ* 58 (1996): 244–63.

Ilan, Tal. "Notes on the Distribution of Jewish Women's Names in Palestine in the Second Temple and Mishnaic Periods." *JJS* 40 (1989): 186–200.

Irvin, Dorothy. "The Ministry of Women in the Early Church." *Duke Divinity School Review* 2 (1980): 76–86.

Jalāl al-Dīn al-Suyūṭi. *Al-Itqān fīʿUlūm al-Qurʾān,* ed. Abū al-Faql Ibrāhīm. Saida: Al-Maktaba al-ʿAsriyya, 1997.

Janzen, J. Gerald. "Song of Moses, Song of Miriam: Who Is Seconding Whom?" *CBQ* 54 (1992): 211–20.

Jones, F. Stanley, ed. *Which Mary? The Marys of Early Christian Tradition.* Atlanta: SBL, 2002.

Jordan, Rosan A., and Susan J. Kalčik, eds., *Women's Folklore, Women's Culture.* American Folklore Society, New Series 8. Philadelphia: University of Pennsylvania Press, 1985.

Joseph, Terri Brint. "Poetry as a Strategy of Power: The Case of Riffian Berber Women." *Signs* 5 (1980): 418–34.

Jugie, Martin. *Homélies mariales byzantines: textes grecs.* 2 vols. PO 16.3, 19.3. Paris: Firmin-Didot, 1922 and 1926.

Kaemmer, John. *Music in Human Life: Anthropological Perspectives on Music.* Texas Press Source-books in Anthropology. Austin: University of Texas Press, 1993.

Kaestli, J.-D. "L'utilisation des actes apocryphes des apôtres dans le manichéisme." In *Gnosis and Gnosticism: Papers Read at the Seventh International Conference on Patristic Studies (Oxford, September 8th–13th 1975),* ed. M. Krause, 107–16. NHS 8. Leiden: Brill, 1977.

Karageorghis, Jacqueline. *The Coroplastic Art of Ancient Cyprus.* Vol. 5B: *The Cypro-Archaic Period Small Female Figurines: Figurines Moulées.* Nicosia: A. G. Leventis Foundation, 1999.

———. *La grand déesse de chypre et son culte.* Collection de la Maison de l'Orient Méditerranéan Ancien 5, Série Archéologique 4. Lyon: Maison de l'Orient. 1977.

Karageorghis, Vassos. *The Coroplastic Art of Ancient Cyprus.* Vol. 5A: *The Cypro-Archaic Period Small Female Figurines: Handmade/Wheelmade Figurines.* Nicosia: A. G. Leventis Foundation, 1998.

Keel, Othmar, and Christoph Uehlinger. *Gods, Goddesses, and Images of Gods in Ancient Israel*. Trans. Thomas H. Trapp. Minneapolis: Fortress Press, 1996.

King, Karen L. "Canonization and Marginalization: Mary of Magdala." *Concilium* 3 (1998): 29–36.

———. "The Gospel of Mary Magdalene." In *Searching the Scriptures*, vol. 2: *A Feminist Commentary*, ed. Elisabeth Schüssler Fiorenza. New York: Crossroad, 1994.

———. *The Gospel of Mary of Magdala*. Santa Rosa, Calif.: Polebridge Press, 2003.

———. *What Is Gnosticism?* Cambridge, Mass.: Harvard University Press, 2003.

———. "Why All the Controversy? Mary in the Gospel of Mary." In *Which Mary? The Marys of Early Christian Tradition*, ed. F. Stanley Jones, 53–74. SBL Symposium Series, 19. Atlanta: Society of Biblical Literature, 2002.

Kinukawa, Hisako. "Women Disciples of Jesus (15:40–41;15:47;16:1)." In *A Feminist Companion to Mark*, ed. Amy-Jill Levine with Marianne Blickenstaff. Sheffield: Sheffield Academic Press, 2001.

Kitzinger, Ernst. "Christian Imagery: Growth and Impact." In *Age of Spirituality: A Symposium*, ed. Kurt Weitzmann. New York: Metropolitan Museum of Art, 1980.

Kletter, Raz. *The Archaeology of the Judean Pillar-Figurines and the Archaeology of Asherah*. BAR International Series 636. Oxford: Tempus Reparatum, 1996.

Klimkeit, H.-J. "Die Kenntnis apokrypher Evangelien in Zentral- und Ostasien." In *Manichaica Selecta: Studies Presented to Julien Ries on the Occasion of His Seventieth Birthday*, ed. A. van Tongerloo and S. Giversen, 149–75, Manichaean Studies 1. Leuven: n.p., 1991.

Koester, Helmut. "One Jesus and Four Primitive Gospels." *HTR* 61 (1968): 203–47.

Koskoff, Ellen, ed. *Women and Music in Cross-Cultural Perspective*. New York: Greenwood Press, 1987.

Kraeling, Carl H. *The Christian Building: The Excavations at Dura-Europos*. Final Report 8, pt. 2. New Haven, Conn.: Yale University Press, 1967.

Kraemer, Ross. *Her Share of the Blessings: Women's Religions among the Pagans, Jews, and Christians in the Greco-Roman World*. Oxford: Oxford University Press, 1992.

———. "Jewish Women and Christian Origins: Some Caveats." In *Women and Christian Origins*, ed. Ross Kraemer and Mary Rose D'Angelo, 35–49. Oxford: Oxford University Press, 1992.

———. "Jewish Women and Women's Judaism(s) at the Beginning of Christianity." In *Women and Christian Origins*, ed. Ross Kraemer and Mary Rose D'Angelo, 50–79. Oxford: Oxford University Press, 1992.

Kutscher, E. Y. "The Language of the 'Genesis Apocryphon': A Preliminary Study." In *Aspects of the Dead Sea Scrolls*, ed. C. Rabin and Y. Yadin, 1–35. Jerusalem: Magnes, 1957.

Lake, Helen, and Kirsopp Lake. *Codex Sinaiticus Petropolitanus*. 2 vols. Oxford: Clarendon, 1911–22.

Layton, Bentley. *The Gnostic Scriptures*. Garden City, N.Y.: Doubleday, 1987.

————. *The Gnostic Treatise on Resurrection from Nag Hammadi*. Missoula, Mont.: Scholars Press, 1979.

————. "Prolegomena to the Study of Ancient Gnosticism." In *The Social World of the First Christians: Essays in Honor of Wayne A. Meeks*, ed. L. Michael White and O. Larry Yarbrough, 334–50. Minneapolis: Fortress Press, 1995.

Layton, Bentley, ed. *Nag Hammadi Codex II, 2–7*. Vol. 1: *Gospel according to Thomas, Gospel according to Philip, Hypostasis of the Archons, and Indices*. NHS 20. Leiden: Brill, 1989.

Layton, Bentley, and Wesley W. Isenberg. "Tractate 3: The Gospel of Philip." In *Nag Hammadi Codex II, 2–7 together with XIII,2*, Brit. Lib. Or.4926(1), and P.Oxy. 1, 654, 655*. Vol. 1: *Gospel according to Thomas, Gospel according to Philip, Hypostasis of the Archons, and Indexes*, ed. Bentley Layton, 129–217. NHS 20. Leiden: Brill, 1989.

Leloup, Jean-Yves. *L'Évangile de Marie: Myriam de Magdala*. Paris: Éd. Albin Michel, 1997.

Lieu, S. N. C. *Manichaeism in the Later Roman Empire and Medieval China*. Wissenschäftliche Untersuchungen zum Neuen Testament 63. Tübingen: Mohr, 1992.

Lord, Alfred B. *A Singer of Tales*. Cambridge, Mass.: Harvard University Press, 1960.

Lowrie, Walter. *Art in the Early Church*. 1947. Reprint, New York: W.W. Norton, 1969.

Lucchesi, Enzo. "Évangile selon Marie ou Évangile selon Marie-Madeleine?" *Analecta Bollandiana* 103 (1985): 366–92.

Lüdemann, Gerard. *What Really Happened to Jesus?* Trans. John Bowden. Louisville: Westminster John Knox, 1995.

MacCoull, Leslie S. B. "More Coptic Papyri from the Beinecke Collection." *APF* 35 (1989): 25–35.

MacDermot, Violet. *The Fall of Sophia: A Gnostic Text on the Redemption of Universal Consciousness*. Great Barrington, Mass.: Lindisfarne, 2001.

MacDonald, Margaret. *Early Christian Women and Pagan Opinion: The Power of the Hysterical Woman*. Cambridge: Cambridge University Press, 1996.

MacGregor, Neil, and Erika Langmuir. *Seeing Salvation: Images of Christ in Art*. London: BBC Worldwide, 2000.

MacRae, George W. "The Jewish Background of the Gnostic Sophia Myth." *NovT* 12 (1970): 86–101.

Madkūr, Ibrāhīm. *Fī al-Falsafa al-Islāmiyya: Manhaj wa-Taṭbīqah*. Cairo: Dār al-Maʿarif, 1947.

Maisch, I. *Mary Magdalene: The Image of a Woman through the Centuries*. Collegeville, Minn.: Liturgical Press, 1998. Translation of *Maria Magdalena zwischen Verachtung und Verehrung: Das Bild einer Frau im Spiegel der Jahrhunderte*. Freiburg: Herder, 1996.

Malbon, Elisabeth Struthers. "Fallible Followers: Women and Men in the Gospel of Mark." *Semeia* 28 (1983): 29–48.

————. "Texts and Contexts: Interpreting the Disciples in Mark." *Semeia* 62 (1993): 81–102.

Mamdūḥ al-Zūby. *Al-Mutanabbiʾūn: Sirat ashhar muddaʿī al-nubuwwa wamuʿtaqa-dātihim*. Beirut: Muʾassat al-Iman, 1995.

Manns, Frédéric. *Le récit de la dormition de Marie (Vatican grec 1982), Contribution à l'étude de origines de l'exégèse chrétienne*. Studium Biblicum Franciscanum, Collectio Maior 33. Jerusalem: Franciscan Printing Press, 1989.

Marcovich, Miroslav. *Hippolytus: Refutatio omnium haeresium*. Patristische Texte und Studien 25. Berlin: Walter de Gruyter, 1986.

Marcus, Joel. *Mark 1–8*. New York: Doubleday, 2000.

Marjanen, Antti. "The Mother of Jesus or Magdalene? The Identity of Mary in the So-Called Gnostic Christian Tradition." In *Which Mary? The Marys of Early Christian Tradition*, ed. F. Stanley Jones, 31–41. SBL Symposium Series, 19. Atlanta: Society of Biblical Literature, 2002.

———. *The Woman Jesus Loved: Mary Magdalene in the Nag Hammadi Library and Related Documents*. Nag Hammadi and Manichaean Studies 40. Leiden: Brill, 1996.

Markschies, Christoph. *Gnosis: An Introduction*. Trans. John Bowden. London: T and T Clark, 2003.

Marshall, David. "Christianity in the Qurʾān." In *Islamic Interpretations of Christianity*, ed. Lloyd Ridgeon. Richmond, Surrey, U.K.: Curzon, 2001.

Marshall, Kimberly, ed. *Rediscovering the Muses: Women's Musical Traditions*. Boston: Northeastern University Press, 1993.

Martin, Dale B. *The Corinthian Body*. New Haven, Conn.: Yale University Press, 1995.

Mathews, Thomas F. *The Clash of the Gods: A Reinterpretation of Early Christian Art*. Princeton, N.J.: Princeton University Press, 1993.

McAuliffe, Jane Dammen. *Qurʾānic Christians: An Analysis of Classical and Modern Exegesis*. Cambridge: Cambridge University Press, 1991.

McGowan, Andrew. *Ascetic Eucharists: Food and Drink in Early Christian Ritual Meals*. Oxford: Clarendon, 1999.

Meeks, Wayne. "The Man from Heaven in Johannine Sectarianism." *JBL* 91 (1972): 44–72.

Ménard, J. É. "La notion de 'résurrection' dans l'*Épître à Rhèginos*." In *Essays on the Nag Hammadi Texts*, ed. Martin Krause, 110–24. Leiden: Brill, 1975.

Mendels, Michal Dayagi. *The Achziv Cemeteries: The Ben-Dor Excavations, 1941–1944*. Jerusalem: Israel Antiquities Authority, 2002.

Mendelsohn, Isaac. "Guilds in Ancient Palestine." *BASOR* 80 (1940): 17–21.

Mernīssī, Fāṭima. *The Veil and the Male Elite: A Feminist Interpretation of Women's Rights in Islam*. Trans. Mary Jo Lakeland. New York: Addison-Wesley, 1991.

Meyers, Carol. "From Household to House of Yahweh: Women's Religious Culture in Ancient Israel." In *Congress Volume Basel 2001*, ed. André Lemaire, 285–96. Vetus Testamentum Supplements, vol. 92. Leiden: Brill, 2002.

———. "Guilds and Gatherings: Women's Groups in Ancient Israel." In *Realia Dei: Essays in Archaeology and Biblical Interpretation in Honor of Edward F. Camp-*

bell, Jr. at His Retirement, ed. Prescott H. Williams Jr. and Theodore Hiebert, 161–70. Atlanta: Scholars Press, 1999.

———. "Having Their Space and Eating There Too: Bread Production and Female Power in Ancient Israelite Households." *Nashim: A Journal of Jewish Women's Studies* 5 (2002): 14–44.

———. "Hierarchy or Heterarchy? Archaeology and the Theorizing of Israelite Society." In W.G. Dever festschrift (as yet unedited), ed. Seymour Gitin, J. Edward Wright, and J. P. Dessel. Forthcoming.

———. "Mother to Muse: An Archaeomusicological Study of Women's Performance in Ancient Israel." In *Recycling Biblical Figures: Papers Read at a NOSTER Colloquium in Amsterdam, 12–13 May 1997,* ed. Athalya Brenner and Jan Willem Van Henten, 50–77. Studies in Theology and Religion, vol. 1. Leiden: Deo Publishing, 1999.

———. "A Terracotta at the Harvard Semitic Museum and Disc-Holding Figures Reconsidered." *IEJ* 37 (1987): 116–22.

Midrash Rabbah. Trans. and ed. H. Freedman and M. Simon. London: Soncino, 1961.

Miles, Margaret R. *Carnal Knowing: Female Nakedness and Religious Meaning in the Christian West.* Boston: Beacon Press, 1989.

Mirecki, Paul Allen. "Peter, Gospel of." In *Anchor Bible Dictionary,* vol. 5, 278–81.

Mitchell, Joan. *Beyond Fear and Silence: A Feminist-Literary Reading of Mark.* New York: Continuum, 2001.

Müller, F. W. K. "Handschriften-Reste in Estrangelo-Schrift aus Turfan, Chinesisch-Turkistan" II, *Abhandlungen der Königlich Preussischen Akademie der Wissenschaften, Philosophisch-historische Klasse.* Jhr. 1904, Abh, 3.

Munro, Winsome. "Women Disciples in Mark?" *CBQ* 44 (1982): 225–41.

Murray, Robert. *Symbols of Church and Kingdom: A Study in Early Syriac Tradition.* London: Cambridge University Press, 1975.

Myres, John. *Handbook of the Cesnola Collection of Antiquities from Cyprus.* New York: Metropolitan Museum of Art, 1914.

Nagel, Peter. "Die apokryphen Apostelakten des 2. und 3. Jahrhunderts in der manichäischen Literatur: Ein Beitrag zur Frage nach den christlichen Elementen im Manichäismus." In *Gnosis und Neues Testament: Studien aus Religionswissenschaft und Theologie,* ed. K. W. Tröger. Gütersloh: Gerd Mohn, 1973.

———. "Mariammê—Netzwerferin und Geist der Weisheit." In *Divitiae Aegypti: Koptologische und verwandte Studien zu Ehren von Martin Krause,* ed. C. Fluck et al., 223–28. Wiesbaden: L. Reichert Verlag, 1995.

Neusner, Jacob. *From Politics to Piety.* New York: Ktav, 1979.

———. *The Pharisees: Rabbinic Perspectives.* Leiden: Brill, 1973.

Newsom, Carol, and Sharon Ringe. *Women's Bible Commentary,* expanded ed. Louisville: Westminster John Knox, 1998.

Niditch, Susan. "Judges." In *The Oxford Bible Commentary,* ed. John Barton and John Muddiman. Oxford: Oxford University Press, 2001.

O'Conner, Kathleen M. "Jeremiah." In *The Oxford Bible Commentary*, ed. John Barton and John Muddiman. Oxford: Oxford University Press, 2001.

Old Testament Pseudepigrapha. Ed. James H. Charlesworth. 2 vols. Garden City: Doubleday, 1983 and 1985.

Orbe, Antonio, S.J., *Estudios Valentinianos*. Vol. 1: *Hacia la primera teologica de la procesion del Verbo*. Analecta Gregoriana 99. Rome: Gregorian University, 1958.

Osiek, Carolyn. "The Women at the Tomb: What Are They Doing There?" In *A Feminist Companion to Matthew*, ed. Amy-Jill Levine with Marianne Blickenstaff, 212–20. Sheffield: Sheffield Academic Press, 2001.

Pagels, Elaine Hiesey. *The Gnostic Paul: Gnostic Exegesis of the Pauline Letters*. Philadelphia: Fortress Press, 1975.

———. *The Johannine Gospel in Gnostic Exegesis: Heracleon's Commentary on John*. Society of Biblical Literature Monograph Series 17. Nashville: Abingdon Press, 1973.

———. "'The Mystery of the Resurrection': A Gnostic Reading of 1 Cor 15." *JBL* 93 (1974): 276–88.

———. "Pursuing the Spiritual Eve: Imagery and Hermeneutics in the Hypostasis of the Archons and the Gospel of Philip." In *Images of the Feminine in Gnosticism*, ed. Karen L. King, 187–206. Philadelphia: Fortress Press, 1988.

Parrott, Douglas M. *Nag Hammadi Codices III,3–4 and V,1 with Papyrus Berolinensis 8502,3 and Oxyrhynchus Papyrus 1081, Eugnostos and the Sophia of Jesus Christ*. NHS 27. Leiden: Brill, 1991.

———. *Nag Hammadi Codices V, 2–5 and VI with Papyrus Berolinensis 8502, 1 and 4*. NHS 11. Leiden: Brill, 1979.

Pasquier, Anne. *L'Evangile selon Marie*. Bibliothèque copte de Nag Hammadi, Section textes, 10. Quebec: Les Presses de l'Université Laval, 1983.

Pearson, Birger A. *Nag Hammadi codices IX and X*. NHS 15. Leiden: Brill, 1981.

Peel, Malcolm L. *The Epistle to Rheginos*. Philadelphia: Westminster, 1969.

Peters, Melvin K. H. *A Critical Edition of the Coptic (Bohairic) Pentateuch*. Vol. 2: *Exodus*, 15, 42. Atlanta: Scholars Press, 1986.

Petersen, Silke. *"Zerstört die Werke der Weiblichkeit!": Maria Magadalena, Salome und andere Jungerinnen Jesu in christlich-gnostischen Schriften*. Nag Hammadi and Manichaean Studies 48. Leiden: Brill, 1999.

Petersen, W. L. "An Important Unnoticed Diatesseronic Reading in Turfan Fragment M-18." In *Text and Testimony: Essays on New Testament and Apocryphal Literature in Honour of A. F. J. Klijn*, ed. T. Baarda et al. Kempen: J. H. Kok, 1988.

Phillips, Victoria. "The Failure of the Women Who Followed Jesus in the Gospel of Mark." In *A Feminist Companion to Mark*, ed. Amy-Jill Levine with Marianne Blickenstaff, 222–34. Sheffield: Sheffield Academic Press, 2001.

Poethig, Eunice. "The Victory Song Tradition of the Women of Israel." Ph.D. dissertation, Union Theological Seminary, 1985.

Preuschen, Erwin, ed. *Origenes Werke*. Vol. 4: *Der Johanneskommentar*. GCS 10. Leipzig: J. C. Hinrichs, 1903.

Pritchard, James B. *Palestinian Figurines in Relation to Certain Goddesses Known through Literature*. American Oriental Studies 24. New Haven, Conn.: American Oriental Society, 1943.

Propp, William. *Exodus 1–18: A New Translation with Introduction and Commentary*. Anchor Bible, vol. 2. New York: Doubleday, 1999.

Quenot, Michel. *The Resurrection and the Icon*. Trans. Michael Breck. New York: St. Vladimir's Theological Press, 1977.

Raḥmān, Fazlur. *Major Themes of the Qurʾān*. Chicago: Bibliotheca Islamica, 1980.

Rapp, Ursula. *Mirjam: Eine feministisch-rhetorische Lektüre der Mirjamtexte in der hebräischen Bibel*, BZAW 317. Berlin: de Gruyter, 2002.

Redmount, Carol A. "Bitter Lives: Israel in and out of Egypt." In *The Oxford History of the Biblical World*, ed. Michael D. Coogan. New York: Oxford University Press, 1998.

Reinhartz, Adele. "The Gospel of John." In *Searching the Scriptures*, vol. 2: *A Feminist Commentary*, ed. Elisabeth Schüssler Fiorenza, 561–600. New York: Crossroad, 1994.

Reisen, H. van. "Verrezen tot leerlinge van de Haer.: Maria Magdalena in de verkundiging Augustinus." *Tijdschrift voor Liturgie* 79 (1995): 98–111.

Renan, Ernest. *Histoire des origines du Christianisme*. 6th ed. Vol. 7: *Marc-Aurèle et la fin du monde antique*. Paris: Calmann Lévy, 1891.

Ricci, Carla. *Mary Magdalene and Many Others: Women Who Followed Jesus*. Minneapolis: Fortress, 1994. Translation of *Maria di Magdala e le molte altre*, La Dracone 2 . Naples: M. d'Auria Editore, 1991.

Richter, Siegfried. *Exegetisch-literarkritische Untersuchungen von Herakleidespsalmen des koptisch-manichäischen Psalmenbuches*. Arbeiten zum spätantiken und koptischen Ägypten, 5. Altenberge: Oros Verlag, 1994.

Ridolfini, F. S. Pericoli. "Il salterio manicheo e la gnosi giudaico-cristiana." In *The Origins of Gnosticism: Colloquium of Messina, 13–18 April 1966*, ed. U. Bianchi. Studies in the History of Religions 12. Leiden: Brill, 1967.

Rigato, Maria-Luisa. "'"Remember" . . . Then They Remembered': Luke 24:6–8." In *A Feminist Companion to Luke*, ed. Amy-Jill Levine with Marianne Blickenstaff, 269–80. Sheffield: Sheffield Academic Press, 2002.

Riley, Gregory J. *Resurrection Reconsidered: Thomas and John in Controversy*. Minneapolis: Fortress, 1995.

Rosaldo, Michele Z. "Women, Culture, and Society: A Theoretical Overview." In *Women, Culture, and Society*, ed. Michele Z. Rosaldo and Louise Lamphere. Stanford, Calif.: University of California Press, 1974.

Rousseau, Adelin, and Louis Doutreleau. *Irénée de Lyon: Contre les hérésies*. 9 vols. SC 100, 152–53, 210–11, 263–64, 293–94. Paris: Les Éditions du Cerf, 1969–82.

Rudolph, Kurt. "Die Gnosis: Texte und Übersetzungen." *Theologische Rundschau* 55 (1990): 113–52.

——. *Gnosis: The Nature and History of Gnosticism.* Trans. Robert McLachlan Wilson. San Francisco: Harper and Row, 1987.

Sagnard, François, and Louis Marie Matthieu, eds. *Extraits de Théodote.* SC 23. Paris: Editions du Cerf, 1948.

Saldarini, Anthony J. *Pharisees, Scribes, and Sadducees in Palestinian Society.* 1988. Reprint, Grand Rapids, Mich.: Eerdmans, 2001.

Sanday, Peggy R. "Female Status in the Public Domain." In *Women, Culture, and Society,* ed. Michele Z. Rosaldo and Louise Lamphere. Stanford, Calif.: Stanford University Press, 1974.

Saxer, Victor. "Marie-Madeleine dans les évangiles: La femme coupée en morceaux?" *RevTh* 92 (1992): 674–701 and 818–33.

Schaberg, Jane. *The Resurrection of Mary Magdalene: Legends, Apocrypha, and the Christian Testament.* New York: Continuum, 2002.

Scheidweiler, Felix. "The Questions of Bartholomew." In *New Testament Apocrypha,* vol. 1: *Gospels and Related Writings,* 5th ed., ed. W. Schneemelcher, trans. R. McL. Wilson. Louisville: Westminster John Knox, 1991.

Schenke, Hans-Martin. *Das Philippus-Evangelium (Nag Hammadi-Codex II,3).* Texte und Untersuchungen 143. Berlin: Akademie-Verlag, 1997.

——, ed. *Das Matthäus-Evangelium im Mittelägyptischen Dialekt des Koptischen* (Codex Scheide). Berlin: Akademie Verlag, 1981.

Schmid, Renate. *Maria Magdalena in gnostischen Schriften.* München: Arbeitsgemeinschaft für Religions-und Weltanschauungsfragen, 1990.

Schmidt, Carl. *Gnostische Schriften in koptischer Sprache aus dem Codex Brucianus,* TU 8.1. Leipzig: J. C. Hinrichs'sche Buchhandlung, 1892.

——. *Koptisch-gnostische Schriften.* Vol. 1. 4th ed. GCS 45. Berlin: Akademie Verlag, 1981.

Schmidt, Carl, ed. *The Books of Jeû and the Untitled Text in the Bruce Codex.* Trans. Violet MacDermot. NHS 13. Leiden: Brill, 1978.

——. *Pistis Sophia.* Trans. and notes by Violet MacDermot. NHS 9. Leiden: Brill, 1978.

Schneemelcher, W., ed., and R. McL. Wilson, trans. *New Testament Apocrypha.* Vol. 1: *Gospels and Related Writings,* 5th ed. (Louisville: Westminster John Knox, 1991).

Schneider, Gerhard. "Maria." In *EDNT,* vol. 2. Grand Rapids, Mich.: Eerdmans, 1991.

Schneiders, Sandra. *The Revelatory Text.* San Francisco: Harper San Francisco, 1991.

——. *Written That You May Believe: Encountering Jesus in the Fourth Gospel.* New York: Crossroad, 1999.

Schüssler Fiorenza, Elisabeth. "The Apostleship of Women in Early Christianity." In *Women Priests: A Catholic Commentary on the Vatican Declaration,* ed. Leonard Swidler and Arlene Swidler. New York: Paulist Press, 1977.

——. *But She Said: Feminist Practices of Biblical Interpretation.* Boston: Beacon, 1992.

————. *In Memory of Her: A Feminist Theological Reconstruction of Christian Origins.* New York: Crossroad, 1984.

————. *Jesus, Miriam's Child, Sophia's Prophet: Critical Issues in Feminist Christology.* New York: Continuum, 1994.

Schwartz, Seth. *Imperialism and Jewish Society.* Princeton, N.J.: Princeton University Press, 2001.

Schweitzer, Albert. *The Quest of the Historical Jesus.* London: A. and C. Black, 1910.

Scopello, Maddalena. "Marie-Madeleine et la Tour: *pistis* et *sophia.*" In *Figures du Nouveau Testament chez les Pères,* 179–96. Cahiers de Biblia Patristica 3. Strasbourg: Centre d'Anayse et de Documentation Patristiques, 1991.

Seim, Turid Karlsen. *The Double Message: Patterns of Gender in Luke-Acts.* Nashville: Abingdon Press, 1994.

Sellew, Philip. "An Early Coptic Witness to the *Dormitio Mariae* at Yale: P. CtYBR inv. 1788 Revisited." *Bulletin of the American Society of Papyrologists* 37 (2000): 37–70.

Sendrey, Alfred. *Music in Ancient Israel.* New York: Philosophical Library, 1969.

Shoemaker, Stephen J. *Ancient Traditions of the Virgin Mary's Dormition and Assumption.* Oxford Early Christian Studies. Oxford: Oxford University Press, 2002.

————. "A Case of Mistaken Identity? Naming the Gnostic Mary." In *Which Mary? The Marys of Early Christian Tradition,* ed. F. Stanley Jones, 5–30. Symposium Series 19. Atlanta: Society of Biblical Literature, 2002.

————. "Rethinking the 'Gnostic Mary': Mary of Nazareth and Mary of Magdala in Early Christian Tradition." *JECS* 9 (2001): 555–95.

Sieber, John H. *Nag Hammadi Codex VIII.* NHS 31. Leiden: Brill, 1991.

Smith, Morton. *Clement of Alexandria and a Secret Gospel of Mark.* Cambridge, Mass.: Harvard University Press, 1973.

Stead, G. Christopher. "The Valentinian Myth of Sophia." *Journal of Theological Studies* n.s. 20 (1969): 75–104.

Stemberger, Günther. *Jewish Contemporaries of Jesus: Pharisees, Sadducees, Essenes.* Minneapolis: Fortress, 1995.

Stempvoort, P. A. van. "The Protevangelium Jacobi, the Sources of Its Theme and Style and Their Bearing on Its Date." In *Studia Evangelica III,* ed. F. Cross, 410–26. TU 88. Berlin: Akademie Verlag, 1964.

Stowasser, Barbara Freyer. *Women in the Qur'ān: Traditions, and Interpretation.* New York: Oxford University Press, 1994.

Subhī al-Sālih. *'Ulūm al-ḥadīth.* Beirut: Dar al-'Ilm lil-Malayin, 1966.

Sundermann, W. *Mitteliranische Manichäische Texte Kirchengeschichtlichen Inhalts.* Schriften zur Geschichte und Kultur des Alten Orients, Berliner Turfantexte 11. Berlin: Akademie Verlag, 1981.

Tardieu, Michel. *Écrits gnostiques: Codex de Berlin.* Sources Gnostiques et Manicheennes 1. Paris: Editions du Cerf, 1984.

Theissen, Gerd. *Sociology of Early Palestinian Christianity*. Translated from the German work *Soziologie de Jesusbewegungs* by John Bowden. Philadelphia: Fortress, 1978.

Theissen, Gerd, and Annette Merz. *The Historical Jesus: A Comprehensive Guide*. Trans. John Bowden; bibliographies revised and updated by Robert Morgan. Minneapolis: Fortress, 1998.

Thomassen, Einar. "How Valentinian Is the Gospel of Philip?" In *The Nag Hammadi Library after Fifty Years: Proceedings of the 1995 Society of Biblical Literature Commemoration*, ed. John D. Turner and Anne McGuire, 251–79. Nag Hammadi and Manichaean Studies 44. Leiden: Brill, 1997.

———. "Notes pour la delimitation d'une corpus Valentinien à Nag Hammadi." In *Les Textes de Nag Hammadi et le Problème de leur Classification. Actes du colloque tenu à Québec du 15 au 19 septembre 1993*, ed. Louis Painchaud and Anne Pasquier, 243–59. Quebec: Les Presses de l'Université Laval, 1995.

Tilborg, Sjef van. *Imaginative Love in John*. Biblical Interpretation Series 2. Leiden: Brill, 1993.

Tischendorf, Constantin von. *When Were Our Gospels Written? An Argument by Constantine Tischendorf—With a Narrative of the Discovery of the Sinaitic Manuscript*. New York: American Tract Society, 1866.

Tolbert, Mary Ann. "Mark." In *Women's Bible Commentary*. Louisville: Westminster John Knox, 1998.

Torjesen, Karen Jo. "The Early Christian *Orans:* An Artistic Representation of Women's Liturgical Prayer and Prophecy." In *Women Preachers and Prophets through Two Millennia of Christianity*, ed. Beverly Mayne Kienzle and Pamela J. Walker. Berkeley: University of California Press, 1998.

Trible, Phyllis. "Bringing Miriam Out of the Shadows." *Bible Review* 5 (1989): 13–25.

———. "Eve and Miriam: From the Margins to the Center." In *Feminist Approaches to the Bible: Symposium at the Smithsonian Institution, September 24, 1994, sponsored by the Resident Associate Program, Phyllis Trible, et al.*, ed. Hershel Shanks, 22–23. Washington, D.C.: Biblical Archaeology Society, 1995.

———. "Miriam." In *Women in Scripture: A Dictionary of Named and Unnamed Women in the Hebrew Bible, the Apocryphal/Deuterocanonical Books, and the New Testament*, ed. Carol Meyers, Toni Craven, and Ross S. Kraemer. Boston: Houghton Mifflin, 2000.

Trigg, Joseph W. "The Angel of Great Counsel: Christ and the Angelic Hierarchy in Origen's Theology." *JTS* n.s. 42 (1991): 35–51.

van Eijk, A. H. C. "The Gospel of Philip and Clement of Alexandria: Gnostic and Ecclesiastical Theology on the Resurrection and the Eucharist." *VC* 25 (1971): 94–120.

van Esbroeck, Michel. "Apocryphes géorgiens de la Dormition." *Analecta Bollandiana* 92 (1973): 55–75.

van Ess, Joseph. "Verbal Inspiration? Language and Revelation in Classical Islamic Theology." In *The Qur'ān as Text*, ed. Stefan Wild. Brill: Leiden, 1996.

Vandenabeele, Frieda. "Has Phoenician Influence Modified Cypriot Terracotta Production?" In *Early Society in Cyprus,* ed. Edgar J. Peltenburg. Edinburgh: Edinburgh University Press in association with the National Museum of Scotland and the A. V. Leventis Foundation, 1989.

Veilleux, A. *La première Apocalypse de Jacques (NH V,3).* Bibliothèque copte de Nag Hammadi, Section Textes 17. Quebec: Les Presses de l'Université Laval, 1986.

Viguera, Maria J. "Aṣluḥu lil-Maʿālī: On the Social Status of Andalusī Women." In *The Legacy of Muslim Spain,* ed. Salma Khadra Jayyusi. Brill: Leiden, 1994.

Waldstein, Michael, and Frederic Wisse, eds. *The Apocryphon of John: A Synopsis of Nag Hammadi Codices II,1, III,1, and IV,1 with BG 8502,2.* NHS 33. New York: Brill, 1995.

Ward, Benedicta. *Harlots of the Desert: A Study of Repentance in Early Monastic Sources.* Kalamazoo, Mich.: Cistercian Publications, 1987.

Weigle, Marta. "Women as Verbal Artists: Reclaiming the Daughters of Enheduanna." *Frontiers* 3 (1978): 1–9.

Weitzmann, Kurt, ed. *Age of Spirituality: Late Antique and Early Christian Art, Third to Seventh Century.* New York: Metropolitan Museum of Art in association with Princeton University Press, 1977.

———. *The Monastery of Saint Catherine at Mount Sinai: The Icons.* Vol. 1: *From the Sixth to the Tenth Century.* Princeton, N.J.: Princeton University Press, 1976.

Wenger, Antoine. *L'Assomption de la T.S. Vierge dans la tradition byzantine du VIe au Xe siècle; études et documents.* Archives de l'Orient Chrétien 5. Paris: Institut Français d'Études Byzantines, 1955.

Werner, Eric. "Music." In *IDB,* vol. 3, 466. New York and Nashville: Abingdon, 1962 and 1979.

Werner, Martin. *The Formation of Christian Dogma: An Historical Study of Its Problem.* Trans. S. G. F. Brandon. New York: Harper and Brothers, 1957.

White, Sidnie A. "4Q364 and 365: A Preliminary Report." In *The Madrid Qumran Conference,* ed. J. Trebolle Barrera and L. Vegas Montaner, 222–24. Studies in the Text of the Desert of Judah 11. Leiden: Brill, 1992.

Widengren, G. "La Sagesse dans le manichéisme." In *Mélanges d'Histoire des Religions offerts à Henri-Charles Puech.* Paris: Presses universitaires de France, 1974.

Williams, Michael A. *Rethinking Gnosticism: An Argument for Dismantling a Dubious Category.* Princeton, N.J.: Princeton University Press, 1996.

Williams, Prescott H., and Theodore Hiebert. "Moses and Miriam: The Song of the Sea." In *Realia Dei: Essays in Archaeology and Biblical Interpretation in Honor of Edward F. Campbell Jr. at His Retirement.* Atlanta: Scholars Press, 1999.

Wilson, Robin McL., and George W. MacRae. "BG,1: The Gospel according to Mary." In *Nag Hammadi Codices V,2–5 and VI with Papyrus Berolinensis 8502,1 and 4,* ed. Douglas M. Parrott. NHS 11. Leiden: Brill, 1979.

Winslow, Donald F. "Logos." In *The Encyclopedia of Early Christianity,* ed. Everett Ferguson, 688. New York: Garland, 1997.

Wire, Antoinette Clark. "The Structure of the Gospel Miracle Stories and Their
    Tellers." *Semeia* 11 (1978): 83–113.
Wisse, Frederik. "The Nag Hammadi Library and the Heresiologists." *VC* 25 (1971):
    205–23.
————. "Stalking Those Elusive Sethians." In *The Rediscovery of Gnosticism: Pro-
    ceedings of the International Conference on Gnosticism at Yale, New Haven,
    Connecticut, March 28–31, 1978*, vol. 2: *Sethian Gnosticism*, ed. Bentley Lay-
    ton, 563–76. Studies in the History of Religions (Supplements to *Numen*)
    41. Leiden: Brill, 1981.
Wright, William. *Contributions to the Apocryphal Literature of the New Testament.*
    London: Williams and Norgate, 1865.
Zwettler, Michael. "A Mantic Manifesto: The Sūra of 'The Poets' and the Qurʾānic
    Foundations of Prophetic Authority." In *Poetry and Prophecy: The Begin-
    nings of a Literary Tradition*, ed. James L. Kugel. Ithaca, N.Y.: Cornell Uni-
    versity Press, 1990.

Contributors

Deirdre Good, General Theological Seminary

Carol Meyers, Duke University

Antti Marjanen, University of Helsinki

Mary F. Foskett, Wake Forest University

Claudia Setzer, Manhattan College

Mary Rose D'Angelo, University of Notre Dame

Diane Apostolos-Cappadona, Georgetown University

Stephen J. Shoemaker, University of Oregon

Hosn Abboud, University of Toronto

J. Kevin Coyle, University of St. Paul

Index

Page numbers in italics indicate illustrations.

DEIRDRE GOOD is Professor of New Testament
at the General Theological Seminary, New York City.